MW00604853

American Tacos

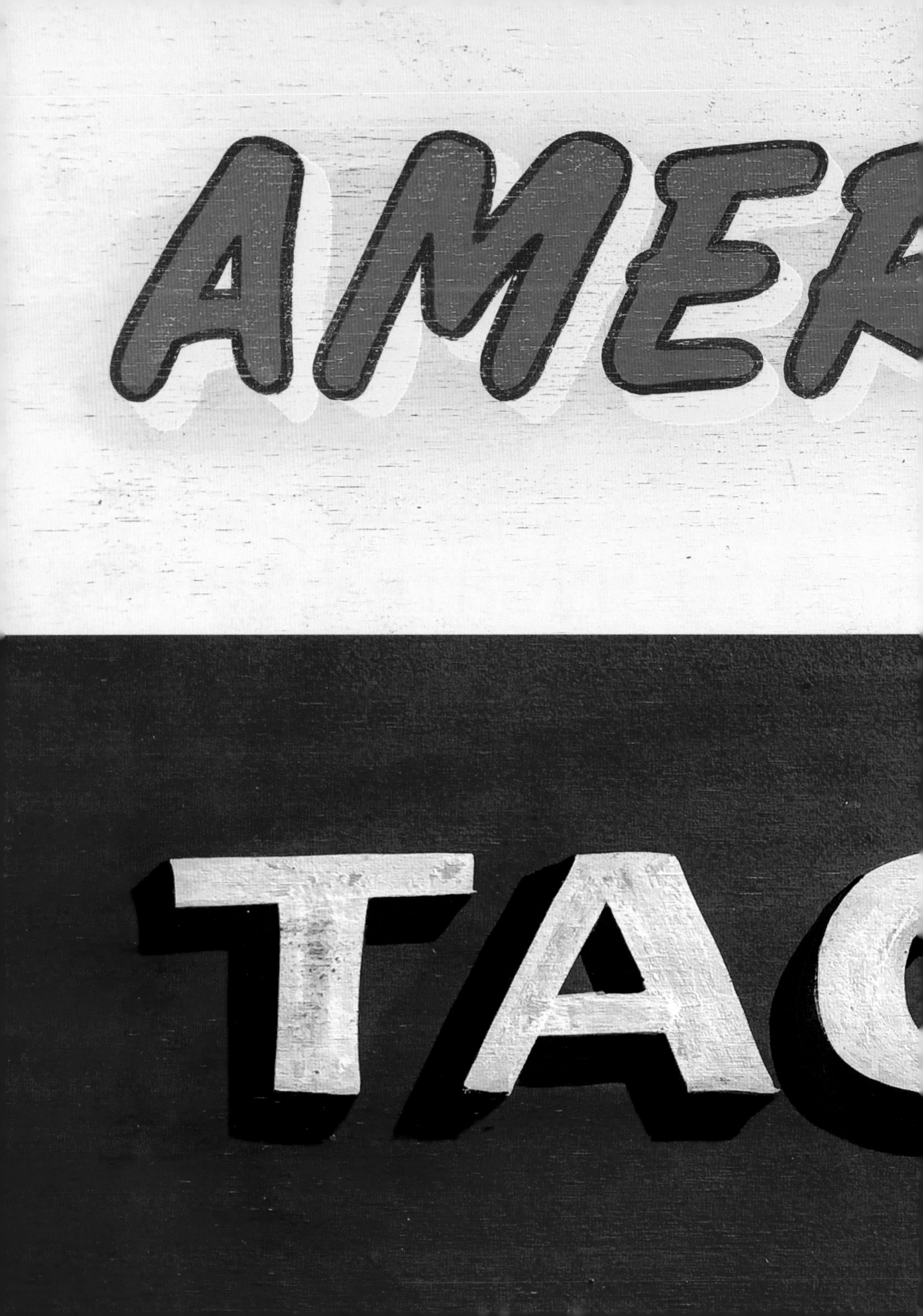
AME
TA

José R. Ralat

American Tacos

A History and Guide

University of Texas Press, Austin

Copyright © 2020 by José R. Ralat
All rights reserved
Printed in the United States of America
First edition, 2020

Requests for permission to reproduce material
from this work should be sent to:
Permissions
University of Texas Press
P.O. Box 7819
Austin, TX 78713-7819
utpress.utexas.edu/rp-form

♾ The paper used in this book meets the minimum
requirements of ANSI/NISO Z39.48-1992 (R1997)
(Permanence of Paper).

Library of Congress Cataloging-in-Publication Data

Names: Ralat, José R., author.
Title: American tacos : a history and guide / José R. Ralat.
Description: First edition. | Austin : University of Texas Press,
2020. | Includes bibliographical references and index.
Identifiers: LCCN 2019026436
ISBN 978-1-4773-1652-8 (cloth)
ISBN 978-1-4773-2099-0 (library ebook)
ISBN 978-1-4773-2100-3 (non-library ebook)
Subjects: LCSH: Tacos—United States.
Classification: LCC TX836 .R35 2020 | DDC 641.84—dc23
LC record available at https://lccn.loc.gov/2019026436

doi:10.7560/316528

For my wife, Jessica, and our son, Diego,
for their patience and humor, and for two of the
best friends and traveling companions a person
could ask for, Jon Daniel and Robert Strickland.
None of this would be possible without you.

Contents

AMER

TAG

RICAN

COS

Your Taco Country Guide

My passion for tacos began when I started dating my wife, Jessica, a Texas native of Mexican American heritage. Each time we called for takeout from the Chinese-owned Tex-Mex storefront along the Sunset Park stretch of Brooklyn's Fifth Avenue, we ordered an extra batch of spongy, made-to-order flour tortillas. It made us feel like we were doing something humorously wrong. After all, my wife and I were living in Sunset Park, a Chinese and Latino enclave in south Brooklyn, where we could order tortas cubana the size of catcher's mitts at the back of bodegas or charred frog legs from a signage-less street cart. But we needed those seemingly contraband flour tortillas. We needed them for breakfast tacos.

It started on a Saturday. That first morning I opened the sliding hollow wood door into the living room–kitchen area of our railroad apartment. A vermillion-stained package of Mexican chorizo lay torn open on the counter. Next to it was a carton of brown eggs. And she made breakfast tacos.

Those flour tortillas—freshly re-heated on the flames of our gas range and bearing the brown-to-black islands to show for it—enveloped a reddish-orange mass of eggs and soft chorizo almost as spreadable as butter. A shot of shredded Longhorn cheese helped to bind the filling. And . . . silence. Saturday mornings were dedicated to breakfast tacos from then on.

Sunset Park was a great neighborhood in which to start my taco explorations. There are taco counters in the back of Mexican bodegas and taco stands on the streets. I remember one, a wood stall that leaned against a bodega, where a woman dished out two-dollar tacos de barbacoa de chivo.

Pay a couple of bucks, get the taco handed to you with napkins—no plates!—and head off to run your errands or to find a stoop and enjoy the gamy strings of bronzed goat meat. Down the street there was a restaurant decorated with crushed velvet that occasionally had a tomato-stewed, queso blanco–stuffed, squash blossom taco that melted herbacious and sweet. It was during a meal at Tacos Matamoros on Sunset Park's Fifth Avenue—where I had already consumed several tacos de cabeza, the beef cheek meat studded with glob-ules of fat demanding to be slurped—that Jessica persuaded me to eat my first taco de lengua. The corn tortilla cradled steamed beef tongue topped with chopped white onion and cilantro to brighten up the meat. And, of course, we had that Chinese-run Tex-Mex delivery joint.

It wasn't as if I wasn't already obsessed with food. Sunset Park also had a Puerto Rican restaurant with Formica booths, white rice good enough to eat by itself, and a streetside walkup window where I ordered pastelillos (Puerto Rican empanadas) filled with cheese or ground beef. One bite and I was thrust, stomach first, back into my maternal grandmother's house in Arecibo, Puerto Rico, the town of my birth. There, mi mamita, Dolores Rivera, would fry up a batch of pastelillos for breakfast because nine-year-old me desperately needed those golden brown, rough-bubbled handpies at seven in the morning.

The restaurant's roasted pig's foot and knuckle, plus half a roll of paper towels, was all I needed to recall the last time I saw José Antonio Maldo-nado, my maternal grandfather, Abuelo Papa. I was five. Both sides of the family, the Ralats and the Maldonados, were gathered at my grandparents' house—the house where my mother grew up, where my folks met and fell in love—for a farewell party. The next day, my parents, my sisters, and I were heading back to Florida. Summer vacation was over. And in walked Abuelo Papa, a whole-roasted pig across his broad, leathered shoulders. He swung it over his head and onto the table in front of me. I was barely tall enough to look over the table, but I was suddenly sitting on it—Abuelo Papa had quickly lifted me onto the table—next to the beast with crackling, tawny-colored skin. "Metelo, Joséito," he said. I reached behind the pig's ears and pulled with both hands. Its face easily separated from its skull in a salty blast of mi isla. I smiled, said "Gracias," and hugged my grandfather. When we got back to Orlando, the call came that the old man had died. Undiagnosed heart trouble, I was told.

It would be years before I launched the *Taco Trail* blog and made food writing my full-time gig. My day job then was as the editor of a now-defunct New York City–based neuropsychiatry journal, but I started freelancing for the *New York Press* (also defunct), writing personal essays, restaurant reviews, and installments for the "Cheap Eats" section. One piece featured what I considered to be the best restaurant along Arthur Avenue in the Bronx's Little Italy, Estrellita Poblana III.

Arthur Avenue, in the Belmont section of the Bronx, is renowned for its indoor retail market, mom-and-pop shops filled with imported goods, and, of course, Italian restaurants slinging pasta a million ways. Mexican food should be the last thing that comes to mind. Yet, just a fried calamari's throw from the likes of Dominick's and Umberto's Clam House II, where a red sauce-soaked plate costs more than a mid-twenty-something writer can afford, the diminutive Estrellita Poblana III caters to the immigrants, most from Puebla or Oaxaca, employed in the kitchens of the aforementioned restaurants. It's a microcosm of the Mexican immigrant community in New York.

Having heard the plaudits for this community for years, my wife and I, along with some friends, trekked an hour and a half on the D train from Brooklyn to the Bronx. We imagined the taste of fresh mozzarella and pancetta on our lips. The line for Casa della Mozzarella was long, but the prosciutto, sorpresseta, and parmesan were worth the wait. The same went for Teitel Brothers Wholesale Grocery. One hundred ravioli ran us $10.50 at another shop. And since food shopping works up a carbohydrate-lusting appetite, off we went for carbonara and matriciana. Everything was out of our budget.

Then we came across Estrellita Poblana III. We got a round of Mexican Cokes (the imported sodas are made with sugar, not corn syrup like its American progenitor). The tamales oaxaqueño, with a slide of mole in the center and banana leaf wrapper on the outside, reduced a friend's speech to monosyllables: "Must. Not. Waste. One. Taste. Must. Have. Again." The cheese enchilada was smothered in salsa and melting chunks of queso fresco piled atop its platter-length size. Two chicken breasts wore a thick shawl of mole poblano, garnished with sesame seeds. The sauce-like mole produced a burn that quickly worked its way up the nostrils, took a break in the sinuses, and rappelled down the throat. The cooks at Estrellita had succeeded where every other Mexican restaurant I had visited in New York had failed: they did mole justice. The accompanying yellow rice was fluffy, soaking up the mole. And the black beans were thick enough to eat with a fork, not a goopy mess. On a small plate was a pile of meat (goat, pork, chicken, and beef), lettuce, and cheese resting on two warm flour tortillas; tomatillo salsa or pico de gallo added a tangy bite.

For our second wedding anniversary, Jessica and I drove across Texas—twice. She wanted to introduce me to her extended family and old friends. I also ate tacos—from Taco Cabana's pearl snap shirt-staining barbacoa in Dallas-Fort Worth to Juan in a Million's signature behemoth in Austin to potato and eggs from H&H Car Wash, owned by grouch Maynard Haddad in El Paso, my in-laws' hometown. We returned to Texas a couple more times before transplanting from New York to Dallas in 2009. My frequent trips to Austin for job interviews and networking events intensified my fascination with the breakfast taco. When we decided to focus our efforts in building a life in Dallas for our family, I shifted my attention to local breakfast tacos, which weren't great. San Antonio and the Rio Grande Valley are the destinations for the best breakfast tacos.

Then came the phone call from *Dallas Observer* editor-in-chief Mark Donald. He asked me if I liked tacos. "Of course," I replied, "Everyone likes tacos."

"Great!" Mark said. "Put together a pitch for an online column and send it to me. We'll go from there."

I had never given much thought to putting regular effort into writing about tacos. I didn't thinkwriting about tacos could be a profession. But I was an unemployed writer with a wife and an infant son—none of us with health insurance—living in my mother-in-law's house. I needed money, and I already had a nominal foundation in tacos.

The original concept was an exploration of the Dallas taco scene via public transportation. I was a New Yorker without a driver's license, so DART (Dallas Area Rapid Transit) seemed as good a method as any to become acquainted with my new city's tacos. Dallas surprised me. The diversity of its tacos surprised me, too. Dallas was a taco city, and I was smitten.

The *Taco Trail* ran for a year on the *Observer* food blog before I went independent and took the name with me. I began eating tacos wherever I could, whenever I could, eventually picking up cookbooks and reference books, thanks to friends. One would return from trips to Mexico City with a book or two for me—among them, *La Tacopedia*, the first comprehensive encyclopedia of the taco. Slowly, I acquired a small library of books that allowed me to delve deeper into the world of tacos and Mexican food. But I was hungry for more. I needed practical knowledge from south of the border to bolster my academic understanding and stateside experience.

Patricia Sharpe, the James Beard Award–winning *Texas Monthly* food critic, brought me on board for what would become the November 2018 cover story: "The 120 Tacos You Must Eat Before You Die." I visited cities across North Texas—Dallas, Fort Worth, Richardson, Addison, Denton, Grapevine—as well as Midland, Odessa, El Paso, and Corpus Christi. I was also responsible for sidebars, co-writing the introduction, and supplemental content. That's where a visit to Mexico City came in.

It was difficult to breathe. I was sitting in the backseat of a cab, inching along the smoggy streets of Mexico City, and I couldn't have been happier. For more than five years, ever since I had dedicated myself to the exploration of tacos under the banner of the *Taco Trail*, I had been trying to get to this sprawling metropolis—the center of the taco-verse. I had eaten so many tacos, written so many taqueria reviews, and read so many Spanish-language reference books, and still I couldn't escape the feeling that I wouldn't truly be taken seriously until I had journeyed to the source. I knew I had to go beyond the books and seek out the elements that had inspired the many tacos I had consumed.

So here I was at last, one January, alongside two trusty companions—Dallas photographer Robert Strickland and Nick Zukin, owner of Mi Mero Mole and Mexican-style pizza place Zapapizza in Portland, Oregon. We had devised a potentially exhausting tasting itinerary: twenty taco spots to visit over two-and-a-half days. Nick, who had been visiting Mexico's capital for fifteen years, is a connoisseur of guisados, the sweeping range of stews, stir-fries, and homey dishes that represent one of the city's most popular street foods. Essentially breakfast tacos, the fillings served from large bowls at taquerias and stands until roughly two in the afternoon daily, guisados can provoke a blissful response from a Chilango (Mexico City resident). Nick had played a critical role in creating our list, which included market stalls, taquerias, and brick-and-mortar restaurants. Our focus would be on two of the city's great specialties: the taco al pastor and the taco de guisado.

We set off in search of guisados, stopping first at Tacos Las Cazuelas. There is no sign, just a white wood-frame stand at the corner of Londres and Havre in Colonia Juárez. To a Texan, some guisados might sound familiar: picadillo, weenies and eggs, and chorizo and potatoes. Others, not so much: cauliflower fritters, rajas con crema, and sardines with nopales. At Las Cazuelas, I ordered a taco with bistec en salsa pasilla. Slices of tender, contorted beef in a dark chile sauce chockfull of coffee and chocolate notes rested on doubled-up corn tortillas with a whiff of a cornfield. It was heavenly, and I began to understand how just the simple mention of a Mexico City guisado could inspire rapture.

Tacos Hola, in La Condesa, has been dishing out guisados for more than forty years. The menu is dozens deep and, as owner David "El Guero" Millan instructed from behind the counter, it comes with one rule: one taco at a time. A smoky rajas con crema—thin strips of roasted poblanos cooked in a light cream sauce on a helping of yellow rice—was all I needed anyway. (And the rice was handy, soaking up the salsa, and therefore saving my shirt, while adding texture.) It's not unusual in Mexico City to see mashed potatoes, French fries, or whole pinto beans piled atop two or three meats in a taco. I had seen those garnishes in photos. But now the lineup was within reach. An American taco purist might shiver at the variety beyond onion and cilantro. I, for one, was practically vibrating with joy.

At a nameless guisado stand on the corner of Tlaxcala and Chilpancingo, an unplanned stop, a taco de albondiga—a solitary meatball with a gauzy tomato salsa over rice—gave off the aroma of a treasured Sunday dinner. It was so mesmerizing that as I bent over to toss the paper liner into the trashcan, I knocked my head on the underside of the stand's metal counter. Later, at Restaurante El Bajío, in the northern Azcapotzalco neighborhood, we got a survey of classic Mexican flavors. This was our break from a strict taco diet, with stellar warm carnitas and pillowy, bluish-green gordas infladas (inflated fatties). Resembling uncrimped puffy tacos, they were made with a masa stuffed with black beans and then flash fried. Every bit as delicate as San Antonio's signature taco, they left me dazzled. (Of course, is there anything quite as magical to a Texan as a puffy taco from the Alamo City? Unlikely.)

We saved the taco al pastor, perhaps the city's most famous taco, for our last night. At El Huequito, one of the taquerias that claims its invention and features homemade tortillas by request, we put in an order, then sat back to watch the trompero, or trompo operator. He turned up the flame for a quick crust on the marinated pork, sliced the meat, and finished our servings with a shot of drippings. This kind of magic show isn't possible in Texas; health departments aren't so keen on open-flame spits. Alongside the al pastor were several tacos con queso. The options included skirt steak, marinated chicken, and chorizo, all with cheese. This was not a mere sprinkle of factory-shredded cheese. No, king-size cheese comforters cover these tacos. What's more, queso fundido (chile con queso's South of the Border antecedent) was available for spooning on to tortillas and tacos.

And then there was la gringa, invented in Mexico City. A gringa is a taco al pastor on a flour tortilla with melted white cheese. It was created in the 1970s, the story goes, because an American college co-ed ordered the customized taco at El Fogoncito, a taqueria in the Anzures neighborhood, so often that the taqueros gave it a permanent berth on the menu, christening it "la gringa," the white girl's taco. Despite its provenance and decades of existence, a taco with a flour tortilla and cheese would be decried by many Americans as inauthentic. Meanwhile, Mexicans continued to enjoy gringas and the campechana, a close cousin composed of longaniza (chorizo) and grilled steak (usually bistec) caught in a net of melted white cheese (usually queso Oaxaca, but sometimes mass-produced mozzarella is substituted). Chilangos in particular and Mexicans in general love cheese. I knew this before visiting Mexico City, but to see the depth of the passion was something else.

Then there was the pyramid of thinly shaved pork al pastor meat atop a house-made corn tortilla, the whole thing draped with cheese. Butting up against this formation were several more corn tortillas. The addition of cheese to the iconic taco al pastor erased the border between Americanized Mexican food and reverently guarded Mexican food. There was no heresy. There was only a taco. An inevitable taco. Here was the comforting synthesis of cherished foods producing something nearly perfect. The centuries of skirmishes over what constitutes legitimate Mexican food—beginning with the Nueva España colonial ruling class branding corn as the food of the uneducated, impoverished poor and continuing through Diana Kennedy declaring Tex-Mex as blasphemy—came to a sticky end.

The American idea of the taco is narrow. We insist on it being "authentically Mexican." "Novelty" and "gringo" are often used to describe anything beyond pork, beef, or chicken—and yet in fewer than three days I had encountered a variety greater than any I could imagine finding back home. I was as content as I could be for the short time I was in the city, more open to possibility and hungry for greater culinary crossover between the United States and its southern neighbor.

Then it hit me: the Abuelita Principle.

Mexican Americans have been known to pump their fists in the air with cries of inauthenticity upon encountering a cheesy taco like the alambres. This El Paso favorite tops grilled beef, soft bacon, and bell pepper with a lacy cap of melted Muenster cheese. "My abuelita made real Mexican food! *That* is not Mexican food," they insist. Everyone's abuelita—Spanish for "little grandmother" and Anglo code for "authentic Mexican cook"—prepared real Mexican food. It's true. It isn't true. Authenticity only exists on paper. Every family tweaks recipes according to their tastes, creating a new, distinct Mexican food that changes with the street address. This is the Abuelita Principle. It simultaneously informs and undermines the dynamic culinary culture that is Mexican food.

The problem is that the Abuelita Principle can dampen the full enjoyment of a gastronomy that is kinetic and expansive. It restricts Mexican food to a nonexistent rigid ideal. Lebanese immigrants—or Iraqi immigrants, depending on whom you ask—are behind the creation of tacos al pastor. Pork isn't indigenous to the New World. Yet, tacos al pastor are seen as an iconic Mexican dish.

The Abuelita Principle is ignorance at best, racism at worst. Let the food go. Revel in its vibrancy. Let it play. When you're ready, take a bite without making a knee-jerk criticism. You might be surprised. And American tacos, in particular, have much to offer in the way of surprises.

It's possible to order chopped steak wrapped in a corn tortilla and adorned with diced raw white onion and cilantro—the common (mis)conception of a street taco—in city, town, and suburb alike, be it American Falls, Idaho, or Miami, Florida. Just like Mexico City, for those stuck on the concept of the street taco. To be clear, though, the only definition of a street taco is a taco ordered on the street—whether it's eaten on the street depends on the consumer. The combination of a tortilla, filling, and salsa is not a foreign concept to Americans. But the traditional taco—by that I mean a classic offering like al pastor—is Mexican. Not American.

Very specific tacos are pegged to very specific places in Mexico. For example, the taco gobernador, filled with a cheese-netted shrimp, is from the Northern Mexican state of Sinaloa. And the ochre-hued pork al pastor belongs to specific regions of Mexico, including, as noted, el capital de los tacos, Mexico City. In other words, tacos are representative and reflective of their time and place. They're regional. That's true on both sides of the US-Mexico border.

So what are America's regional tacos? That's what this book lays out. To put it simply, the evolution of American tacos, like all tacos and beloved dishes, is fueled by regional population shifts, ingredient market availability, and culinary adaptation. There is the old school crispy taco endemic to Texas, the Southwest, Southern California, and the Midwest. Many consider the brittle U-shaped form to be The American Taco. But you already knew that—especially if you grew up experiencing weekly taco nights at home between the 1960s and 1990s.

Cousin to the fried taco shell is the San Antonio–style puffy taco. Light in body and effervescent in appearance and stocked with the Tex-Mex trinity of lettuce, tomatoes, and cheese that obscures the main filling, the puffy taco is a Lone Star State treasure. Just the thought of it induces salivation. Before becoming known as the "puffy taco," it was lumped in with other fried tacos, collectively known as "crispy tacos." Unlike the Texas breakfast taco or the Korean taco, the puffy taco, my favorite of America's regional taco styles, hasn't successfully trekked to all corners of the country. And there are tacos that can't be extracted from their birthplace, like those that are part of the Alta California cuisine.

The chapters in this book are dedicated to styles, charting the stories of tacos through places and people, using newspaper accounts, advertisements, and online information. For older styles, like breakfast tacos and Jewish-style tacos, there is an emphasis on newspaper accounts and advertisements. Newspapers are the voice of the people. Through their pages, we can read what people of a certain time and place cared about, what they embraced or disdained, what they liked to eat, and what they were curious about, both culturally and gastronomically. Newspapers expressed and continue to express—even if the internet has usurped some of the role and influence of print—people's whims, desires, fears, everything. In the case of recently developed or developing styles, such as Los Angeles–born Korean tacos that I call "K-Mex" tacos and the rising Sur-Mex tacos, historical research skews toward online information.

Sidebars and boxes highlighting sub-styles of each featured taco dot the text. Each chapter concludes with a list of restaurants, taquerias, and/or trucks where the style discussed can be enjoyed. It's a curated list of what I consider either the best of the best or vendors of prime examples of a style. In other words, not all the vendors mentioned in each chapter are listed at the end of the respective chapter. Spanish-language words are not italicized. Italicization of non-English words serves to exoticize the culture that breathed the words into existence. Spanish isn't a foreign language in our taco country. Part narrative-driven social history, part taco trail guidebook, *American Tacos* is the culmination of eight years of research that has included traveling across North America to eat what I consider the perfect food and to talk to the people who make tacos and consider them an extension and representation of home.

This is a living document charting the dynamic and developing regional American tacos. Some are further along in development than others. Traditional fried tacos are arguably the oldest style found north of the Rio Grande. Compare these long-established crispy delights to Sur-Mex tacos. Although this blending of Southern US and Mexican cooking has been around since at least the 1990s, Sur-Mex tacos are still moseying along the route to codification. The development of the style has been slowed by Anglo American chefs' propensity for whimsy and a reflexive assertion of control of the Other. Still, the tacos of the American South include locally grown or produced ingredients used in typically Mexican ways. In contrast, K-Mex tacos came into their own only after 2008, but gained an almost immediate national popularity that spurred a quick maturation and entry into the realm of legitimate tacos. If not for that rapid embrace, K-Mex tacos probably would not have progressed beyond ingredients that just happen to be Korean folded in a Mexican tortilla.

"Chef-driven" typically refers to the bending of another nation's cherished cuisine to a (usually Anglo) cook's will or "creative vision." Chef-driven tacos weren't supposed to evolve beyond a forty-dollar entrée compacted into a four-dollar taco concept. Such tacos should have resisted homogenization, but community dialogues between kitchen professionals and the demographics they serve had another thing in mind. Chef-driven tacos evolved into a definable style that occasionally flirts with original free-form expression. In other words, tacos work on their own time . . . and there is no time like taco time.

As I traveled for tacos, I was repeatedly reminded that the culture surrounding this food is rich and surprising and worth deeper and deeper dives. Some of the greatest tacos I've ever had were in Memphis, Tennessee, a city with a rapidly increasing Latino population. I've had awful tacos in Texas, the state I call home, where tacos are the first thing you reach for after turning off your alarm clock each morning.

And then there's Tucson, where I hauled ten pounds of Sonoran-style flour tortillas from Anita Street Market. At Tacos Apson, carne asada is produced in purity, beginning with the mesquite, and at La Indita, an Indigenous Mexican restaurant, the fry bread and the signature melted orange cheese-caked Tarascan tacos are as glorious as the murals. From Micha's "Pattie" Beef Taco, a thin hamburger patty cooked to perfection then wedged into a tortilla before it is fried, to Che West's green-garlic tortilla, Tucson is a dream.

Chicago is no second-class taco city. Immigration has transformed it into a taco capital, with some of the best Michoacán-style tacos outside of Michoacán. (I'm looking at you, Carnitas Uruapan.) Chicago is also keeping alive the tradition of birria, a rich roasted and stewed goat dish, at legendary restaurants like Birrieria Zaragoza. The best seat in the tiny restaurant is at the counter across from the chopping board with a peek at the tortilla press. Thanks to San Antonio transplants Mario and Ana Vela and their taqueria, Amanecer Taco Shop, Chicagoland, as the metropolitan region is called, at last has breakfast tacos. But theirs is not the only breakfast taco operation in the Windy City. Café Tola #2, a corner spot with a painted pink-and-white sign and an exterior decorated with a Voltron mural, serves large breakfast tacos on flour tortillas. An hour or so north of Chicago, Racine, in Wisconsin, has nurtured tacos dorados (golden tacos) so well, it's a shining fried taco city.

And in the greater Kansas City area, the signature parmesan-dusted fried taco, a product of culinary exchange between the region's long-standing Italian and Mexican populations, is disappearing under a double wave of modern and traditional tacos. Kansas City's indigenous taco is something I encountered in Dallas well after I submitted the first draft of *American Tacos*. I had caught word of a pop-up offering Kansas City–style tacos in my neighborhood. What I found was Tacos & Art. Operated by Kansas City native Lisa Martinez, Tacos & Art sold deep-fried tacos that evoke traditional tacos dorados in that the corn tortillas are filled (in this case with ground beef), folded, and sealed with toothpicks before frying. When the tacos are removed from the fryer, the toothpicks are pulled from the tortillas and the filling is garnished with lettuce, a thick salsa, and then finished with parmesan.

Most of all, I've learned that tacos are a gift to be appreciated and enjoyed with friends and strangers. No other food in America brings people together like tacos. Nothing is fully itself until it nestles in a tortilla—and everything ends up in a tortilla. I would like to think consuming tacos makes for better people, making for a better taco country. And America is taco country.

Breakfast taco at Ms. G's Tacos N' More in McAllen, Texas.

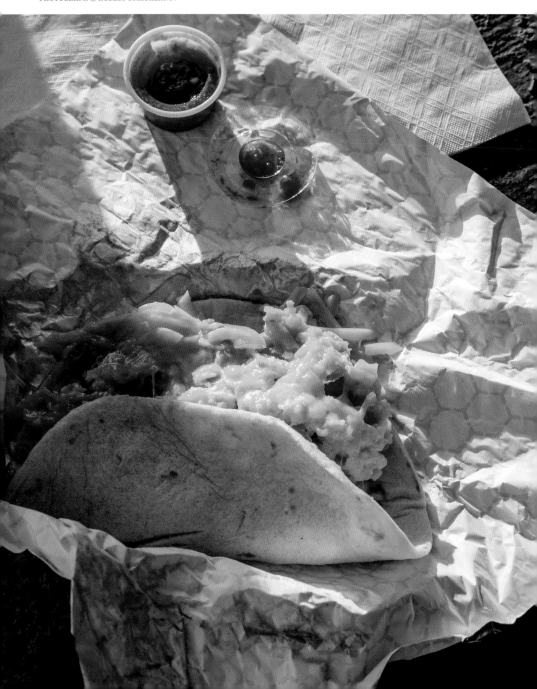

CHAPTER 1

Breakfast Tacos

From dawn until whenever

REGION(S): Texas, with outposts in California, New York, Denver, and a handful of other cities

CLASSIC EXAMPLES: Chorizo and egg; potato, egg, and cheese; migas; and carne guisada

TORTILLA(S): Mainly flour; occasionally corn

LOWDOWN: The breakfast taco is the celebrity of the taco world. Worth fighting for, it is the Helen of Troy of tacos.

You might have heard about a spat over breakfast tacos. It began with a 2016 article by New York–based writer Matthew Sedacca. He claimed Austin was the true home of breakfast tacos—not San Antonio, not Corpus Christi, not the Rio Grande Valley. People freaked. Most of the flame war, however, was tongue-in-cheek outrage. Take the online petition to exile the author of the article that sparked the intrastate conflict: "The subject of tacos, especially in reference to their origin and quality, has long been a sensitive issue and constant source of inter-regional strife within Texas. Without fail, sophomoric claims of taco superiority have been issued from Austin-based brunch-chair experts on a nearly annual basis, threatening the harmony between the city of Austin and the cities with populations of Native Texans greater than 10%." The petition recommended several possible actions, including the "surrender of the offender into custody of the City of San Antonio for mandatory re-education and re-habilitation" or the "establishment of an observed 'San Antonio Day' sponsored annually by the City of Austin, to include [San Antonio NBA team] Spurs-themed parades, statements of praise and admiration for our bicycle community, and the public singing of songs that beg forgiveness for all taco-related transgressions and blasphemies." The hostilities made the newswires. Gustavo Arellano, author of *Taco USA: How Mexican Food Conquered America*, dug into the archives and posted the date of the earliest newspaper print mention of "breakfast tacos": the July 23, 1975, reference to a food tour in San Antonio in the Phoenix-based *Arizona Republic*. (But, as we'll see later, breakfast tacos actually had been noted in print nearly twenty years earlier.)

Wasting no time, Steve Adler, the mayor of Austin, declared war on San Antonio. A treaty summit was held with San Antonio Mayor Ivy Taylor to end "The Great Breakfast Taco War of 2016," as Adler had christened the hostilities. Peace was accorded. Breakfast tacos had united opposing parties.

It wasn't the first time breakfast tacos have been used to bring politicians together. In 2013, in an effort to unify a fractured Texas congressional delegation—one that for decades had found common ground in representing their home state until redistricting drew a proverbial line in the sand—two Lone Star State representatives, Pete Gallego (D-Alpine) and Kevin Brady (R-The Woodlands), called a breakfast taco confab. "This is beyond being bipartisan, this is about being Texan," Brady told the *San Antonio Express-News*. Even Ted Cruz showed up.

This is all neat stuff. It's also pretty much the extent of disseminated knowledge of breakfast tacos. There has been a lot of blogging, internet squabbling, some radio segments, and brief mentions in social history books. In *Taco USA*, his seminal exploration of Americanized Mexican food north of the border, Arellano skims the history and components of breakfast tacos, noting the whiteness conferred on them via their connection to Austin:

> San Antonio also claims the breakfast taco, but Austin has usurped it as its own. No matter who created it, its countenance seems engineered with an eye toward the American palate. Instead of corn tortillas, they're made with small flour ones. The ingredients can occasionally be Mexican, but American morning-time stalwarts dominate. . . . It seems like such a natural meal would be the next great Tex-Mex hit, but breakfast tacos haven't really caught on across the rest of the United States.

Arellano did more digging during the beginning days of the Great Breakfast Taco War of 2016 and pinned breakfast tacos to San Antonio.

Fall 2018 saw a flare-up in what we might as well consider the "Texas Taco Wars." It began with the cover of the *D Magazine* September issue, which declared Dallas a "Taco City" and teased the taco feature I wrote for the magazine. No other city was mentioned on the cover. Or in the tweet that revealed the cover and that pissed off seemingly everyone in San Antonio. The Alamo City mayor, Ron Nirenberg, felt the need to insert himself in the dustup with a tweet that just said, "LOL." Even before the issue hit newsstands, San Antonio media outlets, including TV stations, accused the feature article and its writer, me, of proclaiming Dallas to be the greatest of Texas taco metropolises.

That's right. No one had read the article and yet everyone was claiming that Dallas couldn't have supremacy over anything taco-related in Texas. Folks who had lived in Dallas for a year or so argued they knew everything there was to know about Dallas tacos, and, they said, Dallas tacos sucked. Tim Rogers, the editor of *D Magazine*, and I invited the San Antonio mayor to a private taco tour of Dallas. The politician never responded. Once the issue was publicly available and the article posted online, readers saw that San Antonio was mentioned only once—and then only in passing in the introduction: "It's now possible to enjoy tacos with roots in Mexico City, Monterrey, Sonora, Sinaloa, Oaxaca, Michoacán, Jalisco, Huasteca, the Rio Grande Valley, Tijuana, and San Antonio." The San Antonio tacos I was referring to in the introduction were puffy tacos and breakfast tacos. Wisely, this time, Austinites stayed out of the one-sided spat.

San Antonio fell quiet too, but only after former food and nightlife editor Jessica Elizarraras of the *San Antonio Current* alt-weekly told everyone to chill out. In her column, she tracked the tortilla-based conflicts that started with Sedacca's *Eater* article and Arellano's Arizona newspaper clip find, noting the quiet that followed before San Antonio felt insulted by the "Taco City" cover. "Can we not?" Elizarraras wrote. "To deny other cities in Texas the claim to great tacos is to deny the ingenuity of Mexicans who are bringing their sabores to the states. And to champion the city's tacos over

another city's, as our mayor did, only highlights our inferiority complex."
She also noted that all I wanted was "peace and understanding."

Indeed, ahead of publication, she asked me for comment and included
my response in her essay:

> I appreciate Texans' taco passions. The seriousness with which we hold and
> care for the perfect food, speaks to how fundamental the tortilla—corn or
> flour—is in our daily lives, . . . A city's residents ought to take pride in their
> hometown tacos. If not, why are they even living there? That another city takes
> great pride in its tacos doesn't detract from another city's relationship with a
> food or any object. My hope is that we recognize that tacos are a force for good,
> that tacos unify more than divide, that there is more to the taco experience than
> your immediate experience, and that, whatever Texas town you find yourself in,
> a great taco is not far out of reach. Even in Dallas.

Everybody seemed to take a deep breath and settle down—that is,
until January 2019, when a *San Antonio Current* writer, in an attempt to
ignite another taco war, brought up a November 2018 *Food & Wine* magazine roundup of the top breakfasts in every state. The *Current* writer was
dismayed that a New York–based magazine would describe Austin as the
breakfast taco capital of Texas. This time around, however, no one took
the bait. Readers likely saw that online post's time stamp and moved on.

As we'll see, San Antonio has a rightful claim to early breakfast taco
development, but the provenance of those vittles is the borderland of the
Rio Grande Valley, where breakfast taco flour tortillas can reach the size
of tricycle wheels. In his worldwide survey of the history of Mexican food
in *Planet Taco*, Jeffrey M. Pilcher chalks up the rise of the breakfast taco to
its potential as a fast-food alternative. Still, the full story has yet to be told.

To tell it, however, we need to travel to Mexico, where the taco was born
and where the tortilla became the foundation of the taco. For hundreds of
years, people have filled corn tortillas with nourishment and folded them
for eating at all times of day. That includes first thing in the morning. But
it wasn't until the late eighteenth to early nineteenth centuries that "taco"

began to refer to the food item we know. According to one theory, its origin is tied to silver mines not far from the US-Mexico border. The miners who searched for ore called the small gunpowder-filled rolled paper charges "tacos" ("plugs" in English). Eventually, the word was used to refer to the small filled, rolled, or folded tortillas that the miners ate in the morning. These steamed breakfast tacos de mineros were an energizing foldable exterior containing a dollop of meat or beans with a zap from salsa. (From the beginning, tacos were something to get all fired up about.) Those tacos evolved into tacos de canasta (basket tacos), a Mexico City breakfast favorite prepared by a vendor and placed in a basket (a *canasta*) to be taken by bike to the taquero's usual spot and sold to workers en route to their offices each morning. While in the basket between home and the selling station, the tacos steam.

As the taco evolved and made its way across the northern frontier, there developed tacos de guisados. These home-style stews and stir-fries—ranging from picadillo, chorizo, and potatoes to chiles relleno to eggs and ham and cauliflower fritters—were usually enjoyed in the morning. Along the US-Mexico border are the early examples of what we classify as breakfast tacos. Even now, you can get picadillo or egg tacos on either fresh corn or flour tortillas in Matamoros, Tamaulipas, immediately across the border from Brownsville, Texas. Breakfast tacos are sometimes called "tacos mañaneros" (morning tacos) in border states such as Tamaulipas and Nuevo León. These border breakfast tacos are as Mexican as they are American.

It wasn't until June 5, 1904, in the *San Antonio Light* newspaper, that the taco was first referenced in the Lone Star State, and then it was on a menu alongside enchiladas, tamales, and cabrito asado (grilled, milk-fed kid goat), a South Texas/northern Mexico specialty. Tacos quickly moved from advertised menus to illustrations and dispatches, including the crime beat. In 1906 El Paso, "Candelario Oropeza of Mexico City, a semi-cannibal of the most savage type" cut off his wife's ears and stewed them in a chile sauce before offering the dish to her. It was also said that he rolled the stew into a "taco" for his own consumption. Oropeza had prepared a taco de guisado. Seven years later, the *San Antonio Express* listed a taco de frijole (bean taco) as a standard dish at the Mexican table and included an illustration of a "typical kitchen in Mexico, from a sketch from life." In it, a woman with dark, braided hair is kneeling at a metate, grinding corn for masa. Tortillas are seen cooking on the comal to her left. In February 1915, an article in the Spanish-language *El Paso Morning Times* about Isadora Duncan's theories of child development described "macaroni sandwiches," an unfamiliar food to its readership, as being something akin to "tacos."

There is abundant anecdotal evidence that breakfast tacos—that is, tacos served for breakfast, not always the common stateside concept of breakfast tacos—were prepared by grandmothers and mothers in South Texas, San Antonio, and, later, the Hill Country, decades before Austinites got hooked on them. Then there's the fact that for most of taco history, breakfast tacos—or tacos consumed at any time of day or in any preparation—were just called "tacos." The earliest stateside citation I found is in the May 24, 1959, *San Antonio Express and News*, which describes one Joe Acosta, who opened a small "'taco hut,' on a West Side st. [*sic*] some time ago." Due to poor sales, Acosta, it was reported, "did the next best thing, he 'went to them,' by loading his little Chevy with tasty flour tortillas, and heading for the downtown area." Business boomed. "If you see a citizen munching on a bean or egg taco at the corner of St. Mary's and Travis about noon-time, you can just about rest assured, Joe Acosta made the sale."

San Antonio's West Side is a historically Latino neighborhood and the home of such institutions as the Guadalupe Cultural Arts Center and Ray's Drive Inn. Why Acosta had difficulty selling tacos on the West Side is unclear. It's counterintuitive, actually. Acosta, it would seem, would do gangbusters there. Were Hispanic San Antonians just not that into breakfast tacos in the late 1950s? Were breakfast tacos an Anglo-favored treat in the Alamo City? At this point, that is also unclear.

Breakfast tacos were culturally significant enough in the Valley shortly thereafter that a politician saw the advantage of eating them on a campaign stop, as gubernatorial candidate Don Yarborough did when he visited the Lower Rio Grande Valley in May 1962. Newspapers across the state described Yarborough consuming tacos for breakfast while a mariachi band from Matamoros played for him.

A tracking of newspaper restaurant advertisements and published school cafeteria menus shows that breakfast tacos continued to increase in popularity in San Antonio and in the Valley. Furthermore, the appreciation of these tacos spread up the border to Del Rio, Texas, and into a ring around Austin in towns as far apart as Kerrville in the Texas Hill Country (110 miles from Austin and about 70 miles from San Antonio) and Seguin in Central Texas (approximately 60 miles from Austin and about 40 miles from San Antonio), drawing close to New Braunfels, a small town between Austin and San Antonio. Breakfast tacos had even popped up in Dallas in the early 1970s before scant evidence existed of their production in Austin.

Many of the early breakfast taco joints are gone. In Seguin, Pancho's Taco Villa, Macia's Bakery, and Dandy's Downtown Deli are no longer in business. However, Salazar's Grocery, where Los Primos Mexican Food To Go was once located, remains at its original address, 1104 Avenue D. The business, a third-generation family-run shop, now includes a tax preparation office. In 1977, Los Primos was selling general breakfast tacos, beef barbacoa tacos, and carne guisada tacos for one dollar. Kerrville's breakfast taco pioneers have all but been wiped from the map. The building Maria's Café once called home is abandoned. El Nopalito has been replaced by the Guadalupe Valley Electric Cooperative. So many more Kerrville taco spots are gone. In their place are popular eateries like Rita's Famous Tacos, Del Norte Restaurant, as well as Mary's Tacos, which offers large tacos filled with country sausage, potato, and beans; carne guisada, potatoes, and beans; and potato, egg, beans, bacon, and cheese. Two ought to sate the average customer. In 1985, the Twelfth Annual East Hill Country Tour, a three-day bicycle ride through the verdant Texas Hill Country, treated participants to "South Texas breakfast tacos." Rita Guerra opened her namesake taqueria in 2005, but only after the Kerrville Health Department insisted that she establish

GUAJARDO'S TACO HOUSE

IS NOW OPEN FROM
7:00 A.M. UNTIL 10:00 P.M.
MONDAY TO FRIDAY
SATURDAY WILL BE
OPEN FROM 7:00 A.M. - 2:00 A.M.

MENU
BARBEQUE TACOS
CHORRIZO & BEAN TACOS
EGG & CHORRIZO TACOS
GUISADO TACOS
POTATO & EGG TACO
PORK SKIN & BEAN TACO
MENUDO & TAMALES AVAILABLE DAILY

TRY OUT SPECIAL LUNCH PLATE DAILY

101 AVE. T   CALL IN YOUR ORDER AT **775-7337** FOR HOME DELIVERY

Guajardo's Taco House advertisement,
which ran in the March 10, 1973, edition of
the *Del Rio News-Herald.*

a brick-and-mortar or be shut down. This was shortly after she began selling breakfast tacos to workers and then door-to-door. Now Rita's Famous Tacos is a must-visit Hill Country taqueria.

Approximately two and one-half hours away in the southwest Texas border town of Del Rio, Guajardo's Taco House advertised "Barbeque Tacos, Chorrizo [*sic*] & Bean Tacos, Egg & Bean Tacos, Guisado Tacos, Potato & Egg Tacos and Pork Skin & Bean Tacos," all of which in contemporary parlance are categorized as breakfast tacos. The 1973 advertisement—one of many placed in the *Del Rio News Herald*—simply listed these choices as tacos. (It should be noted that any instance of "barbeque," "BBQ," or "barbecue" tacos could refer to barbacoa. Moreover, notice that guisados get a separate mention.) Guajardo's was well regarded enough in the community that Del Rioans could purchase tickets for city events at the restaurant. The street address of Guajardo's is now a house and is surrounded by other residents and bordered by train tracks. Other notable Del Rio breakfast taco spots included Quick Taco (now a loan office) and Joe's Taco House on Avenue F (the street and restaurant no longer exist). The building once occupied by El Super Taco, which produced homemade flour tortillas and offered border standards, such as tacos rancheros, machacado (pulverized dried salt beef that has been rehydrated), and breakfast tacos, is now a party store. Doc Holiday's, which opened in 1983 as a honky-tonk, is the only remaining business from the city's initial breakfast taco boom. During the country and western nightclub's grand opening party, breakfast tacos were featured as a late-night treat.

From one historical homage to another: the Jimmy Carter Taco was born in 1976. In honor of the legume-farming president's election, San

Antonio Mexican restaurant owner Osvaldo Rodriguez invented the peanut and egg taco. "One customer has grown a liking for them and comes in every morning asking for four peanut and egg tacos," Rodriguez was quoted in the Associated Press article. "If I eat it plain—just peanuts and eggs—and don't drink coffee, it tastes like pork to me."

While breakfast tacos thrived in San Antonio, along the US-Mexico border, and in communities surrounding Austin, breakfast tacos weren't a big deal across the state until the late 1970s and '80s. Breakfast tacos were not yet cause for a culture war. They were not yet an edible commodity. They were tacos you had for breakfast. They just were and needed little explanation, even when there was a question of recent introduction, as is seen in a succinct 1975 ad for the Terrace Restaurant in the *Port Aransas South Jetty*: "Tacos for Breakfast? Yes."

In 1978, advertisements for Lou's Coffee Shop on South Congress and Live Oak in Austin offered a coupon for two-for-one breakfast tacos. But it would be eight years before breakfast tacos were a big deal. And only because Austin said so. It was 1986 and *Texas Monthly* was in full taco mode with "The Great Texas Taco Tour" feature. The importance of San Antonio in the taco landscape is clear from the subtitle: "If You're Not in San Antonio When You've Just Got to Have a Bite, Here's Where to Get Satisfaction to the North, South, East, and West." San Antonio is the taco capital of Texas and the gateway to South Texas, the region where morning tacos and the consumer are inseparable. It is where "if El Pato [a local chain] stopped making its potato-and-egg breakfast tacos, the whole Valley would probably grind to a halt."

The story makes a point of stressing San Antonio's headlining, nuanced role over Austin generally, while puffing up Austin's newest taco craze. "What a difference eighty miles makes: the Capital City's taco repertoire is neither as expansive nor as provocative as San Antonio's," James Beard Award–winning writer and *Houston Chronicle* restaurant critic Alison Cook writes. "In eatery after eatery you find the same offerings—'Austin's short list,' as I have come to think of it. Always most prominent are the breakfast items, the particular taco form on which Austinites dote (some restaurants have taken to advertising 'breakfast all day,' while a few invite you to 'build your own breakfast taco')." Again and again, the feature mentions the status of breakfast tacos in Texas cities. "Dallas isn't enamored of breakfast tacos . . . ." In Houston, "breakfast tacos haven't taken the town by storm . . . ." Of El Paso, Cook writes, "Breakfast tacos? Such newfangled notions have yet to take hold in this strongly traditional, relatively isolated city." The article goes to great lengths to impress upon the reader that tacos are cool, exposing how differently San Antonio and the Rio Grande Valley define breakfast tacos compared to Austin. For San Antonio and the Valley, breakfast tacos just are. For Austin, they're novel and hip. Was "The Great Texas Taco Tour" the first instance of Austin's "Columbusing" (the term for Anglos "discovering" something that is already a fixture in a marginalized culture or a subculture)?

To a certain extent, that is what happened. Look at what Cook sees as "the creeping popularity of the flour-tortilla-wrapped breakfast taco." Flour is the more commonly used tortilla in Austin breakfast tacos. The precise date of the flour tortilla's invention has yet to be uncovered—if it ever will be. But we do know that it developed during the colonial period in Northern Mexico, where the climate is favorable to wheat cultivation. Nineteenth-century newspaper dispatches, travel journals, and other texts are packed with references to a Mexican breakfast that consists of refried beans and other fillings in tortillas. In "A Log of the Texas-California Cattle Trail, 1854," James G. Bell writes that while in New Mexico, he "arrived in camp. . . . Had no regular supper but [ate] a piece of bacon and a flour Tortilla made by the Mexicans . . ." Sounds like a progenitor of the breakfast taco, doesn't it? Maybe.

Part of the reason breakfast tacos, especially ones using flour tortillas, seem like a recent phenomenon in the United States is that after Texas separated from Mexico, segregation and the attempts at ethnic cleansing and the theft of Mexican American ranchlands all but wiped clean the collective memory of tortillas and Mexican food in Texas and the American Southwest. Thereafter, most accounts of Mexican cuisine, often printed in newspapers and travelogues, explained what tortillas were. And when tortillas were defined, they were made of corn. Flour tortillas had seemingly disappeared. "Indian corn bread" was used in place of a spoon at mealtime or as wrappers for foods like beans. We had lost part of ourselves. It wasn't until the mid-twentieth century that flour tortillas reappeared, doing so as a novelty. The El Paso Tortilla Factory, established in 1934, introduced flour tortillas in 1955. They were "new" and "delicious," and the public was invited to the factory to watch the tortillas being made "under the most sanitary conditions." In 1970, the Taxco Food Factory in Bryan, Texas, was already selling flour tortillas to walk-in customers for "breakfast and for tacos." Moreover, at this point, flour tortilla–based tacos were served at almost every restaurant in town.

The story of how Laredo's breakfast tacos came to be called "mariachis," like the story of the origins of the flour tortillas used to make them, is thought lost to history. Specificity is critical here. At one time, a mariachi was not just a breakfast taco; rather, it was a breakfast taco wrapped in a flour tortilla eight to ten inches in diameter, filled with a single item, then grilled and slightly crisped. Now, however, the definition can accommodate more than one filling. According to one interview-based guide, it depends on whom you talk to. "How they came to be called mariachis is folklore, one story passing to the next over tacos," the story goes. "Some say it comes from mariachis playing at 5:00 a.m. in Nuevo Laredo while you eat your early morning tacos; others say eating muy spicy salsa makes you do a big grito [a Mexican yell of celebration typical of mariachi songs]."

Except the mariachi's history is not lost. According to the most reliable source, an ethoautobiographical essay by professor Norma E. Cantú, the Laredo breakfast taco's origins can be traced to Las Cazuelas, once housed in a renovated Market Street gas station. The restaurant has since closed, replaced by Obregon Mexican Restaurant #2. But as the creation tale states, Las Cazuelas was a frequent breakfast taco stop for workers at the nearby railyard. One morning, the cook told a boastful laborer who claimed the tacos weren't spicy enough that she would prepare a special taco, "one that will make him yell out like a mariachi." The very next day, the prankster cook got heavy-handed with hot sauce, the worker requested one of those "mariachi" tacos, and yell he did. The owners of Las Cazuelas were also in charge of the Laredo Community College cafeteria where they sold breakfast tacos christened "rancheros," "Mexicanos," and, yes, "mariachis." Mariachi groups are a fixture of Mexican restaurants and taquerias. I've seen bands dressed in their embroidered regalia running back and forth between eateries during a heat wave. The songs are infectious, enchanting, just like breakfast tacos. So why not christen a taco style after such cultural touchstones?

It became clear during a taco tour of Laredo that the term "mariachi" as it refers to a food is falling out of favor. Menu after menu in the border town listed the morning tacos simply as breakfast tacos. "Mariachi" is old slang, a curiosity, a remnant of a bygone era. If mariachi was ever something other than a fun word for a breakfast taco, something that differentiated Laredo from other cities, there is little evidence to support it—aside from Cantú's work. The mariachi is not long for the taco world. The breakfast taco will transform the mariachi into unfortunate cocktail trivia.

The breakfast tacos of San Antonio, Austin, and Laredo are but a small sample of the styles available across the state. At Ms. G's Tacos N' More in McAllen in the Rio Grande Valley, carne guisada, the rich Tex-Mex beef stew, sizzles with earthy spices and spills out from a small flour tortilla, a little dusty, strong, and with a good chew. An hour away at Los Girasoles Restaurant in Brownsville, diaphanous flour tortillas—go ahead, hold them up to the light—measuring twelve inches or more in diameter are folded around shimmering barbacoa (pit-cooked cow head meat) or machacado con huevo. At Sylvia's, a diner on Southmost Boulevard with an interior completely covered by Dallas Cowboy memorabilia, I ordered two breakfast tacos, one with barbacoa, one with bacon and egg. A reasonable request if you're familiar with the small flour tortillas generally used for breakfast tacos, but here, my order was laughable. Rio Grande Valley tortillas are the size of a child's bike wheel. The waitress told me she would only bring me one at a time. "If you're still hungry after that, I'll be more than happy to bring you another." I had one and I was stuffed.

In Corpus Christi, the flour tortillas are often thicker, but they vary in width. It is here that super tacos stuffed with a ridiculous number of items become common. An extreme example of the super taco is the namesake at Chacho's Tacos: fourteen inches of squishy flour tortilla straining to harness its motley innards consisting of everything else on the menu. It's gloriously, intimidatingly ideal for college buddy dares and famous for treating hangovers. Another option is weenies and eggs. The mixture was commonly employed to create a quick snack, but was associated with Mexican Americans below the poverty line in the early to mid-twentieth century. It was a source of shame, too. The sight of one usually prompted fierce teasing by Anglo classmates, as we see in reports from South Texas and in *Children of Giant*, a 2015 documentary about the making of the classic film in Marfa, Texas, with a focus on the local children cast to play Mexicans. Those children, now elderly, recount stories of racism and prejudice, including the account of Anglos forcing the children to bury a Spanish-English dictionary as a symbolic act. It's a narrative repeated by myriad taqueros and restaurant owners across Texas. But at Chacho's, the weenies and eggs are a salty, snappy filling that perks you up. It's a thing of joy. It also directly links Tex-Mex breakfast tacos with the taco de guisado such as salchicha con huevo, what we know as "weenie and eggs."

Nonetheless, it's in Austin that "tacos for breakfast" became "breakfast tacos." That is, it became a thing. By 1986, nearly ten years after he opened Tamale House on Airport Boulevard, Robert Vasquez had begun selling breakfast tacos at his tiny Austin taqueria. The tacos were dirt cheap. When other old-timers were selling their squishy daybreak treats for two dollars or more, Vasquez and his kitchen were offering breakfast tacos for eighty-nine cents. That price remained constant until Vasquez's death in

Ms. G's Tacos N' More in McAllen, Texas.
PHOTOGRAPH © ROBERT STRICKLAND.

2014, after which Tamale House closed. In an interview conducted before his passing, Vasquez recounted a nascent Austin breakfast taco scene: "A neighbor down the street was selling them, too. So I started a taco war. My tacos went down to forty-five cents each. So he went out of business, and I kept going. About that time, my mother and sister [owners of now-closed Mexico Tipico] started selling breakfast tacos, too. Now, if you look around, everybody's selling breakfast tacos. Everybody. . . . They never used to do it before. It's something that's caught on." Vasquez went on to remark on his customer base and that of other breakfast taco purveyors: "But now, 80 to 90 percent of Anglos eat tacos! I would say 80 to 90 percent of my customers are Anglo. And they eat tacos like they've never had anything before in their life! So things have changed."

Vasquez's sister, Diana Valera, and her children continue the family tradition of classic tacos at Tamale House East, a restaurant with a bucolic side garden and a metal spiral staircase leading to an apartment. It's a serene environment in which to enjoy tacos stuffed with breakfast sausage, egg, and shredded cheese or bean and cheese.

Many of the early adopters of breakfast tacos in Austin came from South Texas and beyond the border. They brought their foods with them, lending further credence to a Rio Grande Valley origin for breakfast tacos. Juan Meza of Juan in a Million is from Laredo. Aurelio Torres of Mi Madre's is also from the Valley. Others are Mexican-born entrepreneurs new to the breakfast taco concept. This includes Sergio Varela, the Papalote Taco House owner from Tejupilco, Mexico. Manuel Lopez Galvan, owner of Taqueria Chapala, is a native of Michoacán state. He opened his restaurant around the turn of the century. Each adapted to the market and was subsequently awarded for it. What is fascinating to me about Lopez and his taqueria is that Michoacán has its own breakfast taco, a taco dorado (fried taco) filled with barbacoa, which is not on the Chapala menu. Jose Luis Perez, also from Michoacán, opened his trailer El Primo in 2005. Originally, Perez says, almost all his customers were Latino. Now up to 70 percent of El Primo's clientele is Anglo. In a 2012 interview, Perez states that he has no idea why breakfast tacos are such a big deal in Austin.

Maybe because so many of the city's tacos today intentionally reflect Austin's quirky eat-local sensibility, many come with a double portion of clever names. Tacodeli is the leader in specialty, Austin-style breakfast tacos. Its main competitor in town is Torchy's Tacos, which opened in 2006. Two of Austin's most popular breakfast taco joints, they feature tacos with names like Space Cowboy (a vegetarian taco from Tacodeli that was named one of the best tacos in Texas by *Texas Monthly* in 2015), the Wrangler (eggs, potatoes, smoked brisket, and cheese), and the Vaquero (eggs, grilled corn, roasted peppers, and cheese), among others.

A Mexico City native, Roberto Espinosa says his decision to open Tacodeli was influenced by his desire to eat what he grew up eating. "There wasn't anything like it in Austin; it was all steam-table stuff. I wanted to cook what I wanted to eat." He did so while adapting his recipes to the Anglo Austin ethos of supporting local businesses and palates. In the process, Espinosa created tacos that represent their time and place. He created Austin-style tacos, and Tacodeli became the quintessential Austin taqueria. There is the Taco Blanco (egg whites and another item), the Frontera Fundido (sirloin, chicken, or portobello mushroom with a Jack cheese glaze and sautéed poblano and onion strips), and specials that reflect the breakfast tacos of Mexico City, tacos de guisados. (Incidentally, former Tacodeli executive chef Joel Fried once told me of the off-menu Meat is Murder taco, the Freakin' Vegan with picadillo. Meat is Murder left with Fried's departure.) Austin is now home to six Tacodelis, and in 2020, more than twenty years after the opening of their first taqueria, Espinosa and co-owner Eric Wilkerson established a Houston branch. It's the second location outside Austin; the first store outside of the Capital City opened in Dallas in 2015. The best in the chain, the Dallas Tacodeli sources Sonoran-style flour tortillas, slightly sweet, almost lucent discs from La Norteña Tortilleria, a few miles from the restaurant. Three women work the dough at that tortilla factory for a clientele that includes most of the neighborhood's northern Mexican-style restaurants. As of this writing, there are several Dallas stores.

Like most Austin taquerias serving breakfast tacos—especially those specializing in the style—Tacodeli and Torchy's Tacos offer the city's signature taco, the migas. Migas in Austin and throughout most of Texas are closer to a Mexican breakfast of chilaquiles—fried tortilla quarters and salsa often served with eggs and various garnishes—than to the original Mexican migas (the word translates to "crumbs"). The original dish is a bowl of soupy, stale bread that was considered a hangover cure. Indeed, the mixture of eggs, jalapeños, onions, tomatoes, and magic carpet-wavy strips of fried corn tortillas in a house-made tortilla can make for a fantastic palliative to the nasty effects of binge drinking.

It's certainly true for the migas taco served at Veracruz All Natural. Established as a food trailer in an East Austin parking lot, Veracruz All Natural is owned and operated by Veracruz, Mexico-born sisters Reyna and Maritza Vasquez. There is now a fleet of Veracruz All Natural trailers and a brick-and-mortar store in Austin and another outpost north, in Round Rock, Texas. Alongside Tacodeli and Torchy's Tacos, Veracruz is a darling of the South by Southwest and Austin City Limits Music Festival out-of-towners. It has received national attention via social media outlets such as Instagram, magazines like *Bon Appetit*, and online food media outlets such as *Eater*. I've heard acquaintances describe the taco as "The. Best. Migas. Taco. Ever." And they are good—a study in contrasting textures. The crunch of the strips stands up against the soft, bouncy eggs studded with hot bites and sweetness.

However, perhaps the greatest breakfast tacos in Austin are served out of a Valentina's Tex Mex BBQ food trailer. Among the best taco purveyors in the Lone Star State, Valentina's melds Austin's great barbecue tradition with owner Miguel Vidal's San Antonio roots. My favorite is the Real Deal Holyfield, a taco of immense fortitude packed with potatoes, refried beans, bacon, and mesquite-smoked brisket or pulled pork, all topped with a fried egg and zippy tomato-serrano chile salsa.

In the beginning, tacos and their tortilla base belonged to the impoverished, the downtrodden, and the criminal before disseminating across the Lone Star State in the mid-twentieth century. Contrary to popular belief, however, Austin's role as the home of breakfast tacos is a recent, albeit critical, development in the food's evolution and national profile. The breakfast taco has always been part of Texas foodways, and its growing cultural significance shows no sign of slowing. Tacos are a part of all Texans. For Austin, the Rio Grande Valley, and San Antonio, they are a matter of not just municipal identity and pride of place but also collective memory and collective genetics. It's soul and the stuff of poetry.

Social media, journalists, and bloggers have reinforced all of this. Some, like *Texas Monthly* writer Dan Solomon, contributed to the dialogue of The Great Breakfast Taco War of 2016 with a blog post spinning the position of breakfast tacos in Austin culture.

> While countless non-Texans get introduced to the concept in Austin every March during SXSW, the claim that the breakfast taco "belongs" to Austin is a controversial one....
>
> People *eat* breakfast tacos in Austin, but that doesn't mean that Austin owns it.
>
> Austin certainly is well equipped to claim ownership of things that didn't originate in the city. It's full of transplants whose first experiences with things like breakfast tacos and barbecue were in the city's limits, and it *does* do those things very well. San Antonio, Corpus Christi, McAllen, and any number of points in between *also* do those things exceptionally well, of course, but people who've visited or moved to Austin from New York, California, or elsewhere don't

always find time to head south on I-35 to experience breakfast tacos in cities that have been serving them for generations.

Furthermore, as a media hub, Austin helps create the narrative about Texas that is disseminated throughout the rest of the state (and the rest of the country), and those voices often don't look south of Slaughter Lane for trends.

Indeed, Austin has an incredible PR machine fueled by its perceived coolness compared to other Texas cities. Austin has barbecue. Austin has SXSW. It has breakfast tacos. And, with the assistance of food writers who have visited during a big festival or lived there for a spell, the city has fooled many into believing breakfast tacos are "Austin-style." In a 2010 *New York Times* piece, John T. Edge wrote of breakfast tacos: "Austin trumps all other American cities." From his days at the *Village Voice* to his current tenure as senior critic at *Eater*, New York's documentarian of ethnic cuisine Robert Sietsema has repeatedly defined breakfast tacos as "Austin-style."

Austin's rising profile is helping the breakfast taco grow into an increasingly nationalized dish. The national taco scene has a lot of Austin connections. Brianna Valdez opened HomeState in the Los Feliz neighborhood of Los Angeles in 2013. A second LA location opened in the Highland Park neighborhood, and a third HomeState outpost, this one in Playa Vista, north of Los Angeles International Airport, opened in 2019. Valdez moved to Southern California after graduating with a business management degree from St. Edward's University in Austin. "I had planned to live abroad to improve my Spanish fluency," Valdez says. "Instead I took a 'brief' detour to LA where my boyfriend received a fellowship at UCLA. I had no idea what I'd do here, but I liked the world of possibilities."

The emphasis on *home* in HomeState is obvious from the first sip of Topo Chico, the salty, refreshing mineral water bottled in Monterrey, Mexico, and a favorite beverage across Texas. A bite of the chorizo, egg, and cheese in a chewy, slightly sweet house-made flour tortilla, and your mind is right back in the Lone Star State while your body remains in Los Angeles. Tacos are named not for main ingredients but for Texas rivers. The aforementioned trio of fillings is the Guadalupe. The Trinity is a classic combination of eggs, potatoes, bacon, and cheddar. The same goes for the Frio, refried charro beans and Monterey Jack. All of them are among my favorite selections at HomeState. Veggie options, another indicator of Austin's influence, are also available, with mixed results. (While the Neches with black beans, eggs, and Monterey Jack is fantastic, the Blanco with egg whites, mushrooms, and Monterey Jack can make for a soggy pocket.) Nevertheless, Valdez and staff make tacos that are the stuff of Texas childhoods. It's confusing, joyous, and, frankly, awesome. And it's in California. "At its roots, this is poor people's food," Valdez explains.

> It's the food I was raised on. It's the food that grandmothers and mothers make for their families. It should be simple. And the intention, loving.
>
> The thing that is most surprising is how excited people have gotten by breakfast tacos! In a city where tacos are kings, I was initially nervous about presenting tacos that are seemingly so simple. Flour tortillas were unheard of and never used. We were presenting something so new to the city that I figured it could go either way: really well, or really poorly.

A smattering of restaurants has joined HomeState in slinging breakfast tacos in California. The Wood Café in Culver City offers soyrizo with scrambled eggs, while The Corner Deli & Grill is in a gas station in West LA. Former Texan Josef Centano's Bar Amá serves up traditional variations, and Angelenos look to be hooked on them.

New York has had an on-again, off-again love affair with breakfast tacos. A few pioneers (e.g., Brooklyn Taco Co. and Whirlybird, both opened by folks inspired by visits to Austin) have since closed, and the current crop of taquerias and restaurants—including Jalapa Jar, which once had a kiosk in a Brooklyn Heights subway station—are more likely to serve breakfast tacos on corn tortillas than on flour. Ostensibly, that confers on them greater Mexican-ness. They might not know that breakfast tacos on both sides of the immediate US-Mexico border are served on flour tortillas. Moreover, if the establishments were truly going for Mexican breakfast tacos, they would be offering tacos de guisado, the Mexico City equivalent, where wet, luscious eggs are mixed with ribbons of ham and laced with a salsa de chile de árbol that tingles the nose as it goes down. Or their menus might include a shrimp fritter that sits on a feathery bed of yellow rice or a taco de chicharrones en salsa verde (fried pork crackling stewed in a green sauce) so fiery that consuming it makes you want to happily claw your eyes out. Or they could be serving Mexico City's other breakfast taco, the taco de canasta.

But that's not what's going on. Instead, there are places such as Downtown Bakery, tucked away in Manhattan's East Village. A busy, long kitchen is partially concealed behind the counter in the tight, one-room restaurant. The menu is listed on the walls above the counter and above the tables adjacent to the counter. The corn tortillas are thick enough that doubling them up seems unnecessary until I notice the volume of food enveloped by the flat bread. Choza Taqueria, which opened in 2010, was an early pioneer of breakfast tacos in the Big Apple. In the Flatiron District, Tacombi Café El Presidente offers northern Mexican-style breakfast tacos with small, nearly translucent flour tortillas made in-house. (Just check out the tortilla machine!) Unfortunately, during my stop at the restaurant, my order came to the table as gut-wrenchingly greasy tortilla packages, including a personal favorite filling, machacado con huevo.

South along the East Coast and Appalachia, taquerias modern and traditional offer breakfast tacos. The Washington, DC, area is home to District Taco, where classic breakfast tacos are abundant. In Blacksburg, Virginia, and Raleigh, North Carolina, Wicked Taco goes the more-is-more route with super tacos like the Moo Eats Two: eggs, Applewood bacon, red bliss potatoes, ancho honey, and jack cheese on a flour tortilla. The Juan in a Million taco pays homage to Austin's legendary restaurant of the same name with an intimidating combination of eggs, rotisserie chicken, Applewood bacon, grilled bell peppers, caramelized onions, habanero salsa, and Hatch green chile queso. They also have a migas tacos on the menu. Meanwhile, in the craft beer-happy hamlet of Ashville, North Carolina, Taco Billy achieves Austin-level success with—you guessed it—a migas breakfast taco. Described as an Ashville favorite, it comes packed with the classic combination of eggs, onions, jalapeños, tomatoes, fried tortilla strips, and cheese. Capital Taco in the Tampa Bay area is unabashedly Tex-Mex and also makes a migas taco. (It's as if breakfast taquerias north of Austin are required by the Austin taco lords to serve migas!) The menu gets a boost from the Caballero (eggs, brisket, jack and cheddar cheeses, and chipotle barbecue sauce), the Texican (eggs, street corn, jack and cheddar cheeses, and chipotle ranch), and the Lean Mean (eggs, pickled carrot, avocado, and queso Chihuahua).

In the Midwest, Taco Circus in St. Louis serves six options (including, of course, migas) all day. In the Chicago area, Laredo natives/former San Antonians opened (or rather rolled out) Amanecer, a mobile breakfast taco joint in a Smart Car that in 2017 moved into a brick-and-mortar store. Amanecer is *puro* South Texas with classic examples of breakfast tacos: bean and cheese, potato and egg, machacado, and carne guisada. Owners Mario and Ana Vela grew up in the land of breakfast tacos, Nuevo Laredo, its sister city north of the Rio Grande, Laredo, and San Antonio. When they moved to Chicago in 2010, they were faced with a life without breakfast tacos. They searched, of course. They followed leads. And they came up empty. "Somebody in Chicago has to be selling them." They asked around. "Oh, yeah, you gotta go far for those," one person told them. "And we'd go, and no one knew what we were talking about," Ana says. "People would connect us to other Texans, and one of the top three topics of conversation between all of us was the lack of breakfast tacos in Chicago." They were constantly talking about it, saying, "Somebody's got to do it. Someone is going to serve breakfast tacos in Chicago. But no one was doing it," Ana tells me.

Wanting their South Texas breakfast tacos, the Velas decided to open their own operation, Amanecer Breakfast Tacos. Ana and Mario held taste tests with friends, learning that Chicagoans were excited about unfamiliar ingredients and names. Machacado was a winner, as were carne guisada and chorizo and egg. The Smart Car hit the road in 2015, and the first day couldn't have gone worse. Ana says she got strange looks. "People weren't used to food trucks or selling food out of cars," she says, noting that when she was growing up, tacos were sold off bicycles, from cars, and from tables set up on the sidewalk. They might have sold only five tacos. "And then the car was towed."

Chicagoans were so unfamiliar with breakfast tacos, the Velas say, that customer education—about tacos, the Velas' South Texas home, and its culture—was a critical component of Amanecer. "An international student at Northwestern had never held a taco before. When she removed the foil and picked up the taco, the filling fell to the ground," Ana says. They did have to make concessions to the market, though. Instead of the thick, flaky San Antonio–style flour tortillas, Amanecer's breakfast tacos were wrapped in a thin, organic tortilla akin to the flour discs of Sonora. (Breakfast tacos with corn tortillas are also available for gluten-free customers.) Still, for the Velas, it's about the flavors. Amanecer became successful as a result of the their hard work on education and catering, the most profitable part of their business. "Someone sets a meeting for nine in the morning, they better bring breakfast tacos if they want everyone to show up on time," the Velas say. As we've learned. That is true even for Ted Cruz.

In November 2017 the Velas opened the Amanecer Taco Shop, a brick-and-mortar grab-and-go store in Evanston, Illinois. The shop's first day, Small Business Saturday of 2017, couldn't have been any more different from the mobile operation. There was a line out the door and by closing the Velas had sold between four hundred and five hundred tacos. "Now, people drive from across Chicagoland for a little piece of home."

Out west, Denver is perhaps the city outside of Texas that is experiencing the biggest breakfast taco surge. It began with Moontower Tacos, a name that references Austin's landmark moontowers, which gained national cred with *Dazed and Confused*, Richard Linklater's 1993 film. Moontower Tacos—which, of course, offered a migas taco—was opened in 2012 by Austin transplant Brent Trash, but quietly shuttered in 2015. It wasn't long before other breakfast taco specialists saw the Mile High City

The original Amanecer taco car.
COURTESY AMANECER TACO SHOP.

as an attractive market. Operations like Tacos, Tequila, Whiskey (AKA Pinche Tacos) gave Denver creative morning eats like the Chicken & the Egg (agave-dipped fried chicken, sweet potato and roasted poblano hash, Mexican chimichurri, and sunny-side up egg) and Queso Relleno (griddled jack cheese, roasted poblano, mushrooms, avocado, pico de gallo, and a sunny-side up egg). Tacos, Tequila, Whiskey misses the point of breakfast tacos. Once broken, the sunny-side up egg yolk coats the hand. It's so sticky, the restaurant should hand out towelettes with each order. Napkins certainly aren't enough. The small tortilla is insufficient for the column of components stacked on it. Before being rebranded as R Taco but after opening in Minneapolis-St. Paul and across the Lone Star State, Rusty Taco opened in Denver, offering classic combos like bacon, egg, and cheese. One of Torchy's Tacos locations (sixteen and counting) calls Denver home. There's another in nearby Fort Collins, Colorado. Torchy's Tacos, R Taco, which has since reverted to its original name, Rusty Taco, and other taco operations continue to announce expansion plans.

Texas-based chains like Torchy's Tacos and Rusty Taco are increasing the breakfast taco's profile outside the Lone Star State. At the same time, Torchy's expansion reinforces the misconception of Austin as the birthplace of the breakfast taco. Austin is instead the breakfast taco's Madison Avenue, its ad agency. This point can't be emphasized enough. Regardless of the state capital's fundamental role in the dish's popularization, the breakfast taco is a South Texas/Rio Grande Valley creation. The people and businesses of that region should get the appropriate credit and acknowledgment.

That being said, truly, there is no stopping breakfast tacos.

Where to Find Them

Amanecer Taco Shop
512 Main St.
Evanston, IL 60202
847-644-3575
amanecertacos.com

Bar Amá
118 W. 4th St.
Los Angeles, CA 90013
213-687-8002
bar-ama.com

Café Tola #2
3324 N. California Ave.
Chicago, IL 60618
773-293-6346
cafetola.com

Chacho's Tacos
3700 Ayers St.
Corpus Christi, TX 78415
361-888-7378

Downtown Bakery
69 First Ave.
New York, NY 10003
212-254-1757
downtownbakerycocina
   mexicana.com

HomeState
multiple locations
myhomestate.com

Los Girasoles Restaurant
5560 E. Ruben M. Torres Sr. Blvd.
Brownsville, TX 78520
956-838-6336

Mi Madre's Restaurant
2201 Manor Rd.
Austin, TX 78722
512-322-9721
mimadresrestaurant.com

Ms. G's Tacos N' More

2263 Pecan Blvd.
McAllen, TX 78501
956-668-8226
msgstacosnmore.com

Obregon Mexican Restaurant #2

303 Market St.
Laredo, TX 78040
956-462-5298

Papalote Taco House

2803 S. Lamar Blvd.
Austin, TX 78704
512-804-2474

3632 S. Congress Ave.
Austin, TX 78704
512-294-2122

yumpapalote.com

Sylvia's Restaurant

1843 Southmost Blvd.
Brownsville, TX 78521
956-542-9220

Tacodeli

multiple locations
tacodeli.com

Tamale House East

1707 E 6th St.
Austin, TX 78702
512-495-9504
facebook.com/tamalehouse.east/

Valentina's Tex Mex BBQ

11500 Manchaca Rd.
Austin, TX 78748
512-221-4248
valentinastexmexbbq.com

Veracruz All Natural

multiple locations
veracruzallnatural.com

Puffy taco at Ray's Drive Inn.

CHAPTER 2

Golden *and* Crunchy

Crispy tacos, taquitos and flautas, fry bread tacos, tacos dorados, and San Antonio–style puffy tacos

REGION(S): Across the United States

CLASSIC EXAMPLES: San Antonio–style puffy tacos, taquitos, old-fashioned tacos

TORTILLA(S): Corn

LOWDOWN: Fried tacos didn't cross the border. The border crossed fried tacos. Assimilated and co-opted, they occasionally forgot how to speak Spanish, but most of the time they developed the advantageous art of bilingualism.

T he traditional taco has to be fried," declared the *Brownsville Herald* in 1950. It might be surprising that a newspaper from a Texas border town with a large Mexican and Mexican American population would print such a statement. But it shouldn't be.

Well before that statement was published, at the turn of the twentieth century and going back to the nineteenth century, there are print references in the United States to filled and folded fried tortillas. In 1900, the *Los Angeles Times* published a reference to fried tacos from a travelogue printed a few years earlier. Bertha Haffner-Ginger included a fried taco recipe in her 1914 *California Mexican-Spanish Cookbook*, and in 1922, a taco recipe that called for frying appeared in the *Castelar Crèche Cook Book*. Scads of published material defined a taco as a meat-filled folded tortilla that is fried. It is perhaps the greatest joke played on know-it-all taco snobs who insist today that a taco starts with a soft corn tortilla.

The first print mention of the taco as a food in the United States dates to an 1887 edition of the Spanish-language *El Fronterizo* weekly newspaper published in Tucson, Arizona. The phrase "echando tacos" is used. Slang for "taco eating," this vernacular remains in use today. A subsequent citation in an 1893 edition of the *El Fronterizo* appears in a recipe for a soup. Neither newspaper passage includes anything about frying. But considering the location—the Southwest—I wouldn't be surprised if the tacos in question were anything but fried and their preparation similar to the description in the *Brownsville Herald*: "It is made with a specifically prepared tortilla, which is folded along the middle and fried in lots of hog fat.

Ground meat, or the shredded meat used down Mexico way, is mixed with whatever sauce or garnishment is on hand. It may be lettuce and tomato, or aguacate salad [guacamole], or the small seed-like chile piquín that burns like acid. A well-made taco is crunchy and delicious."

This stateside characterization of the taco didn't temper the spice of novelty or its allure. As the twentieth century pushed on, the crispy taco proved compelling enough to fill the role of star attraction. Such was the case in January 1965 when El Rancho Restaurant in Amarillo, Texas, celebrated its thirty-seventh anniversary by adding a crispy taco to its menu. "It was new. It was different. It was World Famous."

The boasts of firsts didn't end there. The show was just getting started, and it was going to be refined as it traveled the country. For example, rolled fried tacos were being packaged and marketed as frozen "cocktail tacos," ideal for parties. Crispy tacos were the first tacos to be described as "gourmet," made with "gourmet taco shells." Disagreement emerged over which form of the hard-shell taco was truly highfalutin. "Although the fold-over model is standard fare from Anaheim to Odessa, from Guadalajara (where there are 104 varieties) to Boise, Idaho, the gourmet taco is different, both in configuration and content. The gourmet taco is a rolled taco. It is called a 'flauta' in Phoenix, when you can find one, and a taquito in Los Angeles."

Even the seemingly omnipresent, standard fried taco—what has also been called the Mexican American taco, the Cal-Mex taco, the Taco Bell taco, the old-fashioned taco—is as regional as other taco styles. Order a taquito today in one town, and you're liable to get a folded-over "small taco" (the translation of taquito). Ask for a flauta, and you might get a rolled and fried taco that is three to five inches long, or it could measure ten inches. Adjectives tacked onto the fried tacos—or any taco—complicate matters even further. Specificity matters.

But there are more fried tacos than the aforementioned classic crunchy bites. One must also include the San Antonio–style puffy taco and the fry bread taco. The former is little known outside of South Texas, while the latter, with its dark history, is found across the country at powwows and rodeos. All of these fried beauties will be covered in this chapter, which for the sake of clarity and expediency, will be separated by taco type. Let's start things off with the old standby, everyone's favorite.

The old-fashioned crispy taco

The history of the crispy taco is the history of the taco in America. It involves, as mentioned in this chapter's introduction, the earliest recorded taco recipes. The crispy taco is the taco of family taco night. It's been one of the inspirations for technological advancement in the kitchen. Just look at Juvencio Maldonado, who in 1947 invented an apparatus that allowed a cook to fry several corn tortillas simultaneously while forming them into the classic U shape.

In the Midwest, crispy tacos were embraced as Taco Bell–style fast food franchises opened across the region. Meanwhile, Midwesterners, with the help of a growing Mexican immigrant and Mexican American population in cities like Kansas City, Missouri, began to tinker with crispy taco recipes. In Mexico, tacos dorados, whether folded or rolled, are sealed with toothpicks before frying.

In Kansas City and Illinois and Indiana, residents continued this practice. Kansas City restaurants like Los Corrals, which opened in 1949; Spanish Gardens (now a retail food company); and Manny's Mexican Restaurant dusted their fried tacos with grated Parmesan. This local specialty was a result of Mexican and Italian communities living side by side since the early days of the railroads and ingredient availability. Mexican immigrants and Mexicans wanted cheese on their tacos, and the cheese that was available was parmesan. Since the late 1950s, In-A-Tub has covered their opened fried beef- or bean-filled tacos with mac-and-cheese powdered cheese. These regional specialties endure at neighborhood restaurants, including Manny's and In-A-Tub. But mostly they live on at watering holes such as

The Moonlighter in Chicago, where Topsy's Taco, a freshly fried crispy taco, is served inserted with a slice of American cheese and a packet of Heinz Hot Taco Sauce. On a winter night, when the snow is piercing the air horizontally, drop into The Moonlighter, find a corner in the fireplace nook, and order a Taco Party (a Topsy's Taco, a Miller High Life, and a shot of bourbon) for eight dollars. The menu at R-Bar & Grill in Highland, Indiana, emphasizes the bar's Serbian platters, like cevap, a kebab-style dish, and burek, a filled pastry dish. However, come Tuesdays, fried tacos are the crowd favorites. What's remarkable about these Midwestern crispy tacos is that the lettuce, generally iceberg, isn't watery, limp, or cold. It's chilled, yes, but it comes close to lukewarm and crisp on second bite.

Scooting down to Tucson, Arizona, we find Rollies Mexican Patio. Opened in 2017 by Mateo Otero, Rollies goes all in for the fried. Named for rolled and fried tacos ahogados, this shop, watched over by a mural of a pony-shaped piñata, serves up this specialty topped with ladles of red or cheese salsa and a cap of cabbage and crema. The tacos ahogados don't get soggy and are easily handled without too much of a mess, although extra napkins are recommended. Use the accompanying spoon to drizzle salsa into the center of the taquito after each bite. Rollies also offers Nana's Tacos. These crispy tacos, Otero says, were inspired by all the tacos Chicano grandmothers made for eager, hungry kids. For him, that means a freshly fried shell, ground beef, lettuce, peas (for extra texture), and yellow or Cotija cheese.

Then there's Lucy's Café in El Paso, Texas. It's there we find one of my favorite crispy tacos in North America in the form of Tacos Antonia, a platter of freshly fried crispy tacos dusted in copper-colored seasoning salt and packed with shredded brisket, a citrus-cabbage salad, avocado wedges, and Muenster cheese (a local specialty topping the majority of crispy tacos). Rice and refried beans nudge up against the tacos. These one-of-a-kind treasures are named in honor of founder-owner Lucy Lepe's sister, Antonia, who helped create the dish that was added to the menu in 1979. Hefty with its delightful knotted strings of beef and a solid snap that steers clear of disintegration, the Tacos Antonia are the most popular dish on the menu. "People order them so much, we've had to shorten the name," Lucy's son David Lepe, who manages Lucy's Café West, tells me. "We just call them Toni's Tacos."

I tell Lepe about Stella Taco in Portland, Oregon, a taqueria co-owned by native Texan husband and wife Ian Atkins (Beeville outside of Corpus Christi) and Becky Atkins (Dallas) and their business partner Matthew Fields (El Paso), all of whom knew each other from when they lived in El Paso. Of course, there's a crispy taco on the menu, but it's not the snappy Tex-Mex nosh typical of the Lone Star State. It's not yellow and pockmarked nor is it bubbled. Instead, Stella Taco's crispy taco bears an uncanny resemblance to Toni's Tacos—right down to the seasoning salt—although on my visit to Stella Taco, the cooks only dressed the top edges of the crispy shell with the salt. It's a worthy homage. "Anyone who has spent time in El Paso will know the locals have a sweet spot for crispy tacos," says Ian Atkins. "So many memories are flooding back at the mention of Lucy's. I can taste [the brisket filling]. I played in a band in El Paso and our regular gig was at the attached bar, King's X, so I have eaten at Lucy's more than most people. I had a friend that was obsessed with the Tacos Antonia. He still talks about it every time I see him, even though he now lives in Austin."

Taquitos and flautas: Los rolled tacos

One of the most renowned taquitos can be found in Los Angeles and comes dressed in a heavy shawl of runny guacamole salsa. When Cielito Lindo opened in 1934 on Los Angeles's Historic Olvera Street, the brightly colored restaurant set the standard, and continues to set the standard, for taquitos in Los Angeles. Meanwhile for flautas, Taquizas Gilberto on a nondescript street in West Covina, California, is one of the best and hardest-to-find

Olvera Street in the oldest part of downtown Los Angeles, California.
LIBRARY OF CONGRESS, PRINTS & PHOTOGRAPHS DIVISION, PHOTOGRAPH BY CAROL M. HIGHSMITH, LC-DIG-HIGHSM-21976.

practitioners of the style. Although specializing in sweet, just-this-side-of-gamy barbacoa de borrego, Gilberto also makes flautas de birria, whose ends are bursting with charred, crunchy sprays of goat meat that the fried (and flattop-crisped) rolled tortilla can't contain. These are fetching tacos served hot and, depending on your tolerance for spice, can either dance or scrape across the inside of your mouth and down your throat. I imagine if rock 'n' roll band Jethro Tull front man and flautist Ian Anderson were to pick one up and attempt to whistle out a ditty, the spirited flauta would play him.

To the south in San Diego, rolled tacos also are a local staple—so much so that they have taken the city's name, being called the San Diego rolled taco.

And then we're back to El Paso, where crispy tacos—rolled or folded—are cultural touchstones. Go ahead. Order a taco. The odds are good you'll be served a fried one. Take the border city's most famous taco joint: Chico's Tacos. Opened in 1953, the restaurant has reached such iconic status that, in 2003, the Texas Legislature adopted a resolution honoring the founding Mora family on the restaurant's fiftieth anniversary. It's been showcased on the Food Network and other cable outlets. The signature dish is a basket of rolled and fried tacos (and, yes, they are listed on the menu as tacos) soaked in a sauce so thin its more tomato water than red salsa. For years, these tacos were sprinkled with cheese that resembled shredded orange packing peanuts in both appearance and taste, a fact that didn't seem to discourage the countless locals who wandered into Chico's well after midnight, looking for something to quench their post-clubbing hunger. The chain has changed little since opening, but in 2016, the manufacturer discontinued the hallmark bland cheese. The replacement product is considered "cheesier."

If you're willing to push back against the popular choice, though, there are other, better options in the El Paso area. Ke'Flauta, a small counter service shop decorated with customers' napkin sketches, tops its rolled tacos with guacamole, crema, and queso fresco. But the best place to get taquitos in El Paso is Tacoholics. Jessie Peña opened his taco operation as a food truck in 2010 before transitioning to a brick-and-mortar operation in 2016. The bright flautas ahogadas at Tacoholics are a direct response to Chico's signature dish. "The idea was to freshen up the flauta," Peña says. "I wanted to make it real, with real cheese, real sauce, just real."

In other words, he wanted to create something that was appealing even when you're not glassy-eyed drunk. These flautas can be filled with steak, pork, chicken, or even tofu before getting their baptism of tomatillo salsa. The finished order is a treat of crunchy tortillas that soften as you eat them but never disintegrate. White queso fresco and queso asadero add a salty spike that is cushioned with Oaxacan crema.

Farther down the Rio Grande from El Paso, in the sister cities of Cuidad Acuña, Mexico, and Del Rio, Texas, taquitos are known as "tacos tapatios." (The word "tapatio" is Spanish for "a resident of Guadalajara, Mexico," where folded or rolled tacos dorados topped with salsa and a loose shot of cabbage are a popular snack.) These tacos tapatios are served under a shock of avocado, crema, salsa, cabbage, and/or tomatoes. Drive more than 150 miles north on Highway 277 between Del Rio and San Angelo and find so many walk-up taquerias, restaurants, and shacks serving these taquitos that I recommend renaming the road Tapatio Highway. In Sonora, Texas, there is Taco Grill. Just off 277, along I-10 in Ozona, tacos tapatios are served at Mi Taco. Taquitos are also listed as tapatios at the three Hidalgo's Restaurants, Nacho's Restaurant Cantina & Grill, and Franco's Café, all in

San Angelo. These rolled tacos are also called flautas. Again, we run into how geographically distinct the names of these tacos can be. The same food can have different names, even in the same town.

Fry bread tacos

West Texas is a craggy landscape of broken crispy taco shells. It's the taco trail of that sparsely populated, rich-in-sky region stretching from Eastland to El Paso and Big Bend to Lubbock. The historical record, from oral histories to newspaper clippings, shows us how most of the United States was introduced to tacos as a cuisine—each region's specialty notwithstanding.

One of those specialties—the fry bread taco—was born from one of the darkest periods of this country's history. The taco has a complicated and conflicted (both tragic and community-bonding) history and goes by a few names. Also known as the "Navajo taco" or the "Indian taco" or the "Navajo Indian taco," the dish is a mixture of flour, water, salt, and baking powder kneaded into a dough, shaped into a disc, and fried in oil or shortening. It should come out of frying with a slightly crisped exterior and soft, chewy interior. Traditionally, it is served topped with chili beans, ground beef, cheese, lettuce, tomatoes, and/or salsa and sour cream, evoking its Southwestern United States provenance. Although often too big to eat with one's hands, it retains the name "taco."

The story of the fry bread taco begins in the fourteenth century. It's at that time that evidence of comales, the flattop griddles used to cook tortillas, is first found in the American Southwest at Hohokam sites in Arizona. Edward S. Curtis, the great visual chronicler of Indian tribes in the early twentieth century, snapped photographs of Hopi women grinding maize on flat stone cookware, akin to the traditional Mexican metate, and shaping it into wafer-thin, tortilla-like blue corn piki bread, just as it had been done for centuries. The metate is not the only element piki shares with Mexican corn tortillas. The blue corn powder is nixtamalized—the ancient

Mesoamerican process by which corn is soaked and cooked in an alkaline substance called "cal," and hulled, just like the corn for tortillas—to imbue it with nutrients. Both breads are also time consuming: piki can take up to four days to prepare from grinding to being cooked and rolled. However, although tortillas are a daily food for Mexicans, piki is a ceremonial food for the Hopi, made for important rituals like a wedding.

What we know as fry bread might have originated on the Long Walk, the forced marches led by Colonel Christopher "Kit" Carson and the US Cavalry in 1864. The Long Walk relocated thousands of Navajos from their land in what is now Arizona to Bosque Redondo in New Mexico. Along the way, the displaced tribes were forced to subsist on limited US government-issued rations. Processed flour, salt, and sugar were combined and fried in lard to make a kind of bread that would become part of Native food culture for years to come. This is the story taught in schools. That is, if the history of the Long Walk—not one event but a series of journeys taken by the tribe—is taught at all.

An alternate fry bread creation theory contends that Carson's role in the Long Walk and in the development of fry bread is puffed up. He did not successfully subjugate anyone. His actions played a minor part in a series of events that involved Ute cooperation with American forces and the Navajos' voluntary surrender before Carson's attack on Canyon de Chelly. As the story goes, he cut off the Navajos' escape and razed cornfields and orchards. In the end, however, he is said to have acted benevolently. This supposedly resulted in the surrender of hundreds of Navajos. Instead, one recounting records, only twenty-some Navajos surrendered while the majority escaped via secret pathways.

Whichever story you take as fact, the eventual tribal resettlement at Fort Sumner and the commodities subsistence doctrine of the US Army took a deadly toll. There wasn't enough food for everyone and what government rations there were could very well have been rancid. Eventually, the Navajos were allowed to return to their own lands, but what they returned

The piki maker. Hopi, ca. 1906.
LIBRARY OF CONGRESS, PRINTS & PHOTOGRAPHS
DIVISION, PHOTOGRAPH BY EDWARD S. CURTIS,
LC-USZ62-123456.

to was devoid of life. Long gone were the fertile swathes of canyonlands, the thriving ecosystems that the Navajos and their indigenous predecessors cultivated in balance with the environment.

There is yet another fry bread creation story. It's plausible that its invention occurred concurrently in disparate locations, from Alaska to the Four Corners, as Native communities encountered these unfamiliar ingredients for the first time, brought by the American military and Russian traders, as well as European settlers. In Canada and points north, fry bread takes the name "bannock," based on the Celtic word for a Scottish unleavened barley or oatcake that was brought by traders across the Atlantic. Indigenous North Americans, like the Chippewas, often added dried fruit or spices to the imported flour, then fried the dough in a small amount of oil over a campfire. As the cavalry tore through the West, ingredients like the less healthy flour were substituted for the traditional corn masa out of necessity and survival mode.

All this is to say that fry bread is not a spontaneous creation born from limited resources—that would be too tidy. Instead, it is a synthesis of ancient traditions, one that includes Mexican tortilla preparation, European white wheat flour, and indigenous American food. We know, by the flour tortilla's reach through Northern Mexico after the conquest, that Native American tribes in the area would have almost certainly been familiar with flour as a cooking ingredient well before scouts introduced it. There is also timpsula (also known as "prairie turnip"). Plains Indians, such as the Lakota Sioux, ground timpsula into flour and fried the dough they made with it. Lewis and Clark witnessed Indians cooking with the tuber as early as 1805.

But even if fry bread wasn't simply a product of the Long Walk and internment, the revised history doesn't detract from the significance of the food's backstory. The elements of bread-making were already established when Carson rounded up the Navajos and ripped them from their land. What the captives did was simply use the new provisions of lard, sugar, salt, and flour in a familiar way. They did what they could with what they had and, in turn, innovated something so powerful that it sustained their bodies *and* their identities.

In the twentieth century, at fairs and pan-tribal celebrations—or, as *The Route 66 Cookbook* claims, originally at the Ranch Kitchen in Gallup, New Mexico—fry bread mingled with Southwestern and Spanish-Mexican influences and was transformed into a taco that was equally confectionary and savory. The doughy base evokes a flour tortilla crossed with a zeppole, the powdered sugar-coated fried Italian pastry. When made by experienced hands—and, as with the art of tortilla making, it can take decades to master fry bread—it creates a hearty yet tender basis for a whole range of wet and weighty toppings beyond the traditional beans, meat, cheese, lettuce, tomatoes, and sour cream.

One of the striking characteristics of the Indian taco is that it resembles the San Antonio–style puffy taco, which is made from deep-fried corn masa that's been shaped by a spatula into a shell and dressed with fillings similar to those used in the preparation of a fry bread taco. The puffy taco—whose fans still debate whether it was invented at Ray's Drive Inn in San Antonio, Texas, or at Caro's Restaurant in Rio Grande City, Texas, or on the stovetop of everyone's grandmother—echoes Mexico's tacos dorados, or fried tacos, from which, ultimately, America's crispy tacos are derived. But, let's not forget, a Mexican taco dorado can also be rolled, just like the taquito at Cielito Lindo in LA.

Whatever the Native dish's provenance, today's powwows are inconceivable without a fry bread or Indian taco stand. It's the stuff of proud Native identity and pop culture. Fry bread figures into song, art, and film. For example, in *Smoke Signals*, the film based on a short story by Sherman

Alexie, Thomas Builds-the-Fire (played by Evan Adams) dons a T-shirt bearing the words "Frybread Power." It's also the subject of *More Than Frybread*, a whimsical mockumentary by Holt Hamilton. In many ways, fry bread is at the foundation of modern pan-tribal identity just as corn (and the corn tortilla) forms the bedrock of Mexican culture. Fry bread power, in a manner of speaking, could be the indigenous equivalent of sin maiz no hay pais (without corn, there is no culture).

It may be convenient to think of fry bread in the same way as Mexican taco culture and taco fashion, but a history of the fry bread taco must acknowledge that the specter of oppression continues to hover over this seemingly innocuous food and its toppings. Fry bread carries at least 700 calories and 27 grams of fat per serving, according to the USDA. Researchers at the National Institute of Diabetes and Digestive and Kidney Diseases have been trying to ascertain why Native Americans have incredibly high rates of type 2 diabetes compared to the general population. It is believed that a cultural diet high in processed foods made from flour, sugar, and lard may be partly to blame. In response, some Native writers and artists have turned on fry bread. Creek/Euchee artist Steven Deo went so far as to splash the phrase "Frybread Kills" across a 2004 public service announcement-style poster as part of his *Art of Indians* series.

Meanwhile, fry bread tacos have been experiencing a culinary renaissance, as chefs off the reservation have begun to offer variations from the standard to the upscale. Mitsitam Native Foods Café at the Smithsonian National Museum of the American Indian in Washington, DC, goes the historical route. The taco, which has been on the menu since the restaurant opened in 2004, is capped with a serving of buffalo chili, something that Richard Hetzler, former Mitsitam executive chef, says he felt had to be there from the start. Later, though, the kitchen added a healthier topping option: chipotle chicken. The chic Kachina Southwestern Grill in Westminster, Colorado, and nearby Denver, also has culture in mind. The restaurant and food are "a celebration of the Southwest, both past and present," explains restaurateur Peter Karpinski. "Our overall goal is to highlight, pay respect, and support key attributes that the Native American culture has influenced in Southwestern cuisine, which is displayed through modern interpretations." Of their seven options, the Santa Fe Navajo taco—served with charred tomato salsa, asadero cheese, and caramelized onions garnishing smoked poultry—is one of the most popular. That's as commonplace as Kachina's ingredients get, though. Duck confit, peach-habanero salsa, Gulf shrimp, and cowboy beans are among the other available toppings.

Denver-based fast-casual restaurant Tocabe was featured on the Food Network's *Diners, Drive-Ins and Dives* and contributed a recipe for Osage Hominy Salsa to Guy Fieri's cookbook, *Diners, Drive-Ins, and Dives: The Funky Finds in Flavortown*. Owners Ben Jacobs (Osage) and Matt Chandra dole out a solid collection of fry bread tacos, including some with a ten-spice marinated bison given a thirteen-hour braise. The result is a shredded preparation flavored nutty and sweet and retaining juiciness, as well as a choice of black, pinto, or chili beans. With food customized in the fashion of the Denver-based Chipotle chain and including salsas that run from teasingly candied (maple vinaigrette) to coyly peppery (ancho-chipotle) and with an interior appointed with Native American art, Tocabe is far from a dive. The original location has the feel of a modern proto-chain operation (there is a second Tocabe in Greenwood Village, Colorado, as well as a food truck) and it offers more than fry bread. The menu includes wild rice bowls, blueberry barbecue sauce-glazed bison ribs, green chile stew, and wojapi, an indigenous berry sauce. As many ingredients as possible are sourced from Native American purveyors, such as the Seka Hills Olive Oil from the Yocha Dehe Wintun Nation.

Jacobs has gone on the record stating that he hopes Tocabe in particular and Native Americans in general aren't pigeonholed for fry bread. Indeed, as public interest in Native American food began to increase in 2017, Jacobs joined the movement raising awareness for indigenous ingredients and foodways alongside chefs like James Beard Award–winning Sean Sherman (Oglala Lakota), whose Minneapolis organization, The Sioux

Chef, includes Native American ethnobotanists, chefs, and foragers and groups like the I-Collective, whose members include chefs, educators, and artists. Jacobs is in the vanguard of Native American food revitalization, along with Neftalí Duran (Mixteco), M. Karlos Baca (Tewa/Diné/Nuche), Hillel Echo-Hawk (Pawnee and Athabaskan), and Brian Yazzie (Navajo).

Yazzie is chef de cuisine at The Sioux Chef, a Native American organization dedicated to reclaiming and revitalizing pre-European contact Native American foodways through research, classes, events, and, maybe in the future, a restaurant. He very much sees fry bread as dangerous and works to divorce it from Native American culture. "It's become a part of Indigenous food culture by force through colonialism," Yazzie says, referring to American occupation, Anglo settlement of the Southwest, and the forced relocation of local populations.

> The conditions of reservation life and agreements with the US government have created healthy food deserts via commodity provisions. Many Indigenous people have developed connected memories around fry bread because it is something that was prepared with what was provided when all else was taken away from our ancestors at a time and place. Now we Indigenous chefs have the knowledge and power to share with our tribal communities a healthier alternative route with the use of one of our main staples, corn.

Indeed, the removal of fry bread from not just the Indigenous diet but also from culture overall falls under the concept of food sovereignty: the idea that communities can eliminate colonial ingredients and culinary systems and return to a pre-contact diet. In the case of Indigenous North Americans, sovereignty begins with corn. Of course, what does one make with corn? Tortillas. Yazzie, Sherman, and other chefs in the food sovereignty movement are banishing the fry bread from the taco and replacing it with a corn tortilla to make what they call an "Indigenous taco," which is "a representation of our food culture in a handful of originality," says Yazzie. "Meaning no gluten, dairy, or any ingredients post-colonial contact. There is an endless variety of corn to make tortillas/bread for wild game, fresh vegetables, herbs, and spices, depending on the region."

The fry bread taco inspired the January 2013 Shiprock Pop-Up dinner in Philadelphia. Named after a reservation town in the Navajo Nation and organized by artisan jerky producer Marcos Espinoza, chef Lucio Palazzo, and artist Hawk Krall, the event featured Indian tacos with chili, pork spareribs, chicken ropa vieja, and black beans. Young urbanites and gourmands flocked to the happening.

Marcos Espinoza's Jemez Pueblo-Hispanic mother worked the dinner. "I was back there flapping fry bread—just flapping away," Marcie Espinoza told me, moving her hands in the air in much the same way a pizzeria worker handles dough, as we sat in Navajo Hogan, the restaurant she and her husband own in Salt Lake City. Bill Espinoza was walking between the open kitchen and the cash register taking care of closing operations. "You got here in just time. We're usually closed up or closing by this time on a Saturday," Marcie said. It wasn't yet four o'clock. But there we were, sitting at a large round table, chatting away about the place's twenty-five-year history.

Bill Espinoza originally wanted to open a pinball arcade in the freestanding cinder block building that once housed a print shop. He hoped to attract kids from the nearby high school. Then one day, while Marcie was making fry bread at home, Bill asked, "Why don't we sell them Navajo tacos?" "I remember I said, 'That would be great, but I have a full-time job,'" Marcie explains. The job was with an oil and gas company. She worked the job for more than twenty-eight years while continuing to manage and grow Navajo Hogan. "I'm not a cook," Marcie continues. "I'm just a mom. I mean I really enjoy it, but I'm not a cook."

They tested Bill's idea, and, on the first day, they realized they had underestimated the popularity of fry bread. Even Marcos chipped in. "It was a mess, just a mess," Marcie says. "Marcos—he was in high school at the time—came in to try to flap the fry bread but couldn't keep up. He was covered in flour from head to toe. Then he took off. Just left. I guess he was

Fry bread taco at Navajo Hogan.

overwhelmed," Marcie says in the fond tone of voice only a parent would use. "Eventually we realized this might be something great."

That "something great" is now a small kitchen with a fry station, tubs for the fry bread mix, a sink, and a few tables in the same cinder block building in which we're sitting. That's it. Navajo Hogan wasn't conceived as a sit-down place. "We didn't have bathrooms," cracks Marcie. There were no tables until the 2002 Winter Olympics. Customers were supposed to order and take their food to go. But folks stayed. Health department inspectors ordered the installation of restrooms. The final straw for regulators was finding Kathleen Quinto, one of Navajo Hogan's first employees, working with her one-month-old daughter sleeping in the kitchen.

Surprisingly, the restaurant initially had no name. They didn't know what to call the place. Waiting for inspiration and hoping for something with a personal connection, the Espinozas looked to their roots, to home, and to New Mexico, deciding finally to name their restaurant after a traditional Navajo dwelling. "It's Navajo Hogan: Home of the Navajo Taco." The restaurant found enough success that Bill quit his job to operate Navajo Hogan full-time. Marcie would get up at four in the morning to make sure the kitchen was stocked and would drop in at lunch. She would drive back to work still wearing her scarf scented with fry bread and oil aromas. "I could smell the progress," she says.

For Marcie, the road to this success was built on hardship and hard work in the small pueblos, settlements of Native Americans in New Mexico, one of which is Jemez. It was here that she had to learn to speak English or be hit with a ruler. Although she remains fluent in Spanish, Marcie does not speak the Pueblo tongue of Tewa. "My native language is gone," she says. As a child, Marcie lived with her family on a ranch on the reservation, where they grew their own vegetables, corn, and chiles. "You didn't see hamburgers when we were growing up in the boonies. We were eating healthy: a lot of beans and rice and Jesus Christ."

They slaughtered their own cattle, and her mother would put the meat between two pieces of fry bread grilled on a flattop—no lettuce, no tomato, no anything—and send the kids outside, where Marcie would stare at the brushy desert landscape and tell herself that one day she would be rich enough to buy Wonder Bread. "What I didn't realize back then is that we were eating like kings. Other kids were eating baloney, but I was eating roast beef and this fabulous tortilla fry bread that my mom made with love. We had the things we needed and we worked very, very hard. We had a good work ethic. We had to get up early in the morning to pull weeds in the garden. It would be too hot later. We survived and that's what kept me going."

Now Marcie's customers are treated to dishes made predominately from ingredients from Colorado and New Mexico, with trips to New Mexico for restocking the chile supplies. People are drawn to the "to-die-for" New Mexico chile flavor, as Marcie calls it. Red chile powder is stirred into the flour mix for red chile fry bread, giving the soft, chewy dough a subtle buzz. New Mexico blue corn is added to another batch for a denser order of fry bread that sparkles under incandescent lighting.

No matter the arena, fry bread and the Indian fry bread taco continue to foster community. News about the Navajo Weavers Association rug auctions in Crownpoint, New Mexico, includes details of a fry bread taco school fund-raising dinner alongside details of rug patterns like the Two Grey Hills style and the nontraditional bold designs of a young generation of craftspeople.

Nowhere is the importance of community more on display than at the annual National Indian Taco Championship (NITC), held in Pawhuska, Oklahoma, on the Osage Nation. In the late nineteenth century, the Osage had been removed by the US government from their home in Kansas to Indian Territory in what is now Oklahoma. I made a trip to that far-away-from-almost-everything settlement, two-and-half hours from Oklahoma City and just outside the Tallgrass Prairie Preserve, to see a town that seemed to have stumbled into modernity just as the Old West came to a close. At that time, the Osage were among the wealthiest people in the world, thanks to the oil reserves found beneath their land. A storefront with a "For Rent" sign in the window sits next to a Western art gallery, and a flatiron building stands sentinel over a downtown filled with landmarks on the National Register of Historic Places. Lately, Pawhuska is mostly known as the home of the popular Mercantile Restaurant, owned by author and TV personality Ree Drummond, better known as *The Pioneer Woman* on the Food Network. But at the time of my visit in 2016, the space that would become a one-stop shopping destination for *Pioneer Woman*–curated merchandise and goods in a bakery, deli, and general store was a construction site. Before Drummond, however, Pawhuska was known more for the Indian taco contest.

For the competition I attended, forty food vendors lined downtown Pawhuska, hawking not just Indian tacos but also sticky-sweet fry bread desserts and Indian taco dogs (fry bread–wrapped franks). Salsas ranged from Pace Picante clones to sauces so hot it felt like a nail-spiked gauntlet was stuck around my neck. Some tacos were weighed down by the typical Southwestern garnishes, cheese, lettuce, and tomato. Some allowed the protein—whether bison or beef—to shine. Fry bread thickness varied by vendor, many of whom participated in the blind taste-testing competition. As a judge, I was required to sample twenty entries from folks who traveled from as far as Florida, Minnesota, and Spain. They were exquisite examples of the fry bread taco, with a base bread both golden with a crispiness and chewy on the inside. The toppings ran spicy and cool, light and heavy, but all were a delight. Ultimately, Ramona Horsechief (Pawnee/Cherokee) took first place for her taco, making her the five-time champion.

I chatted with Paula Mashunkashey (Osage), who, with Mike McCartney and Raymond Redbird, established the NITC in 2004. Although Mashunkashey—whose twang is as generous and energetic as she is—retired from the event and moved near her daughter in Kentucky, she makes the trek to northern Oklahoma to check in on the gathering, where, she says, "There's so much love, there's so much culture, there's so much pride." It was about that time that the dance competition powwow caught her attention. She looked at the dancers in their brilliant regalia. "Oh gosh. We've got to do this," she said. She pointed to my recorder and said, "Turn this off. Turn this off." She grabbed my wrist and off we went to join the circle dance. And then I understood.

The question isn't going away: Do we kill fry bread? If we do, what would we be losing? The damage has been done—and it's incredible damage at that. Is mitigation all that's left? These are the difficult questions we face while grappling with food sovereignty, colonialism, oppression, and culinary reparations. What I do know is that it is more than just a problematic piece of bread. When you eat an Indian taco, you're consuming a symbol of persecution and perseverance. But you're also breaking bread with human ingenuity and cultural sustenance.

San Antonio–style puffy tacos

Between the shatter-prone crispy taco and the chewy fry bread taco is the San Antonio–style puffy taco: corn masa dough that is fried and molded with spatulas. Found across San Antonio—from repurposed Dairy Queens to food trucks—the puffy taco is a source of pride among locals, a cumulus-light treasure that elicits a Gollum-like ravenousness. This regional specialty is especially prized at Los Barrios Mexican Restaurant, the San Antonio Tex-Mex standard-bearer. Opened in 1978, Los Barrios was built into and around a former Dairy Queen, and, in fact, regulars call the Section 2 dining area the "Dairy Queen Section." It was here that original owner Viola Barrios and her family "perfected the puffy taco," as co-owner and Viola's daughter Diana Barrios-Treviño is fond of saying. They've certainly perfected their brand of Tex-Mex. Los Barrios, though crowded, is almost silent. If there's music, no one is listening. All you hear is a low, murmuring meditation over combination platters and, of course, puffy tacos.

Tex-Mex scholar Robb Walsh argued in a 2004 *Austin Chronicle* article that evidence suggests that the puffy taco was born in the Texas state capital. (Because spend enough time in Texas and you'll realize that every Texas taco—even if manufactured—is alleged to have a significant connection to Austin.) In Austin, specifically at Amaya's Taco Village, the San Antonio puffy taco is stripped of its geographic indicator and christened the "crispy taco." Of course, as with many Tex-Mex staples, Mexican American and Tejano families insist that their grandmothers invented it. Here's the truth: no one's abuelita invented the puffy taco. (Well, maybe one abuelita did, but we'll get to that momentarily.)

This iconic Texas taco has its roots in the lightly fried salbute, a tortilla that, unlike a puffy taco, is served flat and is not crimped in the center. The salbute, a specialty of the Yucatán Peninsula, is topped with a small serving of meat, usually chicken or turkey, and garnished with pickled red onions, tomatoes, cabbage, and salsa.

The puffy taco also shares a resemblance to the gordita inflada (inflated fatty), a puffed, bubble-like tortilla that can be stuffed with sweet or savory fillings and is usually found in Veracruz, though it is increasingly found elsewhere, including the United States. My favorite is the version sold at Restaurante El Bajío, a legendary restaurant specializing in traditional Mexican regional cuisines. Opened in 1972 in the Azcapotzalco neighborhood of Mexico City, the restaurant boasts sixteen establishments overseen by Chef Carmen "Titita" Ramírez Degollado, the wife of co-founder Raúl Ramírez Degollado. El Bajío's gorditas infladas, a specialty of the chef's native Veracruz, are blue corn tortillas fried on a comal until they inflate, served with a thick salsa flavored with anise and piloncillo, unrefined cane sugar. The deep black salsa is earthy, it's sweet, and it lingers.

Much farther north in the Rio Grande Valley of the Texas-Mexico border is Caro's Restaurant. Situated in Rio Grande City, about forty-one miles from McAllen, Texas, in a beige building with darker beige trim that evokes the most boring adobe, it is as legendary for its puffy taco as El Bajío is for its gorditas infladas. Caro's is one of the restaurants that claim to have invented the puffy taco, the others being Ray's Drive Inn in San Antonio, Texas, and Arturo's Puffy Taco in Whittier, California.

The way Maria Lopez-Rambo tells it, it was her father, Arturo Lopez, owner of Arturo's Puffy Taco and his younger brother Ray Lopez, owner of Ray's Drive Inn, who invented the term "puffy taco." (After 1980, Ray sold his namesake restaurant to his brother for an undisclosed amount of cash and a car.) "Before my dad started calling them puffy tacos, everyone called them crispy tacos," Lopez-Rambo tells me over the phone. "Everyone. My grandmother, who made them in her home, called them crispy tacos." However, it was Lopez-Rambo's great-grandmother who, through consultation with her cousin Frances, invented the look of them, according to a handwritten note from Arturo in which he explains the origins of the Lopez family puffy taco. Arturo's grandmother, Maria Rodriguez Lopez, was making what would have been considered a tostada, but with everything used to make a puffy taco, oil and corn masa, with all the Tex-Mex garnishes at the ready. (Lopez-Rambo says she's not sure of the exact date.) Something distracted her from the frying, and the tortilla masa inflated. "To separate the tortillas, she would use the stick. Something called her attention elsewhere. She unintentionally let the stick slip and the utensil fell on top of what was supposed to be the flat little tostada-type thing. It became puffy around this little item that they threw in there. It was an accident," Lopez-Rambo says.

Although the only thing that changed was the name, the puffy taco as a specific taco style didn't gain renown until Maria's father moved his family to Southern California. It was there that the legendary San Antonio–style puffy taco was born in earnest when Maria's father opened his namesake taco stand. Arturo's Puffy Taco was established in 1977 in La Habra, California, not far from the current location in Whittier. A few years later, Arturo purchased his little brother Ray's place, Ray's Drive Inn on San Antonio's West Side. Arturo would thereafter split his time between his native San Antonio and his home in Orange County,

California. At one point, there were three Arturo's Puffy Tacos, but Ray's Drive Inn never expanded beyond its original location. Arturo passed away in 2015 at the age of seventy-seven. Ownership of Arturo's and Ray's passed into a trust overseen by Arturo's widow, Gloria, and their children. Maria and her older brother John Louis now split their time between the restaurants.

During research trips to Los Angeles, I made stops at Arturo's Puffy Taco a priority. On my first visit, I was able to pay my respects to John Louis after scarfing down two puffy tacos. John was soft-spoken and humble, thanking me for the thoughtful words. But it was I who was thankful. For me, visiting Arturo's and Ray's is always an honor. The Lopez family's puffy taco shacks are churches to me, especially Ray's Drive Inn. Decorated with iconography of the religious and/or the local sort (sports teams and newspaper clippings) with worn furnishings, the restaurants offer a look into the trappings of tradition, with doses of kitsch. In the case of Ray's Drive Inn, a painting of an exotic Mexican lady hangs there, a tourism poster here, an awe-inspiring altar replete with religious candles, fading photographs, and statues of saints with La Virgen de Guadalupe smack dab in the middle define the front dining room. Stories are everywhere. Customers were once able to leave a dime or nickel to light a candle, much like the prayer candles in a Catholic church. The money collected was in turn given to San Juan de los Lagos Parish and Shrine around the corner from the restaurant. Lopez-Rambo says the occasional prayer circle is held in front of the saints and candles.

The backroom at Ray's has more in common with a roadside curio shop than a dining room, crammed as it is with bric-a-brac, such as a taxidermied wildcat and black-and-white photos. There is also a 1926 Ford Model T truck, one of the many classic rides in Ray's automobile collection. The restaurant also houses an upstairs office and the apartment Arturo and Gloria set up for Arturo when he was visiting from California. "He had a little bachelor pad here," Lopez-Rambo says. "He had a Jacuzzi in there, a

The Lopez family in their home on El Paso Street, a few blocks from where Ray's Drive Inn would open in 1956.

COURTESY MARIA LOPEZ-RAMBO/RAY'S DRIVE INN.

big living room, and it was beautiful, a beautiful apartment. I know my mom loved it, too."

Three houses across the street belonged to Arturo. Ray and his family lived in one. In Arturo's later years, the Lopezes returned from California to put down roots in Texas. The houses sit adjacent to the restaurant's second parking lot, a patch of gravel. There are loads of classic cars, including a 1928 Falcon Knight, a 1953 Chevrolet pickup, and a 1954 Corvette convertible, just to name a few. These are holdovers from Ray Lopez's classic car collection and a reminder that Ray's, the restaurant, is in fact a drive-in. The restaurant is within walking distance from the old Lopez family home on El Paso Street. It is there that the five Lopez brothers and five Lopez sisters were raised and where the family's entrepreneurial spirit was born. Basillia Lopez, Arturo's mother, operated a mercantile goods store out of a kitchen window. The Lopez family history is part of the history of San Antonio's West Side.

Throughout my interviews with Lopez-Rambo, she is clear that these stories are the ones she has lived or that have been passed down to her. "By the time it gets to the fifth person it's a whole other story," she says. But she is firm about the coining of the term "puffy taco." It's even etched into Arturo's gravestone, Lopez-Rambo says.

While the Arturo Lopez branch of the family claims to have invented puffy tacos, what is known as the "San Antonio puffy taco" was popularized at Henry Lopez's Henry's Puffy Tacos Express in the Alamo City. Ask Imelda Lopez Sanchez, Lopez's daughter and vice president of general business operations at Henry's Puffy Tacos. "My father was making puffy tacos at his brother Ray's restaurant, Ray's Drive Inn, in the 1950s," she says. But, as noted, back then, puffy tacos were crispy tacos. Puffy tacos were only being sold as "puffies" in California. The name "puffy taco" didn't come into common usage until Henry's Puffy Tacos Express began serving them in 1978. The term was created as a marketing tool, Sanchez says, to highlight the 1,700-square-foot building.

Lopez-Rambo remembers the matter was decided via telephone. "My Uncle Henry calls and asks my father, 'Hey, do you mind if I use the name puffy taco because you're in California and nobody's using the name puffy taco out here in Texas.' Henry said, 'We're a couple of states apart. Would you mind?' So that's how I heard it. So my dad basically said, 'Well, sure, baby brother, you can have the name.'" The name stuck. Puffy tacos became hugely successful in San Antonio through the 1970s and '80s. Then everybody started calling them puffy tacos. Eventually, Arturo's wife persuaded him to apply for the trademark and the term "puffy taco" remains trademarked. A small plaque near the cash register at Ray's Drive Inn commemorates the trademark. The puffy taco continues to hold the family together.

Discrepancies in this timeline exist beyond the Lopez family tale. The Tamale & Taco House of Monroe, Louisiana, ran an advertisement in the city's paper in 1970 and 1971 that notes puffy tacos. A 1977 ad for Fiesta Patio in an edition of the *San Antonio Express* describes the restaurant's food as "Mexican health food" that is "naturally delicious" and lists two-dollar "Melt-In-Your-Mouth puffy Tacos [*sic*]."

Whatever the origins of the puffy taco, the iconic Ray's Drive Inn taco has since become a matter of pride. The Lopez name and the puffy taco are synonymous. One can't be mentioned without the other. And they're protective of it. It's easy to see why. The original Henry's Puffy Tacos location on West Woodlawn Avenue, a squat, counter-service establishment, produces a tortilla with a crispy, just shy of flaky, exterior. The center is chewy, which, in concert with the ground beef, lettuce, tomato, and cheese, cools and heats,

Ray's Drive Inn neon sign.
PHOTOGRAPH © ROBERT STRICKLAND.

giving the palate crunch, salt, and a touch of sweetness from the tomato. It's a masterpiece.

The puffy tacos at Ray's Drive Inn are even better. If they were any lighter, they would flit away into the firmament. Order the fajita, and, more importantly, don't forget to flash your lights for car-side service. It's not a drive-in for nothing.

But, really, it's Henry's that has embraced the puffy taco and leveraged it, capitalizing on its iconic status. Take the San Antonio Missions minor league baseball team and its Henry the Puffy Taco mascot created in 1987 by Henry's Puffy Tacos CEO Jaime Lopez.

Two other San Antonio family establishments rate a visit on a puffy taco tour. All have locations fairly close together north and west of downtown. In 1949, Rudolph and Adelfa Quiñones opened Jacala Mexican Restaurant. Its current location, the second, has the trademark Tex-Mex establishment look: wrought-iron chandeliers, brick archways with inlaid mirrors, and Christmas lights. The walls are lined with out-of-chronological-order Fiesta San Antonio framed posters. On the tables, cheese enchiladas share real estate with the iconic fried treat. Jacala's puffy tacos are easily consumed in two to three bites and, like Henry's version, are satisfyingly chewy. Although officially the order is a platter of three with the same filling, it doesn't hurt to ask to have the plate customized.

The puffy tacos are customer-customized at the aforementioned Barrios clan's restaurants, Los Barrios Mexican Restaurant, Viola's Ventana, and La Hacienda de Los Barrios—the last a gastronomic megaplex that includes playgrounds and an expansive, live oak–shaded patio that has been featured several times on the Food Network. "You want it with queso Chihuahua, shrimp, or only guacamole? Sure. Anything the customer wants," Diana Barrios-Treviño tells me before lifting a plate holding a fresh-from-the-fryer puffy taco shell to her lips. "Mick Jagger's lips," she jokes as she points to the shell. It's the only time Barrios-Treviño's arms and hands cease gesticulating during our conversation at La Hacienda. Her passion led her to Washington, DC, where—at the invitation of White House Deputy Social Secretary Ebs Burnough—she made San Antonio puffy tacos on the White House lawn for the 2010 Congressional Picnic attended by President Barack Obama.

"I'm the first to say I'm not a culinary-trained chef," Barrios-Treviño told the *San Antonio Express-News* after the event. "It's just what we've done forever. To be invited all the way to the top is a testament to the great food San Antonio has to offer."

Indeed, the puffy taco has traveled far. The Gorgon at Otto's Tacos in New York City was first available as an off-menu special before news of its peculiarity—and girth—hit the local food blogs and the owners moved it to the official menu. It's an unfortunate taco, too large and too hot to hold. What's more, waiting for it to cool results in a soggy base. The Gorgon is closer to a fry bread taco in that utensils are required for its consumption.

A better bet in New York is the pork puffy taco at Javelina. The Tex-Mex restaurant offers classic puffy tacos that are crispy but light, crunchy on the outside and chewy within. Pickled red onions and dabs of saltiness from queso fresco lend a tang to the heavily seasoned pork wedged into the fried cradle.

Tucked away in Wichita, Kansas, El Patio Café, a small restaurant with a rough wood and dark green interior appointed with romantic paintings of Aztec figures, sells two large, light puffy tacos per order. These Tex-Mex specialties are bolstered by chimichangas and burritos.

These options notwithstanding, the puffy taco has resisted exportation on the level of the classic crunchy taco or the breakfast taco. When found outside its heartland, the puffy taco usually isn't more than a special. At Resident Taqueria in Dallas, puffy tacos aren't listed on the chalkboard menu. Rather, the special is only available when co-owner and chef Andrew Savoie is in the kitchen, as he personally wants no one else to fry up the treat. Savoie has become so adept at cooking the puffy taco shells, he'll turn his back to the fry station to chat with me. Served glistening but not oily, the Resident Taqueria puffy taco is so delicate that it can't contain Savoie's upmarket quality ingredients and plating. Elements of the picadillo—namely the whole olive, confit tomato, and cilantro sprig placed just so—roll off the side of the taco onto the aluminum plate. There's little time to snap a photo or scoot the spilled filling back into the shell. The structural integrity of any puffy taco is brief—maybe two minutes—and then the fried shell begins to turn to mush due to the weight of the fillings and any collected moisture.

In an age when foods are advertised as convenient, puffy tacos aren't quick and easy. Perhaps that's why they aren't found in many towns outside San Antonio. "Good food shouldn't be easy," Barrios-Treviño says. That hasn't stopped myriad restaurants and taquerias from selling what are advertised as puffy tacos or puffed tacos—even in Texas. At Dos Comales Café y Cantina in Corpus Christi, the puffy tacos are inflated but not formed into the familiar taco shell shape. Rather, they are served flat with a hole cut in the top, where a filling—usually picadillo with an abundance of lettuce, tomato, and cheese—is placed. These puffed tacos echo the infladitas of Mexico.

For now, though, most of us will have to content ourselves with trips to San Antonio, where a Lone Star treasure is found at home plate or on the dinner plate.

Where to Find Them

Crispy Tacos, Flautas, and Taquitos

Caro's Mexican Restaurant

607 W. Second St.
Rio Grande City, TX 78582
956-487-2255

Chico's Tacos

4230 Alameda Ave.
El Paso, TX 79905
915-533-0575
multiple locations

Cielito Lindo

E-23 Olvera St.
Los Angeles, CA 90012
213-687-4391
cielitolindo.org

In-A-Tub

4000 N. Oak Trafficway
Kansas City, MO 64116
816-452-2149

8174 NW Prairie View Rd.
Kansas City, MO 64151
816-436-5888
in-a-tub.com

Jacala Mexican Restaurant

606 West Ave.
San Antonio, TX 78201
210-732-5222
jacala.com

Ke'Flauta

5100 Doniphan Dr.
El Paso, TX 79932
915-581-4028
keflauta.com

Lucy's Café

El Paso, TX
multiple locations
lucysrestaurants.com

Manny's Mexican Restaurant

207 Southwest Blvd.
Kansas City, MO 64108
816-474-7696
mannyskc.com

The Moonlighter

3204 W. Armitage Ave.
Chicago, IL 60647
773-360-8896
themoonlighterchicago.com

R-Bar and Grill

9521 Indianapolis Blvd.
Highland, IN 46322
219-922-8008
r-barandgrill.com

Rollies Mexican Patio

4573 S. Twelfth Ave.
Tucson, AZ 85714
520-300-6289
facebook.com/rolliestucson

Stella Taco

2940 NE Alberta St.
Portland, OR 97211
971-407-3705

3060 SE Division St.
Portland, OR 97202
503-206-5446

stellatacopdx.com

Tacoholics

1506 N. Lee Trevino, Ste. B-1
El Paso, TX 79936
915-929-2592
tacoholics.com

Taquizas Gilberto at Leyva's Bakery

551 E. Francisquito Ave.
West Covina, CA 91790
626-917-4095

Fry Bread Tacos

Kachina Southwestern Grill

10600 Westminster Blvd.
Westminster, CO 80020
303-410-5813
kachinawestminster.com

1890 Wazee St.
Denver, CO 80202
720-460-2728
kachinadenver.com

Mitsitam Native Foods Café

National Museum of the
   American Indian
Independence Ave. SW &
   Fourth St. SW
Washington, DC 20024
202-633-6644
mitsitamcafe.com

Navajo Hogan

447 East 3300 South
South Salt Lake City, UT 84115
801-466-2860
navajohogan.biz

Off the Rez

Seattle, WA
offthereztruck.com

Tocabe, An American Indian Eatery

3536 W. 44th Ave.
Denver, CO 80211
720-524-8282

8181 E. Arapahoe Rd. C
Greenwood Village, CO 80112
720-485-6738

tocabe.com

Puffy Tacos

Arturo's Puffy Taco
15693 Leffingwell Rd.
Whittier, CA 90604
562-947-2250
arturospuffytaco.com

El Patio Café
424 E. Central Ave.
Wichita, KS 67202
316-263-4490
facebook.com/elpatiocafeks

Henry's Puffy Tacos Express
6030 Bandera Rd.
San Antonio, TX 78238
210-647-8339

3202 W. Woodlawn Ave.
San Antonio, TX 78228
210-433-7833

henryspuffytacos.com

Javelina
119 E. 18th St.
New York, NY 10003
212-539-0202

1395 Second Ave.
New York, NY 10021
917-261-7012
javelinatexmex.com

Los Barrios Mexican Restaurant
San Antonio, TX
multiple locations
losbarriosrestaurant.com

Ray's Drive Inn
822 SW 19th St.
San Antonio, TX 78207
210-432-7171
raysdriveinn.net

Resident Taqueria
9661 Audelia Rd. #112
Dallas, TX 75238
972-685-5280
residenttaqueria.com

Tacos at Davila's BBQ in Seguin, Texas.

CHAPTER 3

Barbacoa *and* Barbecue Tacos

Out from the pit

REGION(S): Mainly Texas, the American South, and California, but also found across the country

CLASSIC EXAMPLES: Smoked brisket, barbacoa de cabeza (whole beef head), cachete (beef cheek), lengua (beef tongue)

TORTILLA(S): Corn and flour

LOWDOWN: Smoke 'em if you got 'em—preferably in an earthen oven, but an offset smoker will do. Why? Because barbacoa is barbecue.

Armando "Mando" Vera is likely the last of his kind. The stocky, mustachioed, pitmaster owns Vera's Backyard Bar-B-Que in the border town of Brownsville, Texas. Grandfathered in after the city reformed its health regulations, Vera's is the only known restaurant in the Lone Star State where traditional barbacoa de cabeza de res en pozo—translated as pit mesquite-smoked cow head barbecue—is legally prepared.

Now that most commercial barbacoa cooks have been forced to take their cow head cooking indoors into large stove-top steamers or ovens, I'm thankful for Vera's underground exception as I sample a pinch of cachete, or beef cheek (the most common form of barbacoa), from a red-and-white paper boat set in front of me. There is an almost imperceptible scent of smoke, like the barely visible waves of heat rising above the pit. The fat has melted away in the long, slow cooking process, leaving the meat glistening.

This is Texas, specifically the Rio Grande Valley, where chips and tortillas are considered necessary utensils. So, using my fingers, I lift two helpings of barbacoa the size of a pair of limes into fresh corn tortillas, give each parcel a shot of homemade salsa, and finish with the traditional garnishes of cilantro and chopped white onion. I take a bite and am silenced.

My day's drive to South Texas, which began at three o'clock in the morning when my traveling companion picked me up at my house in Dallas and ended at lunchtime in Brownsville, was worth it just for those first bites. The city itself, however, makes for an odd mecca of barbecue.

Mando Vera, owner of
Vera's Backyard Bar-B-Que.

Chain restaurants and big-box stores frame Interstate 69E into Brownsville; mom-and-pop shops and restaurants branch out from there. The frame houses along the Rio Grande are dilapidated. Farther north, newer middle-class homes peek out from side roads. Whole stretches of land have been cleared and reduced to dirt, while downtown storefronts, once abandoned, are slowly being reoccupied. It is nothing like the verdant agricultural hub described to me by friends and family. The soul of Texas, the heart of beef country, the birthplace of Tex-Mex, the bridge between old Mexico and new Texas—this place is worn around the edges.

It's hard to say whether the city is on the upswing like neighboring McAllen to the west or barreling toward desolation à la Harlingen to the north. But whichever way Brownsville and the Valley are going, culinary traditions continue to prevail, and none is as significant to the region as barbacoa.

Barbacoa is barbecue. In fact, the word "barbecue" is the English interpretation of the Spanish word. What we know as barbecue in the United States was originally encountered by Europeans in the Caribbean Basin and on what is the modern Latin American mainland. As Spanish explorers and missionaries noted at the time, barbacoa was used to describe a grain store or a stick framework upon which meat or fish was grilled or roasted. In a letter to the Spanish king dated 1520, Hernán Cortés described it as meat cooked under the ground and sold by vendors in the main market of Tenochtitlan, the capital of the Aztec empire. The sixteenth-century explorer of the American Southwest and northern Mexico Álvar Nuñez Cabeza de Vaca claimed that human flesh was among the meats suitable for barbacoa.

Early interactions between Europeans and Indigenous communities left barbacoa with a "barbaric" connotation, says Andrew Warnes in his book, *Savage Barbecue*. This negativity continued through the sweeping reforms of the food science movement of the late nineteenth century and early twentieth century, which couched its actions in racist language and symbolism and made villians of street vendors. Selling food on a public square was labeled unhygienic and less than human. Cooking food in a hole in the ground was even worse and health regulations were eventually changed to ban earthen-pit cooking unless, as current law requires, the pit (or pozo) is lined in concrete.

But the shadow of barbarism continued to darken barbacoa's name well into the twentieth century. Take, for example, the seemingly innocuous *Gordo* comic strip. Created, written, and drawn by Chicano artist Gustavo "Gus" Arriola and commended as building a bridge between Mexican and American cultures, the *Gordo* series ran from November 24, 1941, to March 2, 1985. Through its titular character, the Mexican bean farmer and tour guide Perfecto Salazar "Gordo" Lopez, and the supporting cast, the comic strip introduced stateside audiences to Spanish-language phrases like "hasta la vista" and occasionally included recipes. One 1953 strip saw a taquero chatting with Gordo about a stubborn donkey. "Nothing would make that obstinate ass move!" says the taquero. "Finally . . . someone suggested I build a fire under him! . . . That's how I got started in the barbecue business." Gordo's reply was to choke on his taco. This punchline braids the long-running suspicion of Mexican meat preparation provenance and a negative attitude toward barbacoa.

Not all Americans looked down, as it were, on barbacoa. It was described as "fit for the table of a king," by Austin, Texas, author Fanny Chambers Gooch in her 1887 recounting of her time in Mexico, *Face to Face with the Mexicans*. Gooch goes on to describe the laborious cooking process she witnessed. The protein used wasn't beef, though. Once done, it was "a delicious, brown, crisp, barbecued mutton." And considering the hard work that went into preparing barbacoa, it wasn't something made for a family dinner; rather, it was purchased at the local market ready to eat.

Although evidence of earthen-oven cooking in Texas goes back several thousand years, South Texas barbacoa de cabeza practitioners trace at least to the time Americans began immigrating to Texas in the nineteenth century. When Anglo cattle ranchers butchered beef, they would pass on the unwanted cow heads—brains, eyes, and all—to their Mexican ranch hands and vaqueros. These workers would do what they could with the scraps.

They cleaned the discarded skull and meat, wrapped it in maguey leaves and/or burlap, and placed the head into a pit heated by mesquite coals. The pit would be filled with maguey and soil, and the head would be left to cook overnight or longer.

This method of preparation is given a modern update at Vera's Backyard Bar-B-Que, where the family's barbacoa customs date back to Vera's uncle, who was taught the process by a gentleman from Mexico and then went into business with Vera's father. Later, in 1955, Vera's father opened his own restaurant.

"It started across the street," Vera says, pointing to a parked red pickup truck. His parents' store was a meat market that cooked and sold barbacoa in the same way that storied Texas barbecue joints like Kreuz Market in Lockhart and Louie Mueller Barbecue in Taylor trade in brisket, ribs, and sausage. Born in 1960, Vera grew up in the business and takes his father's lessons to heart.

"First, I clean [the heads]," he says. "I soak them in water and wash them. I take the blood off—not all of it, but most of it. Then we wrap them in foil." Once protected in extra-heavy-duty aluminum foil, the unseasoned cow heads—up to ninety, but usually only forty to fifty—are placed in his brick-lined barbecue pit and covered by stainless steel sheet metal, which is in turn covered with packed soil. There they'll smoke for eight to twelve hours. I ask Vera how he knows the mesquite coals are hot enough for the beef and when the heads can be removed. "Like this," he says, extending his bare forearm out over the pit.

Vera's is only open Friday, Saturday, and Sunday, but preparations begin much earlier. His weekly process entails gathering his materials on Wednesdays, cleaning the heads on Thursdays, and starting the fire on Fridays. The barbacoa is then ready to be removed from the five-foot-deep pit on Saturday morning for weekend consumption—which is important because barbacoa is a festive dish, one that is most commonly served on Saturdays and Sundays when there is ample time to savor it.

As Vera and I sit at a picnic table inherited from a long-shuttered barbecue joint, we're not at all concerned with the past or the process of our meal. We're simply digging in to all that is barbacoa. In front of us are lengua (tongue), paladar (palate), and mixta (a chopped mix of leftover meats from the head). What's not included on the table is an ojo (cow eye), a delicacy Vera describes as "Mexican caviar." I call it "something you sample once." I did so two years ago, when a friend presented me with one cooked in a West Dallas backyard. Its texture is of a firm grape that pops under concerted effort. Vera says the eyes are the most popular cut, but he isn't much for it either. Like me, Vera has had eye once. "But I prefer something else," he explains.

While we sit eating our preferred cuts, chatting and gingerly trying to remove twists of beef and flecks of cilantro from between our teeth, I point out customers, both Hispanic and Anglo, all local, stopping in for their usual takeout orders and ignoring the menu. (No one but us outsiders, the ones who make pilgrimages to meet the last of his kind and to taste something of a traditional preparation that is in danger of disappearing with the pitmaster's passing, stays to eat at Vera's.) Business is just fine, the pitmaster says. In fact, it is picking up. Business can increase by 40 percent after Vera's Backyard Bar-B-Que is mentioned in a magazine or newspaper story.

He leads me outside to the corrugated metal smokehouse behind the restaurant. The pit room is not much larger than the five-foot-square space that stores the cow heads that have kept Vera's in business for decades. It's small. That a singular Texas barbecue style is coaxed from such tight accommodations is a wonder. It's downright magical.

Indeed, there is an element of alchemy and mystery to barbacoa. While eating more beef at another Sunday session at the restaurant, the buddy who drove down to the Valley with me was doing backroad reconnaissance. Upon his return, he reported spotting a small but promising place, its gravel parking lot jammed with pickup trucks and a line of people out the door. An hour later, we drove to the establishment and found a wood frame building

Barbacoa pit at Vera's Backyard Bar-B-Que.
PHOTOGRAPH © ROBERT STRICKLAND.

and attached carport brimming with baseboards, trim, window frames, and planks that had ostensibly been removed from an interior in the process of demolition. A meek Chihuahua guarded an open door to the side yard. But there was no longer any sign of food or customers. So we cut our losses and hit several joints along and near Southmost Boulevard, the border-skirting road on which Vera's sits.

All these restaurants prepare barbacoa according to current health regulations, by steaming it. And it's everywhere on weekends—even at the place where Vera gets his tortillas, Capistran Tortillas & Bar-B-Que. There, barbacoa is ordered at a drive-through kiosk where the menu is painted directly on the walls.

Marcelo's Tacos, another stop down the street, offers barbacoa from a stove-top steamer. When I asked the people behind the counter for the size of the vessel, an elderly gentleman stretched his right arm over his head, his left toward the floor, and laughed.

Not all that I would call barbacoa is prepared in pits or cookware, nor is it always beef. Unlike the fare at Sylvia's, Vera's, and Capistran, El Pastor Mexican Grill, a restaurant in McAllen, Texas, specializes in cabrito al pastor (shepherd-style kid goat). The animal is butterflied and spit-roasted over coals, in the same manner as the barbacoa witnessed by Spanish conquistadors and missionaries. Guests are offered their own view of the foods at El Pastor as the cooking is done behind glass near the eatery's front entrance. And the results are delightful. Gaminess spears my taste buds. Crispy skin snaps. The urge to order some of the offal creeps up. Perhaps some machito—tripe stuffed with heart, liver, and sweetbreads. It was one of the few non-beef meals I would consume. Yet, in this part of the country at least, barbacoa is all about the cow—specifically the head—and the traditions passed down for generations. And Vera's is the last bastion of the old ways.

It doesn't have to be the last pit-smoking restaurant standing, though. In Dallas, when Four Corners Brewing Company purchased the land on which they would build their current location, the owners included a concrete-lined barbacoa pozo. It's protected by a metal grate. Anyone can look into it. I have done so many a time, Four Corners beer in hand. Most visitors probably walk past it without noticing it. So why would a craft brewery install a barbacoa pit? Because Four Corners was founded in part by a Texas Chicano, the company's beer labels are inspired by Mexican Loteria cards, and its brand identity embraces Latino heritage, right down to the name of its beers, including my favorite, the El Chingón IPA.

The idea of a barbacoa pit in such a case seems like an obvious choice. But pouring concrete into a hole to create a barrier between earth and meat isn't easy, though it's not exactly difficult. The Four Corners pozo took three days to finish. It's simply a delicate procedure that requires patience, which is how a supervisor at the Brownsville Public Health Department put it when I asked him why there was a prohibition on in-ground preparation of barbacoa de cabeza. As he put it: "It's not that we no longer allow it. We're just more stringent. It's a delicate matter."

Before Mando Vera's father was packing cow heads into an in-ground oven, barbecue joints across Texas—from Wilson's Barbecue in El Paso to the Bar-B-Que Pit in Brownsville—peddled tacos. With each passing year, more barbecue and Mexican restaurants sold barbacoa and barbecue. They were offered at taco shops and disseminated as newspaper recipes nationwide—even in Wilmington, Delaware, and Sheboygan, Wisconsin, where "the Mexican 'barbacoa' has been adapted and taken over North of the Border, becoming the favorite for family cookouts and casual entertaining in the summer months." According to a 1966 recipe printed in several newspapers across the country, the meat of choice in the case of "Barbacoa Mexicana" is chicken—key to which is the marinade of dry vermouth, cinnamon, honey, lime juice, garlic, and salt.

Most businesses—for example, Guajardo's Taco House, a breakfast taco emporium in Del Rio, Texas—didn't differentiate between barbacoa and barbecue per se, listing what they sold as simply "BBQ." But others, like Taco Village in McAllen, Texas, distinguished between the two. In 1967, the restaurant sold orders of three tacos with tomatoes, white onion, and lettuce for twenty-five cents, including "Bar-B-Q" and barbacoa. The menu reads like a smoked meat connoisseur's wish list. Cabrito and Polish sausage were available as twenty-five-cent tacos and barbecue was available in burger form as "pit ribs and Bar-B-Q Meat" and lamb. Farther down the Lower Rio Grande Valley in Brownsville, the Bar-B-Que Pit sold "Bar-B-Que Tacos" for a dime in 1964. Barbacoa and barbecue were familiar to Americans, but the heart of the preparations was in the Lone Star State.

It continues to be so with Valentina's Tex Mex BBQ in Austin where Central Texas barbecue (brisket, ribs, sausage) is served alongside the South Texas–type barbecue with cushy flour tortillas. Like many Mexican American and Mexican restaurant stories, the tale of Valentina's begins with the absence of a childhood dish and the desire for it. In this story, the person behind the barbecue is Miguel Vidal. Raised in San Antonio, where his restaurant experience began as a dishwasher at the age of fifteen, Vidal moved to Austin in 1999. He relocated to attend St. Edward's University on a soccer scholarship and worked at his cousin's restaurant, Ranch 616. "I wanted to play soccer professionally," Vidal says. "I played semi-pro. I played for Austin Lightning and here and there after college. But I had some injuries."

At the time, Vidal says, he was also missing the way he ate with his family. "When I was eighteen years old, coming from San Antonio to here in Austin, the tacos were different, the Mexican food was different," Vidal explains. "I was always yearning for what I grew up around. When my family would get together, when we would barbecue, it was sliced brisket and whole and half and quarter chickens with rice and beans and salsa and tortillas. That's the spread!" The kind of communal or familial feast has long been a part of barbacoa and barbecue. They are party foods, meant for special occasions—from holiday feasts to quinceañeras to the botanas of Del Rio, Texas, the big community barbecues that afforded candidates a chance to meet one another and voters.

It was that spread that Vidal wanted to showcase, but it took him a few tries to get there. "I was always working with something." He started a T-shirt company. In an effort to promote a friend's band, he played with them a little bit, and argued they should play art shows and sell food. "I thought, there should be a San Antonio–style taco shop; the kids would kill it. The idea was always there and the first idea was tacos. I wanted to bring what my mom made at home. Not barbecue, nothing like that. The first real kind of idea was to do tacos better than anyone."

When he told his parents the plan to showcase the family's food traditions from a truck, they were unconvinced. "My father was especially skeptical," Vidal tells me. But the future pitmaster was undaunted, assuring them that "no one will make tacos like this here. No one is doing it. No one has. No one is showing the love that we get in the backyard, bringing it into the culinary world, into a restaurant, and sharing it with people."

Vidal notes that his first job in Austin was formative. It wasn't at a restaurant. It was at the Four Seasons Hotel where he worked the valet stand. "I didn't know what it was like to stay at a five-star hotel," Vidal says with the feeling of a man who hasn't forgotten where he comes from, what he wants, and what he has sacrificed.

> I didn't know what it was like to give that level of service and the level of experience. Meeting those people, going into the kitchens, seeing the dishes that were coming out of their kitchens, seeing the level of service they were expecting out of a doorman or valet parker—that kind of was what was hitting me. That level of service and the level of food and the creativity and the work. So I was sort of trying new things. But every time I would go home and eat my father's brisket and eat flour tortillas and eat enchiladas, make tacos out of the food, I thought, "You cannot get food like this back in Austin." This food was as good as eating a five-star meal. When I was throwing around the idea later on in life to my dad and my family, they were like "Are you sure people are going to want to eat that stuff?"

The first location of Valentina's Tex Mex BBQ trailer was along Austin's downtown West Sixth Street nightlife corridor. There was an initial price pushback. Vidal recalls it originally came from the Latino community and blue-collar workers. "We had some construction workers come in and they were like '¿Cinco dollares por un taco? ¿Qué pasó, papá?' I said, 'Look, just take them. And you tell me it's not worth it.' Then they started coming back. They'd buy our stuff." Here and there people would remark that it seemed like a high price for tacos. But when customers see the barbecue pit and learn that Vidal spent sixteen hours working the brisket—that is, out of a twenty-four-hour process that includes trimming meat, the sixteen-hour smoke, and a six-hour rest before he can cut and slice the brisket—they come to understand the quality that makes Valentina's one of a kind. "Then we make the tortillas [four hundred in a shift]. Make the salsa fresh. So we have this twenty-four hours that I put on a tortilla and I charge six dollars for it now. And it's gone." Vidal swishes his hands in the air like a magician whose assistant has vamoosed. "When the people eat, they get it."

Vidal and I are discussing the genesis of Valentina's Tex Mex BBQ in what is the realization of that vision: the third location for the food trailer operation. We're in a corrugated steel-covered and -sided picnic-style dining area decorated with Texana and soccer memorabilia on the southern outskirts of Austin. English soccer is on the televisions hung nearby. Johnny Cash, Jimi Hendrix, and Led Zeppelin tunes play over the sound system. One side of the dining space leads to the future brick-and-mortar home of Valentina's. Work is ongoing and measured. Vidal is in no rush. His mesquite-fired barbecue pits are within view as are supplemental rigs and the main trailer, where customers order the brisket, chicken, whatever smoked meat preparation strikes their fancy from either the Tex (sandwiches and meat by the pound) or the Mex (tacos, elotes, daily specials) sides of the menu.

Then there's the Real Deal Holyfield, a signature taco Vidal first served to his father. "His favorite thing was huevos rancheros," the younger Vidal recounts. "That was his plate. We were serving breakfast only on the weekends at that time, and he came up on a Friday. And he said, 'I could really go for some huevos rancheros. Make some right now.' I shot back, 'Man, I'm getting ready to open for lunch. I'm busy.'" It's at this point in the story that Vidal turns his shoulders down and in toward the table, a physical reaction I've witnessed in Latinos that signals resignation in the face of a potential curse brought down on you by a parent. It's a fear that the angels would smite you and baby Jesus would weep if you did not do exactly as you were told. "'All right, Dad, I'll see what I can do,' I said."

So I started digging around. Since we were going to serve breakfast on Saturday, we had the eggs on Friday. I had some potatoes, some produce that had come in. We were getting ready to prep for the next day. So I had all the elements to make it. I had the charro beans. So I fried up some bacon. Put the bacon aside. Used the grease from the bacon to add to the smashed-up charro beans. And I cut up some potatoes—a small amount—fried them up really quick. So in my head, I'm going to make him huevos rancheros. But then, I thought, "Hey, I'm going to make him a taco instead—a huevos rancheros taco for him." I press out the tortilla and apply a little more pressure so it can be bigger than our normal ones. I put the beans on top of it, I put the potatoes on, I put on the bacon, I put the eggs with our red salsa on top of that. And then I was thinking that it just needs a piece of brisket because the brisket looks pretty good today. So I cut him a nice fat piece of brisket to put on top of that. And I put it in front of him. And at the time I was making it, I was listening to Snoop. That line was in my head. It was that line he was rapping, "It's the real deal Holyfield." So I put the plate in front of him, and he asked, "What's this?" It was automatic. I said, "It's the Real Deal Holyfield." It just sort of came out. He ate it and said, "That was good."

Vidal is telling me this story with the mischievous grin of a child who is going to do what he was told, but not the way his parent expects.

"'It was badass, right?'" the younger Vidal shot back. "'Tomorrow we're going to do that taco.' It started to do well right away. Damn, people will pay this kind of money for this kind of taco, I thought. There's a lot of food in this. One and you're good. So we started doing it every Saturday, and people began requesting it. When we moved to South Austin from downtown, it went on our menu every morning."

Vidal and I are sitting for the interview on a Sunday, which—and this was completely intentional on my part—means smoked barbacoa de cachete tacos are available as a special. The shredded beef, punctuated by tender, glistening chunks with just enough fat to keep the meat from drying out, is topped with onion, cilantro, and salsa, eliciting declarations of "Thank God, it's Sunday!" In Texas, it's not really Sunday if there isn't barbacoa, and Vidal puts his own spin on Sunday barbacoa. First, it's only cheek meat and it cooks for twelve hours. Nothing about that is unusual. What differentiates Valentina's barbacoa from others is that, like all the meat served from the trailer, the beef cheek is cooked on the pit using a braising method that calls for onions, salt, pepper, garlic, and a beer-water combination. The collected juices from the smoked braising go into the house-made salsas, giving everything that goes on the customers' trays a bit of the work and heart that goes into Valentina's food.

> Could this have worked anywhere else? I don't know. I really think that this had all the right timing and elements coming together for it to really work. I personally think if I had opened up in San Antonio, it would have been a lot harder at the time. It was on the cusp of the huge wave of barbecue that was coming in, the cusp of new-school barbecue and people breaking some traditions. It's funny. People say, you're fusion food, but this is how I always remember eating. I see it being something that was there before there was a name for it. Taking old traditions or primitive types of cooking and basic necessities of living life to create what we are serving.

To hear Vidal tell it, he would never have thought of opening Valentina's any place other than Austin. "If I wanted to show my family's food to other people and do it around the best, I wanted to be the best. And in Austin and the surrounding area, in my opinion, that's where the best are." Indeed, Valentina's counts James Beard Award–wining barbecue pitmaster Aaron Franklin of Franklin Barbecue among its loyal customers.

Even with all his success, Vidal isn't one to stray far from the smoker. Sure, he'll take the Valentina's Tex Mex BBQ brand to food conferences and festivals like the Southern Foodways Alliance fall symposium in Mississippi or the Charleston Wine and Food Festival in South Carolina or to catering events, but you're more likely to see him hauling mesquite logs from the storage rig to the smokers, his face intent on the task of making kick-ass barbecue. It's a look that has one wishing to never meet Vidal in a shadowy alley after crossing him. But then the man smiles and even his spiky black hair seems charged with joy.

In a culinary field dominated by popular white male pitmasters, Vidal's barbecue has occasionally been seen as novel. Although perhaps

Barbacoa in the city

From its Central Mexico cradle, barbacoa spread north and came to thrive in the United States, perhaps nowhere more emphatically than in Philadelphia, where Cristina Martinez and her husband, Ben Miller, have been serving barbacoa de borrego (lamb barbacoa) since 2014. Although South Philly Barbacoa started as an informal word-of-mouth, out-of-the-home operation, Martinez and Miller moved into a storefront in the City of Brotherly Love in 2015. Their barbacoa is a labor of love, sure, but it's a labor of necessity born from the couple's need to send money to Martinez's daughter in Capulhuac, Mexico. The financial support is why Martinez traveled north. She could not provide her daughter with the education she wanted without crossing the Rio Grande, which she did as an undocumented immigrant. She worked her way up kitchen ranks, gaining enough professional culinary experience to open her own place with Miller. It's a daring endeavor not only because South Philly Barbacoa offers customers borrego prepared using the method Martinez learned at age six in her native Mexico, but also because she is, as previously mentioned, undocumented.

Martinez is arguably the most famous undocumented immigrant in the United States. In South Philly Barbacoa's first year, *Bon Appetit*'s Andrew Knowlton named it one of the best new restaurants in the United States: "They're not just restaurateurs but also community organizers, encouraging Philadelphia chefs to acknowledge the contributions of undocumented restaurant staff. But

# of brotherly love

they don't need a megaphone; they have barbacoa.... The steaming barbacoa is chopped to order, so tender it looks ready to melt."

In the wake of the accolades, articles and features focusing on Martinez, Miller, and South Philly Barbacoa began running in newspapers and magazines. Martinez and Miller gained opportunities and gained a voice. Miller has spoken at international food conferences such as the MAD Symposium in Copenhagen and advocated for immigration reform. And in 2018, Netflix dedicated an episode of *A Chef's Table* to Martinez. All the while, Martinez and Miller have continued to prepare and share the same luscious lamb barbacoa to everyone who wants it—undocumented or not—because as Martinez says, "It brings joy to my heart."

South Philly Barbacoa
1140 South Ninth St.
Philadelphia, PA 19147
215-360-5282
southphillybarbacoa.com

new in presentation and unabashedly Central Texas in style, Valentina's Tex Mex BBQ very much specializes in keeping with tradition and is now among the best—if not the best—barbecue spot around. It certainly offers the quintessential Texas taco. I dream about the chicken taco with its thin scarf of surprisingly subdued tomatillo-habanero salsa balanced by a batch of house-made guacamole, and I never skip out on the Real Deal Holyfield when I make it in time for breakfast. I request the brisket sliced to reveal the bark as dark as a bedroom shielded from sunrise by blackout curtains.

Valentina's used to be the first stop on an annual Austin Black Friday family taco tour. We eventually made it the last stop because kicking off a taco crawl at Valentina's meant everything else left us dejected. There is nothing in Austin that measures up to the Valentina's standard. Its influence is felt east toward Houston and down into San Antonio.

Valentina's helped prompt the slow move from white bread to flour tortillas as the starch accompaniment of choice for Texas pitmasters. It's a welcome change. Tortillas should be the obvious choice. 2M Smokehouse in southeast San Antonio serves traditional Texas barbecue—unabashedly smoky with pronounced black pepper, coarse black bark, and an embracing smoke ring that fades into the meat. There's a Mexican American touch, too. Taco choices, served on fluffy, slightly dusty house-made flour tortillas, are limited to lean brisket, pulled pork, or turkey. The serviceable brisket is improved by a dose of pickled nopales (chopped cactus pads) and pico de gallo—too much though and the vinegar's tang overpowers the beef and flour tortilla. Better is the pulled pork: a substantial serving of juicy, threaded smoked meat comes with islands of bark that add to the textures and remind the customers that they're eating barbecue. Then there's 2M's smoked serrano chile and queso Oaxaca sausages. Although they're not available as tacos, the sausages are worth ordering and adding to another taco. Not too spicy, with a milky white cheese strong enough to withstand a long rest in a smoker without distentegrating, the sausage is snappy and delightful, and when it finally hits your tray, it makes waiting in line before 2M Smokehouse opens at eleven worth it.

For co-owner Esaul Ramos, 2M is the culmination of experience that began in high school when barbecue went from hobby to obsession. Ramos then decided he wanted to spend his life working in smoked meat. He quit his job and drove to Austin from his hometown of San Antonio to apply for a job at La Barbecue. A week after applying, he got a call offering him a job as a cook under La Barbecue's then pitmaster John Lewis. Working there, Ramos says, helped him hone his skills and taught him how to cook on a larger scale, as opposed to the typical backyard barbecue setup.

It also gave him the confidence and foundation to open his own place in his old neighborhood, the heavily Hispanic Southside of San Antonio, with his friend Joe Melig. Before they could open a brick-and-mortar spot, Ramos and Melig ran a series of pop-ups at a church in Lytle, Texas, about thirty minutes outside San Antonio. The pastor had given them access to the church's kitchen with space enough for tables and chairs inside and out. It wasn't long before the city of Lytle shut down the operation. "From that point, I just said, you know what? Screw it," Ramos explains. "We got to find a building. So I got on Craigslist and I found this building."

The place was originally for sale, but there must have been something the owner liked about Ramos or what Ramos said because the young pitmaster persuaded the owner to lease them the building. "I told him, 'You won't be sorry. Eventually we'll buy it from you.' I gave him my word and that was enough. Maybe I just talked to them the right way or maybe it gave him a good vibe. And he said, 'OK.'" Ramos and Melig threw more pop-ups at the building that would one day house the restaurant to help generate cash and pull together their savings to open 2M. "Thankfully, we were able to hold up our end of the bargain."

From the beginning, 2M Smokehouse—the name derived from Marquez, Ramos's grandparents' surname, and Melig—was to be built on a Mexican American sensibility. It began with flour tortillas. "I grew up eating everything with tortillas. So yeah, tortillas and barbecue, go hand in hand. I wanted to bring them in. It's not new. We're not reinventing the wheel. We're just adding our twist to barbecue. It's a lot of the flavors that I grew up with as a kid and that's what I try to impart into the products that we have at 2M. The early days were rough, to put it mildly. In the beginning we were staying here 24/7," Ramos says, noting there is a bed in the pit room. "We would get here on a Wednesday and we wouldn't go home until Sunday evening. Now it's just a couple days, here and there."

The Chicano-style barbecue doesn't stop at tacos, sausage, and tortillas. On the first Sunday of the month, Ramos and Melig offer beef-cheek barbacoa seasoned with salt, pepper, garlic and onion powders, cumin, and coriander. Because cooking the barbacoa in a pozo is prohibited, Ramos does everything else he can to get the classic barbacoa taste and texture with a touch of Central Texas barbecue. The meat is wrapped in banana leaves and foil before being placed in the El Mexicano smoker—"because it works hard like one," Ramos chuckles—"which gives the beef a cover of smoke before it's placed in pots for braising, which is also done in the smoker. That allows the meat the opportunity to break down and impart the fine texture San Antonians like in their barbacoa." The preparation is proving so popular, Ramos and Melig might consider offering barbacoa more than just once a month.

This Mexican American style of Central Texas barbecue—Tex-Mex barbecue, for short—is having a moment, and Ramos couldn't be happier or prouder. "Other people are starting to see that a lot of these Hispanic base flavors are where you get your bold flavors and that's where you introduce barbecue into Mexican dishes. They just marry very well together. I'm actually all for it. I think it's great. But for me, it's different growing up in San Antonio. It's predominantly Hispanic here. So I already knew that I was going to bring that here to speak to the customers." It wasn't until people from non-Chicano majority cities or cities with increased Latino influences began to flock to 2M, which sits on what is essentially a backcountry road, that Ramos says he truly understood that barbecue and Mexican food belong together.

The Pit Room in Houston serves beef tallow-infused flour tortillas in taco form. Among the best of those tacos is a lightly smoked chicken, with charred garlic cloves and a cylinder of crisped Monterey Jack, soaking in its own juices. It's a barbecue delight. Tejas Chocolate + Barbecue in Tomball covers brisket, sausage, pulled pork, turkey, and pork belly as sandwiches with a brioche bun or as two tacos with flour tortillas.

Before Valentina's, 2M, Tejas, and other Mexican American–inflected Texas barbecue, there was Davila's BBQ. Established in 1959 by Raul Davila in a segregated Seguin, Texas, Davila's BBQ is now run by Raul's grandson and third-generation pitmaster Adrian Davila. If the elder Davila experienced racial discrimination as a Mexican American man opening a barbecue restaurant and welcoming African American customers before desegration, Adrian Davila isn't aware of any details. But it's not for lack of trying. Davila acknowledges that it wasn't unusual to see a Mexican American as a kitchen or restaurant worker, but not as the head of a kitchen. He put questions to his grandmother, Raul's widow. "How did y'all get the money? Why did grandpa want to work in a kitchen?" His grandmother's answers involved the family's long history in commerce. Adrian's great-grandfather owned a general store in nearby Luling in the 1940s. When Raul Davila and his brother Adolph were old enough, the pair took a train to Kerrville to work at a restaurant, instead of taking over for their old man. They were twelve and fourteen years of age, respectively. What restaurant? Adrian doesn't know: "I never could really figure that out." His grandmother was mum on the subject.

Davila thinks his grandfather was able to open and successfully run his operation because he and Adolph proved themselves in barbecue, beginning in a local processing plant in Luling, where they were butchers and made sausage. In the 1950s, Adolph left the plant and opened his own business—a gas station-grocery store-restaurant combination that sold cigarettes, beer, and dry goods alongside barbecue sandwiches of sliced brisket and other smoked meats, including sausages. The Davila brothers also sold those sausages to area businesses and restaurants as far away as San Antonio and Austin, as well as in Seguin. It was there in 1959 that Raul

Davila decided to open his own business in an abandoned schoolhouse. The two backrooms provided living space for Davila, his wife, and their four kids. The cash register and a couple of tables were in the front. Raul built his own pit and began using the recipes that are still used today. "The toughness of the labor of barbecue and making sausage or breaking down animals—I think that is how they were able to find a common ground. The skills learned while working in that processing plant and the barbecue knowledge they gained is universal," Davila says.

Barbacoa, an occasional special at Davila's BBQ, was featured in a June 2018 *Man Fire Food* episode. The lamb barbacoa, prepared in a pozo at Davila's ranch, was offered in taco form. The meat was loaded with chiles, dried oregano, and dark spices. It was a reminder of the importance of tradition and culture to Davila. "I remember we'd go to school and the other little kids would show up with their greasy bags for tacos and other kids would say, 'Ew, you're eating brains.'" He notes that nose-to-tail eating is en vogue now, but Mexicans were always eating nose to tail. "It was efficient food. It was eating and using all the ingredients. When you harvest an animal, that's doing the animal respect." Davila's continuing the tradition. "We don't have to move toward it because we're already in it. This is what we're doing." The seasoning they've been using for their barbecue for sixty years is the same as that going into the tacos they've been making for forty years. "It's embedded in us."

Davila calls his family's style of smoked meats "vaquero barbecue," which links the barbacoa tradition, starting in the early days of Mexican ranch hands and cowboys, and the use of mesquite, which the Davilas have used since the beginning, to Central Texas barbecue brisket and the resurgent interest in open-fire cooking.

The brisket may be the same and the tacos are still tacos, but Davila is having fun with them on his catering and lunch truck. Purchased in 2017, the truck is what Davila considers his food lab. It's where he serves a mesquite-smoked brisket taco loaded with flavor and heat. The tortilla

Davila's BBQ in Seguin, Texas.
PHOTOGRAPH BY ROBERT STRICKLAND.

parcel is packed with brisket, pico de gallo, a touch of barbecue sauce, a slice or two of avocado, and a crema of Sriracha, garlic, and mayonnaise.

Davila's BBQ is as invested in barbecue as it is in the community, sponsoring local sports teams and selling tickets for events like the Noche de Gala and Fiesta Patrias, celebrations of Seguin's Mexican heritage. It's the kind of hometown place that you wish you could keep to yourself, but it's too dang good not to share. The history is rich, as is the food, which clearly skews to the regional style of smoking while being unique enough to set it apart from the local barbecue temples that regularly draw an hour or longer wait. The catering business that Adrian's father, Edward, launched in 1973 also helped distinguish it from other barbecue operations. Adrian joined the business in 1991 at age nineteen, but long before then he had seen the community that barbecue, specifically Davila's BBQ, had created. He had watched his grandfather break down the meat, whether a whole animal or quarter of a cow, transform it into food, cook it, and send it to the front room. Customers were laughing while eating the barbecue. Barbecue creates memories. And it starts with something as primal as a bloody animal. "When you barbecue, you're expressing yourself and who you are," Davila says. "That expression is creating memories for other people. That's what got me into it."

Texas barbecue restaurants aren't the only barbecue spots using tortillas in tacos or interpreting barbecue through a Latino prism. Podnah's Pit Barbecue in Portland, Oregon, tops house-made flour tortillas with brisket, ribs, eggs, and cheese for breakfast tacos. Its sister restaurant next door, La Taq Cantina & Taqueria, is a Tex-Mex wonderland, serving killer puffy tacos. Meanwhile in Brooklyn, Morgan's Barbecue offers cornmeal-crusted catfish tacos with a gum-tingling jalapeño-cabbage garnish. Queso-slathered brisket tacos with pickles and ranch-dipped pulled pork tacos are available at Hometown Bar-B-Que, also in Brooklyn.

In Nashville, whole-hog pitmaster Paul Martin, owner of Martin's Bar-B-Que Joint, offers tacos two ways. One puts standard smoked meats into tortillas. The other is a taco that is not a taco. It's the Notorious Redneck Taco, served since the restaurant opened in 2006. Subbing a hoecake bigger than your hand and too firm to bend for a tortilla, the Redneck Taco is held down by saucy, messy barbecue pork and capped with a slaw that is more texture than layered flavor. I asked Martin why use a hoecake? "Nashville traditionally has served its barbecue on top of a hoecake. We added slaw on top [because *all* barbecue sandwiches should be topped with slaw] and we called it the Redneck Taco." It now ranks as one of the top five menu items at Martin's Bar-B-Que Joint. In 2017, 55,088 Redneck Tacos were sold. More novelty than novel, the Redneck Taco is yet another barbecue taco—a taco in name only as it refuses to accept a definition of a taco that isn't Martin's—that can't touch Valentina's Tex Mex BBQ.

Something else sets Valentina's apart from Martin's: the environment. Although Valentina's is open and friendly—it's not unusual to see Vidal making the rounds in the back dining patio offering customers a can of beer from the twelve-pack under his arm—the front dining room at Martin's BBQ felt down right marginalizing for this brown boy. No sooner had I finished my meal, put down my fork and knife, and crumpled the last of five napkins on the cafeteria tray than a young man of color appeared to my right prepared to clear my setting. That's when I noticed several young men and women standing against the perimeter ready to swoop in to attend to customers' needs, chillingly evocative of house slaves at their stations. I got out of there as fast as I could.

Where to Find Them

Capistran Tortillas & Bar-B-Que

Brownsville, TX

multiple locations

Davila's BBQ

418 W. Kingsbury St.

Seguin, TX 78155

830-379-5566

davilasbbq.com

El Pastor Mexican Grill

600 W. Expy 83

McAllen, TX 78501

956-627-3929

Hometown Bar-B-Que

454 Van Brunt St.

Brooklyn, NY 11231

347-294-4644

hometownbbq.com

La Taq Cantina & Taqueria

1625 NE Killingsworth St.

Portland, OR 97211

971-888-5687

lataqpdx.com

Marcelo's Tacos

3305 E 26th St.

Brownsville, TX 78521

956-546-0021

Morgan's Barbecue

267 Flatbush Ave.

Brooklyn, NY 11217

718-622-2224

morgansbrooklynbarbecue.com

The Pit Room

1201 Richmond Ave.

Houston, TX 77006

281-888-1929

thepitroombbq.com

Podnah's Pit BBQ

1625 NE Killingsworth St.

Portland, OR 97211

503-281-3700

podnahspit.com

Tejas Chocolate + Barbecue

200 N. Elm St.

Tomball, TX 77375

832-761-0670

tejaschocolate.com

2M Smokehouse

2731 S. WW White Rd.

San Antonio, TX 78222

210-885-9352

2msmokehouse.com

Valentina's Tex Mex BBQ

11500 Manchaca Rd.

Austin, TX 78748

512-221-4248

valentinastexmexbbq.com.

Vera's Backyard Bar-B-Q

2404 Southmost Rd.

Brownsville, TX 78521

956-546-4159

K-Mex taco.
COURTESY CHI'LANTRO.

CHAPTER 4

K-Mex

Korean tacos go on a roll

REGION(S): Los Angeles, nationwide

CLASSIC EXAMPLES: Short rib with kimchi, tofu with kimchi, kalbi (or galbi)

TORTILLA(S): Corn

LOWDOWN: Although relatively new, K-Mex tacos are the template for the codification of a regional style on a national scale. The K-Mex taco godfather, Roy Choi, is credited with jump-starting the gourmet food truck movement.

The spring rain had let up in downtown Austin, Texas, but the humidity, fed by damp concrete, was inching ever higher. It was enough that wrinkles straightened out during a short walk from the house to the car and then to Chi'Lantro BBQ, a food truck shelling out Korean-inspired tacos and dishes like kimchi fries. It was 2010, and the truck had rolled out earlier that year.

A sprinkle of sesame seeds dots an order of Korean short rib and pork tacos spiked with kimchi and tempered by ribbons of fresh green lettuce. At the helm of the operation is Jae Kim, a native of South Korea who moved to the United States when he was eleven, graduated from California State University, and established his first business, the Foothill Café coffee shop, at the age of twenty-one, before relocating to Austin.

Jae Kim did not grow up reaching for corn tortillas with one hand and a spicy pork-Asian pear combo with the other, nor did he call the lettuce wraps jammed with kalbi (marinated short rib), jalapeños, and kimchi "Korean tacos." Though he was born and raised in South Korea, he admits that when he was living in California and he and his family craved Mexican food, they would take their carne asada or burritos home and immediately take all the traditional Korean side dishes, or banchan, out of the fridge. "It was just what you did," he says. Consider banchan the garnishing possibilities for tacos. There's kongnamul (soybean sprouts dressed in garlic, sesame, soy, and scallions). There's danmuji (pickled daikon radish paired with onion). There's a litany of stir-fried greens. There's pajeori (loops of

Jae Kim, owner of Chi'Lantro.

green onion salad). And, of course, there is olfactory-scraping kimchi joining the hundreds of side dishes. The whole lot of them are ripe for tortilla nestling.

But now Kim was in Texas, where tacos are as essential to the local diet as kimchi is to Korean foodways. He found inspiration in what was happening in California with Roy Choi and the Kogi BBQ to Go food truck. Choi is the classically trained chef whose food truck, Kogi, gave rise to the K-Mex taco possibilities. We'll get to Choi and Kogi's story shortly.

But first, more about Jae Kim and his idea. Chi'Lantro was a fully formed concept from the start. Yes, the development in California was exciting, but Kim was interested in what he calls "Korean Tex-Mex." Torchy's Tacos and Tacodeli were direct inspirations. He wanted the bulgogi-style rib eye to mirror carne asada. Carne asada is key. But so is pork. Kim wanted thinly sliced pork bathed in a deep red gochujang chili paste to look like al pastor. It was all about the look and feel that the tacos and burritos would evoke.

So he pulled together the capital—which included $30,000 in savings—needed to jump-start his new enterprise and shelled out his first tacos on a frigid day in February 2010 at the Dobie Mall, near the University of Texas at Austin. Nobody came. Then one gentleman, who Kim thinks felt sorry for him, bought something. The next day, the same guy brought a friend. Eventually, Kim realized that Chi'Lantro did well late at night. "We were just the perfect drunk food truck at two in the morning," Kim says. A second truck followed in 2011 and with it, a popular service at Fort Hood in Killeen, Texas, where soldiers noted the use of fresh cilantro—"I like that it has cilantro in it. It's hard to get a dish with fresh herbs here," one soldier said—and Chi'Lantro's vivifying mayo-based sauce. "It's good on everything they've got here," another soldier said.

The rain shower that had stopped just before lunch on the day I first visited Chi'Lantro kept the line manageable for customers and made for good people watching from my space on an adjacent concrete retaining wall. What struck me most about the folks excited about K-Mex was how many asked

Kimchi fries.
COURTESY CHI'LANTRO.

to have the kimchi left out of the order. Kim had noticed this, too. Tired of having to throw out so much kimchi at the end of a day of service, he set out to find a way to repackage the spicy fermented cabbage for customer attraction. "As it gets more fermented, it's much more intimidating to somebody who is trying kimchi for the first time," Kim says. "I had to throw it away, and it was such a waste of money." He called what happened next as coming from "a very desperate place." The first thing he did was throw kimchi on the grill to allow the aroma of the cooking cabbage to flow from the truck. He was betting the smell would lure customers, especially the late-night drunk crowd that was his early core demographic. Second, he dunked fries in the fryer. Kimchi and kimchi fries are now among the top-selling items. Customers request an extra piling of kimchi on their orders.

For Kim, this popularity is inspiring, and his Korean Tex-Mex is a gateway in a corn tortilla. Chinese and Japanese foods in this country have been historically geared toward the white American palate, but not Korean food. It's stayed under the radar and has been served to Koreans, not white Americans. But the rise in popularity of K-Mex food has exposed the American public to possibilities. "When customers realize that what we serve is Korean food, they get excited about it and become curious about what kimchi is and what traditional Korean barbecue is. When they begin to research traveling to Korea, I get excited about that. It's absolutely rewarding," he says.

I met Kim a couple of times before interviewing him for this book. The man is a smiler. The smiles he has had during our face-to-face interactions compel me to return to Chi'Lantro. I want a taste of Kim's smile-inducing K-Mex tacos whenever I'm in Austin. The tacos dazzle and are a tad prickly with spice. They swell with sweet, tangy kimchi above swirls of meat.

These tacos—and kimchi—drive him to work harder and grow, not just as a business, but as a person. Chi'Lantro's first brick-and-mortar location opened on Austin's South Lamar Boulevard in 2015. Seven other outposts have opened since then. Chi'Lantro was also an inaugural vendor at the first annual Taco Libre Austin held on Mother's Day weekend 2017. This quick growth is due in part to Kim's appearance on *Shark Tank*, the TV series that puts entrepreneurs in front of a panel of venture capitalists, including owner of the Dallas Mavericks basketball team, Mark Cuban.

In the episode, which aired November 11, 2016, Kim tells his story, beginning with the move to the United States with his sister and mother after his parents' divorce, through the successful early years of Chi'Lantro. He is tenacious. During his ebullient pitch for $600,000 and a 15 percent stake to the potential investors, Kim notes that the appearance marks his third attempt to make it on *Shark Tank*. He walks one of the panelists through the creation of a Korean rice bowl and serves the other four investors prepared rice bowls. Everyone loves the food! But, one by one, they all decline his proposal for funds. All except real estate mogul Barbara Corcoran, who offers Kim the requested money in exchange for a 30 percent stake. Kim counters with gratitude and a 20 percent stake. Corcoran accepts, adding, "You're a straight shooter; I'm crazy about you."

Kim's story as a food truck and restaurant owner is linked to Kogi BBQ and Kogi's chef, Roy Choi. Like many of the entrepreneurs and chefs he has inspired, Choi was born in South Korea and immigrated to the West Coast as a child—in his case, at the age of two in 1972.

The United States wasn't completely foreign to the Chois. His Korean-born parents had spent time in their youth in the United States. Choi's father moved to the states to study politics and diplomacy at the University of Pennsylvania, the University of Colorado at Boulder, and later UCLA. His mother moved to the United States to attend art school. Choi's parents met in 1967. Two years later, they moved back to Korea. Their return to the United States after the birth of their son came in the midst of increased Korean immigration that occurred between the relaxing of Asian immigration regulations in 1965 and the 1979 assassination of South Korean President Park Chung-hee. We'll get to that part of the tale later, but, first, Roy Choi's story.

Choi was thrust onto the streets and into the kitchen at a young age. His parents moved him and his little sister across Southern California, beginning with a stint in Koreatown in Los Angeles, where the Chois owned a liquor store, and later at Silver Garden, the Korean restaurant his parents opened in Anaheim. He was then "adopted by the city streets," as he writes in his autobiographical cookbook, *L.A. Son: My Life, My City, My Food*. Choi "discovered the urban forest of old palms and sycamores right below Olympic Boulevard. Made my way into alleyways and onto their broken sidewalks." He encountered tamales and kimchi, and, this is integral, he got a taste of carne asada.

His parents struggled with alcoholism. And Choi struggled with fulfilling his role as a dutiful son in the Korean tradition—excellent grades and aspirations of a career in medicine or law being among the expectations—managing his life as a child of the Los Angeles streets, and attempting to assimilate. The intersectional life of 1980s and '90s Southern California, a Korean American upbringing, and street life, which included a heavy dose of music, Latino culture, and low-rider culture, "was all a jumble."

There was hope in cooking. He attended and graduated valedictorian from the Culinary Institute of America in Hyde Park, New York; did a stint at the Michelin-rated Le Bernardin in New York; and wound up working at California country clubs and hotels. His culinary career in a rut, Choi was open to an idea his friend Mark Manguera shared. It wasn't a fleshed-out concept. There was no business plan. It was a Korean barbecue-filled taco. "Wouldn't it be delicious?" Choi remembers Manguera asking. That was enough. The recipe testing began, and a vision of a Korean taco began to coalesce. As the chef remembers, it involved his parents' old restaurant, his childhood fridge, Orange County, and memories of kicking around the streets. "Los Angeles on a plate. . . . The flavor tasted like the streets. And the look said home." A 1980s catering truck was acquired. He was home.

As Choi understood it, for a fusion taco—an American taco—to be a true taco, the elements must bridge seemingly disparate components to create something that understands both cultures. As he told NPR's Terry Gross during the 2013 promotion of *L.A. Son*, Choi believes his K-Mex taco is culture and identity:

All the pieces of my life started coming together. It was almost like an avalanche. And so it was growing up, it was being around low-riding, it was being around growing up in Korea, the immigration, being around the American school system, all the snack food and junk food that I've eaten, all the tacos that I've eaten. And so it was all these things, and then I really wanted to make it feel like Los Angeles. I felt like it had to be just like a street taco in LA. So it was on a four-inch tortilla, two tortillas griddled really nicely. And the meat—I wanted to do Korean barbecue, but then I was thinking carne asada. So it was this feeling that I wanted the meat to be cooked, then chopped, like it's been chopped all day, and then thrown back on the plancha, so it gets crispy again. And then I thought of that feeling you get—it was like trying to capture everything in one bite—right before you eat Korean barbecue. You get a little salad. So I was thinking of that salad, and if I could put that in there, and then cilantro and onion, which come on true Mexican tacos, and then a salsa roja. But then the salsa roja we would combine with the dry chile árbol and the smoked flavors and the roasted garlic, but then also with Korean chili paste, lime juice, and soy sauce. And all that just came together, just whirled together, and then sesame seeds on top. And then, in the slaw, it has green onions, cabbage and Romaine lettuce. So it's like this whole meal in one bite.

The Kogi truck debuted in Los Angeles in late 2008, introducing customers to Korean-Mexican food (aka K-Mex) and gaining almost immediate traction via social media, specifically Twitter and blogs. *L.A. Taco,* a local news and lifestyle website, took notice in 2008: "Is there anything more Los Angeles than a Korean BBQ taco truck that cruises the streets delivering high quality cuisine to the city's taco lifestyle hubs?" Word of what Choi and company were doing with Kogi earned the attention of journalists and bloggers across the country. Periodicals such as *Newsweek,* the *Wall Street Journal,* even the *New York Times* ran Choi profiles and articles about the K-Mex trend. "We salute the Kogi truck and hope it is the inspiration for many more," *L.A. Taco* wrote in the first of many posts highlighting Choi and Kogi. Indeed, Kogi is credited with kicking off the gourmet food truck trend that continues to this day.

Fewer than two years after Kogi was founded, K-Mex dining establishments, whether truck or brick-and-mortar, were opening across the country, from New York to Portland, Oregon to, yes, Austin. K-Mex was heralded as a novel culinary hybridization, and Choi was anointed its architect, expanding the Kogi brand into a fleet of trucks, a storefront location, a short-lived airport counter, as well as other food concepts. He also consulted on Jon Favreau's film, *Chef,* about a frustrated fine dining chef who finds personal fulfillment in opening a Cuban food truck.

As charmed and glitzy as this chef life appears, Choi is more interested in the intersection of social issues and food. More importantly, he's never forgotten his LA roots. In response to a 2014 *Reddit* Ask Me Anything (AMA) question about the food truck culture he inspired, Choi wrote:

> i never imagined anything other than making tacos for the people in front of me. but the energy then gave me and my team the imagination to dream and trust our instincts. of course, it's here to stay because it was here before twitter. It's the way the whole latino culture eats and working-class citizens enjoy their lunch. and now it's spread its wings to involve everyone. It's a beautiful thing that helps small business in america and beyond. Grassroots underground independent love [*sic*].

Wanting to do more, Choi worked with Thomas Jefferson High School kids in Watts in South Central LA to open a campus café. Then, at the 2013 MAD Symposium in Copenhagen, he announced he was undertaking an effort to use healthy fast food to alleviate hunger and nutritional deficiencies in the food desert of Watts, where, Choi noted, 44 percent (65,000) of children have parents who make approximately $22,000 or less and live in poverty. He went on to run through ever-worsening statistics of poor academic scores for school children, including those at Thomas Jefferson. As he went through other chilling statistics, Choi's voice occasionally cracked under the sadness of truth.

Next, he addressed the hunger epidemic in a city rife with farmers' markets, showing slides of liquor store after liquor store, noting there are no chef-driven restaurants or organic establishments in neighborhoods like Watts. There are fast food joints and a few supermarkets, the latter usually taking the form of rebate shops selling expired food. "Our neighborhoods with the highest crime rate and the highest drop-out rate and the least jobs are getting the worst foods," Choi said to a room full of the world's best chefs—René Redzepi, David Chang, Margot Henderson, and others—as he paced nervously around the stage.

Then he said, "Chefs can do anything." What if, he asked, classically trained chefs were required to open a street cart in inner-city neighborhoods for every sit-down restaurant they established? Chefs need to apply their maternal, caretaking characteristics to those who desperately need it, he said, not just to those who can afford it. Do chefs have the guts to break this cycle?

Choi, dressed in camo-print pants, spotless Nike kicks, an extra-long Stüssy shirt, and Los Angeles Dodgers cap, wasn't speaking intellectually. He wasn't spouting hypothetical musings. He backed up his words, having gone into neighborhoods and served the public from his Kogi trucks. He admitted he had achieved hero status. But he needed to do more for those who needed it. He began working with the kids at Thomas Jefferson High School. Still more needed doing. Food deserts didn't need to exist. Choi's presentation cut to my core. My parents skipped meals so that my sisters and I would not go hungry. Now, I'm privileged enough that my son wants for nothing. I'm privileged enough that I can carve out time to write a book about tacos. (I know I can do more, too.)

In 2014, Choi and chef-partner Daniel Patterson announced they would open Loco'l, an alternative fast-food restaurant that adapted the chef-driven aesthetic to the McDonald's model. They hoped to challenge the status quo. Loco'l opened in Watts in 2016. The next year, the *Los Angeles Times* named Loco'l the restaurant of the year. A second location in Oakland, California, set up operations in 2017. But all Loco'l outposts were closed in 2018, and the business transitioned to a catering service model. That year was a dynamic one for Choi. In June, the chef shuttered his restaurants in the Line Hotel in Koreatown in Los Angeles. He opened a new restaurant, Best Friend, in the Park MGM in Las Vegas in December 2018, and he set out across America to film *Broken Bread*, a TV series exploring community food systems. The series aired in spring 2019 on KCET and was co-produced with *Tastemade*, a food and travel website with video-focused content.

Why do I bring this up? Choi communicates in the vernacular of street food. Tacos are street food. They are the food of the everyday. Tacos happen and then they trickle up. It's essential that we remember this. Never forget where the taco started: the street. That's true for Mexico. That's true for Los Angeles.

Choi remains directly involved in Kogi's operations, but he's more than K-Mex. K-Mex is more than Roy Choi. Yes, Choi showed the consumer potential of fusion eats and inspired other Korean Americans and Korean immigrants to introduce their cuisine through quickly established orders like bulgogi and galbi to a wider audience via the approachable vessel of the corn tortilla. He was the internet megaphone that alerted the country to a local style of cooking thick with the fragrance of corn and chili pepper hot sauce that preceded him. Unfortunately, after several attempts, I was unable to connect with Choi for an interview while I was writing this book.

For Cecilia Hae-Jin Lee and others in the Southern California Korean community, K-Mex was a natural evolution fueled by proximity to and interaction with the region's Mexican and Mexican American community. No one invented Korean tacos, she says. It was as clear as any day in the 1980s that her family spent grilling at Griffith Park. "There would be a Mexican family barbecuing next to us. The Mexican family is looking at our food. We're looking at their food. The next thing you know we're sharing each other's food," says Lee, a food and travel writer and photographer and the author of several cookbooks, including *Quick & Easy Korean Cooking* and *Quick & Easy Mexican Cooking*. "They would put our kimchi in their tortillas. We would put their carne asada in our rice and kimchi. We were doing that while growing up in the early '80s. We were eating Korean tacos then," she explains, adding that anyone who worked at a Korean grocery store or a Korean restaurant in the LA area absolutely put kalbi in a tortilla. Tortillas were and continue to be a Southern California fixture. You see a tortilla. You put that tortilla in your hand. You fill that tortilla.

But throwing something into a tortilla doesn't automatically make it definable as a taco. Choi understood that. The entrepreneurs featured in this chapter who have been inspired by Choi understand that. Lee understands that.

In addition to her writing, Lee is also the owner of Nabi Korean Restaurant, the Los Angeles Union Discount Swapmeet counter eatery serving

Korean-inflected dishes—among them, tacos with a house-made salsa verde. Tacos weren't on the menu until a January 28, 2018, *Saveur* magazine profile of the restaurant accidentally stated that Nabi sold tacos. "I think there was a typo. We sold tortas, not tacos," Lee says. "'So, damn,' I said. 'Now I got to make Korean tacos.'" Shortly after she added tacos to the menu at Nabi, Lee began offering Korean burritos due to customer demand. Tamales brimming with kimchi and cheese in cornhusk envelopes are available at Christmas.

That a modern, Asian take on tacos was introduced to the American public through a Los Angeles food truck and captured our appetites with the similar trucks and restaurants that followed is striking enough, but when the size of the Korean community in Los Angeles County is revealed, it's incredible that something gained national attention and canonization so quickly. The Korean population of LA County, as of the 2010 census, stood at 216,501. That's a 16 percent increase from 2000 census data, which reported that population at 186,350. During the same time period, there was a 32 percent increase in the total Korean population in the United States. Between the censuses, California saw a 31 percent increase in its Korean population.

For most of the twentieth century, Korean immigration to the United States was sporadic and the data on the number of immigrants are unreliable. Koreans who immigrated were counted in the Japanese quota and were required to get permission from the Japanese passport bureau. In 1939, the Korean population of LA County maxed out at three hundred. Then the legislation that tightly controlled Asian immigration to the United States was repealed, leading to increased movement from the Korean Peninsula to the United States, mostly to Los Angeles. In 1970, there were 39,000 Koreans living in the United States. But, according to the next census, which followed the 1979 assassination of South Korean President Park Chung-hee by the director of the Korean Central Intelligence Agency and subsequent increased movement to the United States, there were 290,000 Koreans residing in the United States in 1980. Cecilia Hae-Jin Lee's family was part of the 1970s diaspora. Ten years later, there were 568,000 Koreans in the United States. It was at that time, Lee remembers, that Mexican corn-dough flatbread and Korean fermented and pickled cabbage came together

But it would take nearly twenty years for the term "Korean taco" to appear in print independent of K-Mex as a culinary category. The earliest appearance I can track dates to the September 1, 1996, *Los Angeles Times* restaurant review of 2424 Pico by S. Irene Virbila. The longtime food critic describes what the menu calls Korean tacos as marinated beef in "frilly lettuce cups." (Never mind that a taco requires a flatbread to be a taco.) Years later, in a review of Tabletop Grill & Sushi in Phoenix, Arizona, Carey Sweet describes a plate of romaine lettuce for the construction of "Korean tacos." The phrase was used with creative license.

David Choi and Andy Heck originally opened Seoul Taco in St. Louis as a food truck in 2011, but established a brick-and-mortar the following year in the eclectic Delmar Loop neighborhood. The K-Mex operation has since expanded across Missouri and has locations in Chicago. Sue Wong Shackelford, who grew up in a restaurant family, opened Kalbi Taco Shack in 2016, also in St. Louis. Although named for a Korean pork preparation, Kalbi hawks more than K-Mex. Tacos stuffed with jackfruit or teriyaki chicken are also popular.

TaKorean in Washington, DC, slings five taco options, from chicken seasoned with a ginger-popping marinade, ever-present bulgogi, and hoisin-washed tofu to seasonal vegetarian choices, which have included seared cauliflower simmered in a concentrated, prickly chili-lime glaze. The slaw here isn't standard, and kimchi isn't a given, although it is an option. A balanced vinaigrette of rice vinegar and sesame oil dresses romaine. Soy sauce and gochujang (red chili paste) wash purple cabbage, ruffled kale, and carrots. Other toppings mirror the complementing concept of banchan. There's pickled daikon with turmeric, avocado with a touch of ginger and rice vinegar, scallion swirls, salsas aplenty, and a poached egg.

Pan-Asian tacos

K-Mex-peddling taquerias and trucks weren't the only tortilla-based operations established in the wake of Roy Choi's success. Waves of Asian fusion food establishments have found inspiration in the Los Angeles chef's application of heritage flavors. In New York, Takumi Taco serves Japanese-inflected options, including a fried gyoza taco filled with a chilled slap of big-eye tuna sashimi brambled with jicama, avocado, and cucumber. Takumi also sells a Sapporo-braised short rib taco with taut, rich beef, tangy Japanese mustard, prickly-yet-mellow yuzu-avocado salsa, Napa cabbage, and black sesame seeds on corn tortillas. Nom Mi Street food truck offers a Vietnamese-inspired fish taco in Houston, Texas, a city with a sizable Vietnamese population. You might think Fort Lauderdale, Florida–based Box of Chacos slings tortillas with a Middle Kingdom spin, but the mobile food vendor cooks up a Thai red curry beef taco with a bleu cheese slaw, an ancho chile-seasoned chicken perked up with Korean-style ranch dressing, and a shrimp tempura taco.

Takumi Taco
75 Ninth Ave. (and various locations)
New York, NY 10011
212-989-4200
takumitaco.com

Nom Mi Street
Twitter: @NomMiStreet

Box of Chacos
35 SW 19th Avenue
Fort Lauderdale, FL 33312
954-648-6535
boxofchacos.com

Just outside DC, at Taco Ssam, tacos start with house-made corn tortillas and are available with Korean components or familiar Mexican options, meaning a customer can nosh on a kimchi-bursting pork taco before moving on to a lengua taco. Taco Ssam ups its bona fides Mexicano with chilaquiles, tamales, and menudo. Menudo!

Farther north, in New York City, Phillip Lee opened his taco truck in spring 2011. Like Jae Kim, Lee sees Kimchi Grill as a vehicle (no pun intended) by which to share Korean cuisine with a non-Korean public. A brick-and-mortar location opened the following year in the Brooklyn neighborhood of Prospect Heights and there is a kiosk in the Harborside Terminal Building food hall. Addictive and snappy Korean fried chicken is a surprising and welcome menu option here.

Before Chi'Lantro and other K-Mex rigs and restaurants, there was KOI Fusion. The Portland, Oregon, truck and brick-and-mortar operation was born from the 2008 decline of the building and architecture industry to which Bo Kwon, KOI Fusion's owner, sold architectural imaging software. "The writing on the wall was that the whole building sector was going to have a big, big hit," Kwon says. "The architects were saying, 'Not only can I not buy this software, I have to shut down my firm and I have to fire all my architects and go back to working for myself.'"

While considering his next move, Kwon picked up a side gig as a nightclub host. That's when his future culinary venture began to take shape. Hanging out at Portland's burgeoning taco truck scene after the clubs let out for the night—when trucks and carts were the only things open—Kwon decided that operating a truck seemed like a viable option. "I'd go eat at taco trucks with all the industry employees, all the bartenders, and all the bouncers, and we'd all just get together and the only things open were the taco trucks. I thought, I know where to park, and I know there's not much competition at night." His parents weren't keen on the idea of Kwon going into a high-risk field. "I was explaining to them, 'Hey, I want to start a food cart, but do it with Korean food.' At that time, Korean food was not popular.

And so my parents really thought I was just a little bit crazy. They said, 'No one knows our food.'" Then Kwon's parents saw a segment on Roy Choi and Kogi BBQ on a Korean-language television station. It was a fateful moment for Kwon and his folks. "Roy was a Los Angeles Koreatown native, and so they just supported it." Kwon's father said, "Look at this guy. He kind of has your idea and he's doing it, you know? Wow. How cool is that?"

Kwon tried to connect with Choi from Portland, but his attempts didn't get anywhere. So he called in sick to work, took a red-eye flight to Los Angeles, and began asking around for Choi at the restaurant where the chef worked at the time. Everyone told Kwon that Choi wasn't available to talk. "You can set up an appointment," he was told. Kwon was undeterred. Feigning the need to use the restroom, he ducked into the kitchen door, saw Choi, and yelled his name. "He turned his head. I was like, 'My name is Bo, from Portland, Oregon,' and he totally remembered all my messages. 'I took a flight just to meet you.'" The way Kwon recounts the episode, Choi was blown away by his move, said he could give him five to ten minutes, and asked how he could help. Kwon explained his idea for the truck, which by then had morphed into franchising Kogi, and told Choi that he even had recipes.

Choi could see Kwon's passion about the project but noted that the timing wasn't right. So he encouraged the budding entrepreneur to share Korean food through the prism of his own influences. That's what Kwon saw the chef was doing, having grown up in Koreatown next to South Central and Latino neighborhoods. Both just happened to have Latino influences in their lives. After all, Choi wasn't just trying to build a brand. He was trying to create a blueprint, a movement for Koreans. "Half my fridge was always Korean food because my parents were there and then half of it was by influence," Kwon says. "So I would have quesadillas and peanut butter and jelly and different cold cuts that my parents would never use. What would happen is I would run out of food, and we'd have to make items all the time when my friends would come over, and we'd make kimchi quesadillas and turkey bulgogi sandwiches. It's how I grew up. It made sense to do that."

Kwon's parents threw themselves into the project alongside their son, coming up with recipes and different concepts. They had long-term relationships with Korean vendors, and they began to source products from these contacts. What would be KOI Fusion became a family business and, for Kwon, born and raised in Portland, a way to connect with his cultural heritage. "It gave me an identity going to a predominantly non-Asian school, growing up in a non-Asian community where the only time I got to see a lot of Koreans was at church."

Tenacious Kwon next walked up to the first food truck he saw on the side of the road, Rosie's Grill, and approached Rosie, who was working in the truck, with a business proposition. He wanted to buy the truck, but Rosie didn't want to talk. She refused to speak English to Kwon, even though she speaks English. "So I just sat there and ordered food." By the end of the experience, after asking her probably four times if she would sell her food truck, Rosie waved Kwon over, saying, "I can see you're serious. I'll talk to you about this truck, but it's not mine. It's my son's." She called her son, and he was there within five minutes. As they explained it, Rosie and her husband had purchased the truck for their son, and the son had decided he did not want a food truck. As a result, Rosie was stuck running the truck. Rosie's son told Kwon if he had the money, the deal could be completed that day.

There was a problem, though. Kwon had never made a taco. He had never made salsa. He had never made pico de gallo. Rosie began to laugh. "She was probably thinking, 'This crazy, crazy Korean,'" Kwon chuckled. He told them he wanted Rosie to continue working. He would watch and learn, and he would pay her. She would keep the money made on the truck. "OK. Come back at three in the morning," was Rosie's immediate response. "That's when we start." For three weeks, she made Kwon show up at three to make pico de gallo and salsa. He did everything Rosie told him to do.

"I'm soaking it up, and actually, I'm having fun doing it, and she's now getting to know that I'm not trying to do this for the wrong reason," Kwon tells me. Over the long hours in close quarters, Rosie began to see how passionate Kwon was about the taco truck. He was serious. Rosie's workload began to lessen. She was making more money, getting paid hourly, and she got to keep the profits of the truck. A month later, Rosie told Kwon to bring his Korean barbecue to the truck. They would start selling his meat recipes with her ingredients—and not tell anyone. The pair stuck to their usual routes and sites, shelling out bulgogi and kalbi short ribs, and were met with instant praise. "Everyone came back saying, 'Whatever you guys did to your meat, keep doing it,'" Kwon recounts.

In April 2009, the truck's name was changed to KOI Fusion, which has nothing to do with the fish. Rather, it's an acronym for "Korean Oregon Infusion," and it represents Kwon, a Korean American born in Oregon. Rosie worked for Kwon for two years and retired. The first brick-and-mortar opened in September 2010.

Today, KOI Fusion is spread out across six outposts, selling the same tender bulgogi that Kwon passed through the truck window alongside Rosie. Each meat and the tofu get a tangle of rice wine vinegar-bathed slaw and a smattering of crunchy bean sprouts with a small pile of cucumber sticks and shots of pico de gallo and cilantro. The cap of salsa is up to the customer, and the default tortilla is of the corn variety. This configuration, Kwon says, is born of the balance and layers, physically and figuratively, that characterize Korean and Mexican foods. For one, the base is the tortilla. For the other, the base is rice. Rice holds everything together and is accentuated by the banchan that offer juxtaposing flavors and textures, be they sweet, hot, sour, soft, mushy, crackling. It might not make sense to eat them individually, but composed in a tortilla, they achieve a tasty equilibrium. Take mole, for example. For as varied as they are—for example, mole poblano, pipian, mole de manzana, mole amarillo—moles share a balance that is greater than their individual parts. Perhaps that explains

K-Mex's almost immediate legitimacy. Taqueros and restaurateurs, like Rosie's crazy Korean, took what could have been a quick fad and helped fan a fiery hunger. Much like kimchi, whose flavor and aroma deepen as it ages, K-Mex's popularity is only intensifying.

Where to Find Them

Chi'Lantro BBQ
Austin, TX
multiple locations
chilantrobbq.com

KOI Fusion
Portland, OR
multiple locations
koifusionpdx.com

Kimchi Grill
766 Washington Ave.
Brooklyn, NY 11238
718-360-1839
kimchigrill.com

Seoul Taco
St. Louis, MO
multiple locations
seoultaco.com

Kogi BBQ
Los Angeles, CA
multiple locations
kogibbq.com

Fried chicken taco at El Mero Taco.

CHAPTER 5

Sur-Mex

Tortillas with a drawl

REGION(S): Gulf Coast, American South

CLASSIC EXAMPLES: Catfish, chopped smoked pork with jalapeño coleslaw and tequila BBQ sauce, and fried chicken, with a lot of cheese—whether cheese dip, queso fresco, or pre-shredded cheese mix.

TORTILLA(S): Corn and flour

LOWDOWN: Like Tex-Mex—and, really, all American tacos—before it, Sur-Mex is a regional American cuisine born from population shifts, industry, and ingredient availability. Although it can be traced back to at least 1990s Atlanta, Georgia, and the Sundown Café, this taco style remains in the earliest stages of development and codification. In that way, Sur-Mex is a Southern drawl—it's taking its sweet, sweet time.

E l Mero is us," say Jacob and Clarissa Dries, owners of El Mero Taco, a Memphis, Tennessee, food truck specializing in the intersection of the culinary traditions of the American South and Mexico, two of the world's greatest corn cultures. El Mero takes its name from Spanish slang for "the best." A way to express something is the best of the best in Spanish is to say "el mero mero." The Drieses met while attending culinary school in Austin, Texas, and relocated to Jacob's native Memphis after the city permitted the operation of food trucks. They specifically wanted to open a taco truck that was an extension of themselves. This Sur-Mex—the blending of Mexican and Southern cooking—is best experienced in the buttermilk fried chicken taco. Light and tangy with a blanket of queso blanco—melted warm white cheese dip beloved in Texas, where the dip is often made from orange cheese—the truck's signature taco is a marvel of incorporation on corn tortillas made at Tortilleria La Unica, also in Memphis. The disc is sturdy yet pliant. When crumpled in the hand, it blooms anew when the hand opens. It's certainly strong enough for the bird and the dressing. Sweetness pervades the taco, but there are reminders of spice in slices of house-pickled jalapeños.

I visited El Mero for a Thursday lunch at Court Square downtown. Other trucks join the Dries's rig on Thursdays, but none draws a downtown business crowd like El Mero. Jacob and I talked near the truck, watching the fried chicken tacos flit out of the window. As Jacob told me about how he and Clarissa met and then made the deliberate jump to a food truck, I chowed through a sweet potato taco in a helix of queso blanco and a side of smoked cheddar grits made from heirloom Tennessee corn and pumped with roasted poblanos. The same corn goes into the elotes side dish bobbing in Parmesan cheese-punctuated peppery mayo: all of it recognizably Mexican, all of it recognizably local. "It's basically me and my wife if me and my wife were a menu," he reiterates. There's a little from both sides. Some of it is amalgamation. Some of it is more Mexican. Some of it has Southern twang.

They've come a long way from their initial foray into food business ownership. For the first six to eight months while work was being done on the truck, El Mero Taco operated as a burner-and-home-kitchen-deep-fryer enterprise under a tent, serving its developing Sur-Mex style at art galleries and breweries. Once the truck was ready for service, Clarissa took the lead—only one of them could be dedicated full-time to El Mero—while Jacob worked at a Memphis Whole Foods Market as the prepared foods department manager. He got the barbecue counter up and running and was smoking everything from brisket to duck. Jacob made sausages while in the meat department, but as El Mero business picked up, he decided to demote himself in an effort to give the food truck greater focus. Eventually, he left his day job to commit himself to El Mero Taco. That was fall 2017, several months after I visited with the Drieses and enjoyed their tacos. "She took the handle on it big time," Jacob says with pride and excitement for Clarissa. "She was killing it."

Under such focused dedication, El Mero's tacos developed and are continuing to mature. One example is the albondigas and collard greens taco. Hand-rolled meatballs stewed in a chipotle-tomato concoction, a classic Mexican preparation, are coupled with a mess of straight-up collard greens before getting a shot of coleslaw and a splash of melted queso blanco. It's the stuff of homey soul food. It's gravy. Some new customers mistake it for Italian food. So maybe it's Sunday gravy.

But there isn't anything foreign at El Mero Taco or in Sur-Mex. Familiarity keeps popping up. There are similar flavors, like corn itself, as Jacob points out. Yucatán Peninsula achiote-and-citrus-clutching cochinita pibil is smoked underground. In the South, pork is also smoked—not underground, but smoked nonetheless. In 1980, the Memphis population clocked in at 646,356 with the Latino community only numbering 5,225. Thirty years later, the Latino population had increased to a whopping 41,994. During the same period, the non-Hispanic white population decreased from 331,779 to 177,735. Mexican food and tacos are not alien to the residents of Memphis. Interaction has cultivated a new perception and appreciation for Mexican food and led to the integration of Southern and Mexican cuisine.

Jacob and Clarissa Dries are an example of that integration. Take what each thought of the other's cuisines before they met: "I didn't know good Mexican food before I met my wife," Jacob admits. It was all nachos and crunchy tacos. Dinners with Clarissa at her aunt's house in Austin changed everything for him. Among the first Mexican dishes he ate was chile en nogada, a stuffed poblano chile draped in a walnut sauce accentuated by pomegranate seeds. The dish is a traditional platter served on special occasions and the holiday season. "Prior to that, my understanding of Mexican food was really the Tex-Mex-type of Mexican. After that, I thought, this is what it was all about." For her part, Clarissa thought Southern food was little more than barbecued pork. She had tried Texas barbecue while visiting family in the Lone Star State. "I don't think I had really good ribs until I moved to Memphis," Clarissa says. "But it's not just the barbecue for me. I love sides like grits. I had never tried grits before. I love them now. I love the richness of Southern food."

For Clarissa, being in a kitchen—mobile or otherwise—is following in her parents' and grandparents' footsteps. Her grandfather owned and operated the Casa del Sol restaurant in Juarez, Mexico. There he served American presidents, Mexican presidents, and culinary luminaries like Julia Child. After marrying, Clarissa's parents relocated to Oaxaca and opened three restaurants. Among them is Los Portales, open for about thirty years, a beacon of borderland eating in Oaxaca. Alongside the moles indigenous to the southern state, Clarissa's father cooks up alambres and cabeza.

Taco plate, El Mero Taco.
COURTESY CLARISSA AND JACOB DRIES
OF EL MERO TACO.

With recognizable ingredients, Sur-Mex tacos can seem safe and approachable, and there's certainly an element of culinary passport into the greater world of tacos through the menu. But El Mero embodies a new South, one whose communities are warming to the immigrants who over the last decades have begun calling it home. With the immigrants come their restaurants, unequivocally Mexican restaurants like Taqueria El Kora serving up birria on handmade corn tortillas. Marciel's Tortas and Tacos dishes out tortas, a style of Mexican sandwiches, and fried tacos (known as tacos dorados) filled with potatoes, refried beans, and chipotle-bathed chicken tinga, plated up and pressed with more refried beans between them. The concept of soul food isn't immune to the blender of Sur-Mex. Soul Fish Café—a restaurant that wears its name on its walls with trophies, images of impressive catches, and decorative fish—serves ample, spicy blackened catfish rolled in flaky flour tortillas.

My time in Memphis coincided with the 2017 Day Without an Immigrant, the nationwide boycott designed to call attention to the importance of immigrants to the United States. I realized that only the day before my trip and knew that several of my planned stops would likely be closed. Tacos Los Jarochos was shuttered behind a chain-link fence, and Taqueria Guadalupana #3 was dark. But Las Tortugas Deli Mexicana was open. A fast-casual shop specializing in tortas, Las Tortugas offers both a deep list of tacos and misleading propaganda meant to indoctrinate customers to owner José "Pepe" Magallanes's rigid idea of authentic Mexican food. Attached to the walls and glass in the restaurant are sheets of paper noting that sour cream, cheese, and—best of all—flour tortillas are "not Mexican." The sheets also describe menudo (tripe stew) and beef tongue as "very low end" Mexican food. A small cup of sour cream was served with my batch of tacos, which I ordered at the front counter and fetched from another counter on the side of the kitchen.

The addition of sour cream made me chuckle. The restaurant owner makes such a big deal about defining "true Mexican food" versus what he interprets as poverty foods and as Americans' tainted version of Mexican food, yet he serves sour cream, a thicker, heavier analog to Mexican crema. The irony of the sour cream was too rich for me.

Memphis is the home of Sun Records, barbecue ribs, and the Lorraine Motel, where Martin Luther King Jr. was assassinated in 1968 and which now houses the National Civil Rights Museum. Memphis is a city of color—colors, really. Through its Mexican and Mexican American population, the restaurants catering to those individuals, and other restaurants inspired by or clearly capitalizing on the popularity of Mexican food and tacos, Memphis is becoming a taco capital. And if you're in the mood for Sur-Mex, it's a required stop on a cross-country taco tour, and, once there, your first visit should be to El Mero, truly one of the best taco operations in the country.

I would be remiss here if I didn't mention the work of the Southern Food-ways Alliance (SFA). Under John T. Edge, the institute has commissioned oral histories and published articles on, among other topics, Latinos, food, and the transformation of the South. "El Sur Latino" was the theme of its 2017 fall symposium. The event convened chefs, scholars, journalists, and restaurateurs to discuss the next transformation of the American South. Professor and poet Steven Alvarez spoke about Atlanta's Plaza Fiesta, a space that more closely resembles a sprawling, colorful Mexican market than a suburban American mall. The shopping center is anchored by restaurants serving exquisite examples of Mexican food, and it lives, as Alvarez says, as a symbol of the rise of brown consumer power. At the SFA 2017 Food Media South conference in Birmingham, Alabama, Alvarez spoke about the course, "Taco Literacy," that he taught at the University of Kentucky in Lexington. The class investigated culture (including immigra-tion) and writing through the local Mexican community and its foods. Also present was Eddie Hernandez of Taqueria del Sol. The small chain with locations in Georgia and Nashville opened its first restaurant in 2000 with executive chef and co-owner Hernandez at the helm in the kitchen where the Sur-Mex regional style of tacos quietly developed.

I visited the soft-spoken Hernandez and business partner and co-owner Mike Klank at the original Taqueria del Sol on Atlanta's Westside, which is among the earliest restaurants to offer the fried chicken taco. Of course, it's not like anyone hadn't plopped breaded and deep-fried poultry into a tortilla before Hernandez. The Towne Crier Chicken restaurant (sister to the steakhouse that closed in 2018) in the West Texas city of Abilene adver-tised a fried chicken taco in 1972. "No one's inventing food," Klank says. The Taqueria del Sol version is unassuming: breaded and fried chicken tenders with lettuce and tomato. The poultry remains juicy beneath the lightly crisped exterior. The garnishes add cooling touches. It has a zinger of a companion in the Memphis Hot Chicken taco, an occasional special that, although fiery, keeps the spice at a manageable level. You might begin to sweat, but you won't begin to hallucinate or crawl across the ceiling.

Fried chicken taco at Taqueria del Sol.
PHOTOGRAPH © ROBERT STRICKLAND.

For Hernandez, this blending of cuisines simmered throughout a life that included a stint in a rock 'n' roll band in his native Monterrey, a two-year term as the mayor of Rosebud, Texas, and, ultimately, royally screwing up a batch of turnip greens while cooking at an early Mike Klank restaurant, Azteca Grill. "Those turnips were a mess," says Hernandez, who soon learned to properly prepare the greens for cooking. "We don't have turnip greens in Mexico!"

In 1991, the pair opened Sundown Café. It was there that the Sur-Mex taco unwrapped itself to the world with Taqueria Sundown, a thrice-weekly lunch service that Klank and Hernandez modeled after a taco truck. "We sent [the tacos] flying like you do at a food truck," Klank says.

One of the tacos developed for the lunch service remains on the Taqueria del Sol menu. Hernandez created a masa breading for a fish taco they were developing. A Mexicanized Southern-type tartar sauce went with the taco. Out went the pickled relish, in came the pickled jalapeños and poblanos. Fried seafood appears on the weekly taco special, one being The Bob, a fried shrimp package given crawfish mayonnaise, and, of course, pickled jalapeños. But for me, and many others, it's about the fried chicken taco. It's the restaurant's number-one-selling taco. I imagine that the line I saw form during my visits to the original Taqueria del Sol and the Decatur, Georgia, spot was for that blessed taco.

After the devastation of Hurricane Katrina in 2005 in which 80 percent of New Orleans flooded, the Crescent City saw an influx of Mexican, Mexican American, and Central American laborers, some of whom put down roots. It wasn't the first time the sudden surge of a Latino low-skilled workforce—dubbed "hurricane chasers"—occurred after such a natural disaster. In the decade following Hurricane Andrew in 1992, the non-Hispanic white population segment of Broward County in south Florida dropped from 75 percent to 49.9 percent, a significant difference for a region with a large Cuban and Puerto Rican population.

In the wake of Hurricane Katrina, the US government temporarily suspended the Davis-Bacon Act, which requires that workers be paid the prevailing local wages for public works projects. From September 2005 to November 2005, contractors were no longer required to pay market wages. Inspections to determine whether businesses were employing legal workers were deferred. The Mexican army crossed the US border and marched across Texas to New Orleans to assist in reconstruction. Some people, including laborers, stayed. However, the city's population shrank by more than half between April 2000 (484,674) and July 2006 (230,172), and the population hasn't exactly bounced back. The New Orleans population was up to 386,617 in July 2015, according to the independent Louisiana-based Data Center. Overall, the Latino population increased from 14,826 in 2000 to 21,929 in 2016. Put another way, it's almost doubled from 3.1 percent of the total population in 2000 to 5.6 percent in 2016. An even greater jump in population is in adjacent Jefferson Parish, part of the New Orleans metro area, where the Latino population increased from 32,418 in 2000 to 63,136 in 2016. That's more than 14.5 percent of the parish population.

Commerce hasn't recovered either. In 2005, there were 31,401 businesses counted. In 2016, that number had decreased to 29,002. A decade after Hurricane Katrina, the formal business enterprises in New Orleans numbered 29,794. In that total are Mexican-, Mexican American-, and Latin American–owned and operated businesses, included eating establishments.

To some, increased presence might have seemed like a new phenomenon, but New Orleans has a long history with Latin American cultures and food. It's where Benito Juarez sought refuge on the two occasions he was exiled from Mexico in the mid-nineteenth century. At one point, he worked as a roller in a cigar factory. Since the eighteenth and nineteenth centuries, ships carrying trade goods and people have traveled between New Orleans and Latin America. Although most Mexicans escaping the brutality of the Mexican Revolution in the 1910s crossed into the United States via Texas, some did flee to New Orleans. The majority of those Mexicans who ended up in the Crescent City were from Mexico's Gulf states. Moreover, many Mexicans who settled in New Orleans were able to move within Anglo social circles. They passed as white and were welcomed as white. As the families assimilated, their stories were largely lost to history.

One element stuck, though. The South, especially the Mississippi Delta, had become enamored with tamales, adapting them and creating a style specific to the South. As early as the 1890s, tamales and their vendors were mentioned in the crime beat pages of newspapers. The history of Latin Americans in New Orleans was rediscovered after Hurricane Katrina with the influx of Latino workers and the immigrant-owned food trucks catering to the immigrant workforce that needed fast, cheap, familiar food in reconstruction zones and along the city's periphery.

Then, in 2014, New Orleans experienced a taco boom with what the *Times-Picayune* called "a new breed of serious New Orleans taquerias," discounting, whether intentionally or due to deadline, all the food businesses that came before them. Maybe the critic Brett Anderson was referring to establishments that offered taco fillings of the pork-beef-chicken variety and suggesting that now Anglo-owned taquerias were exploring new territory. Maybe. It certainly doesn't come off that way. Local chefs were opening their own taco shops and Mexican restaurants—and fast. Among the restaurants that began selling tacos was Del Fuego Taqueria on Magazine Street. Former Commander's Palace and Jacques Imo's Café chef David Wright knew what he was getting into. "Most people have an idea of what Mexican food is before they walk in the door," Wright told me during a spring visit to his Magazine Street restaurant. "And we try to do some different things that you don't get at a lot of Mexican restaurants in America. . . . Some people are like, 'I don't even know how to pronounce that word, so I'm just going to skip over it because I have no idea what it is.' And that kind of sucks sometimes as a chef because it's delicious and you want them to eat it."

The vibrant Del Fuego tacos are planted on mismatched dinnerware that could easily have been pulled from your Aunt Mabel's grits-and-greens kitchen. My order arrived on gleaming plates with sylvan wreath prints. The taco's spice-rippling sausage was offset by queso fresco. The cheese adds pleasant saltiness to the dish. Another floral-decorated plate carries a jumble of cactus strips under more queso fresco. The battered Gulf fish rests under a spirited Baja-style cream sauce. These tacos are the stuff of joyful times—so much so that I returned the same day to the taqueria.

John Besh, another New Orleans chef, also got into the Mexican restaurant business in 2014. The local boy and legendary celebrity chef, whose restaurants include Luke and August, teamed up with friend Aarón Sánchez, also a celebrity chef with multiple cooking shows and restaurant stints under his toque. Johnny Sánchez combined their names and craft to offer a contemporary Mexican food through a Crescent City lens. The New Orleans

Times-Picayune downplayed the Mexican part of that aesthetic: "Mexican dishes from Sánchez's heritage get extra refinement from Besh and his team." Here we again see how a restaurant with an appearance of "safeness" offers customers a secure port of entry into Mexican food and tacos. Johnny Sánchez is a dazzling space with a large mural that melds Dia de los Muertos iconography with the stylings of American tattoo art focusing on the Virgen de Guadalupe. The albondigas taco, two small meatballs in smoky salsa chipotle with a light shawl of pickled onions and the slightest dusting of queso fresco, is a favorite of mine. Also worth tacking onto a meal is the catfish taco gussied up in a masa wrapping and carrying a sliding scale of textures and flavors from avocado to a jalapeño tartar sauce.

It should be noted that during the research for and writing of this book, Besh was accused of sexual harassment and assault and for fostering an environment where such behavior was permissible. The story broke in an October 21, 2017, report by Brett Anderson in the *Times-Picayune*. Besh subsequently stepped down from his role in the operation and the restaurant company changed its name from Besh Restaurant Group to BRG Hospitality. In February 2019, Sánchez gained new partners, Johnny Sánchez's chef Miles Landrem and former Johnny Sánchez manager Drew Mire.

On the mobile front is the Taceaux Loceaux food truck. Rolling out in 2010, the truck is decked out in a Dia de los Muertos interpretation of Leonardo da Vinci's *The Last Supper* with a Danny Trejo–resembling Jesus. The truck's owners, Alex and Maribeth del Castillo, wanted to honor the world's cuisines as well as the city's cooking. They found inspiration in clever names. There's the truck's name, for starters. And then there are the tacos. Southern Decadence offers twice-fried chicken skins. The Kermit's BBQ pork taco is named in honor of legendary local musician, founder of the Rebirth Brass Band, and barbecue cook Kermit Ruffins. There is also a braised greens taco and a shrimp taco.

But Taceaux Loceaux is more than tongue-in-cheek menu items on wheels. Maribeth del Castillo is a trained chef with local culinary bona fides, having worked for a time at the original Emeril's New Orleans and moving into the corporate side of Emeril Lagasse's restaurant company. Taceaux Loceaux was among the New Orleans restaurants that pitched in after Hurricane Harvey hit Houston. In late May 2019, they opened a brick-and-mortar establishment, while continuing to operate the food truck. I spoke with Alex del Castillo ahead of the restaurant's opening. Ideally, he told me, Taceaux Loceaux would like to nixtamalize corn and produce its own tortillas at the restaurant. They would continue using only Gulf shrimp, but would go to the dock directly and have staff peel and devein the catch. Expect shrimp po-boy tacos, del Castillo told me, as well as "whatever is around that's good. That's what tacos are in Mexico. That's what they are in New Orleans."

Of course, New Orleans had Mexican restaurants and taquerias before the taco boom of 2014. Juan's Flying Burrito opened in 1997, going for a San Francisco Mission–style approach of fat flour tortilla wraps and tacos like the vegetarian Mardi Gras Indians and the hard-shell Mexicanos with chorizo. The year after the 2008 recession, the Rum House on Magazine Street began serving Caribbean-inspired tacos. It's a popular marvel. Unfortunately, the tacos aren't as appealing in execution even while brimming with flavor and myriad ingredients. During my visit, the tacos arrived cold and over-sauced. Still, there are great ideas in the Rum House use of curries and jerk seasoning in their tacos. (More about that in the West Indian Tacos sidebar.)

The abundance of taquerias isn't always welcomed. "If there's one thing that rubs me the wrong way, it's that it's become easier to find a taco in New Orleans than it is a po-boy, and I say that only half-joking," Frank Brigtsen, owner-chef of Brigtsen's, told *Eater New Orleans* in a February 2016 post. Although Brigtsen's dissenting voice is in the minority, it does bring to light a question of how the new demographics have settled vis-à-vis the city's cherished culinary delights like muffulettas, oysters, and po-boys. What prejudices there are, they have no effect on the popularity of the food. In 2017, the Big Easy hosted Top Taco NOLA, a taco festival welcoming restaurants (not all were Mexican restaurants) and tequila brands alike.

Cajun tacos (taceaux?)

The EaDeaux's Cajun Cocina trailer sits rickety, bright, and quiet on a front corner of the EaDo Hand Car Wash. There is little in the way of relief from the elements save for the misters under a covered picnic area adjacent to the trailer. That's nice and all, but they're unlikely to beat back the steady, simmering spice from EaDeaux's gumbo taco, a flour tortilla bearing liberal scoops of the namesake Louisiana stew generous with wheels of Andouille sausage and fragrant with the Bayou State's holy trinity of vegetables (celery, onions, and bell peppers).

But this isn't the Bayou State. It's the Bayou City, Houston, Texas, where Cajun cuisine meets the Lone Star State's affinity for swaddling everything in a tortilla, corn or flour. This mishmash isn't a left-field head scratcher. Gumbo is a stew, and there is a long tradition of stew-based tacos: they're called tacos de guisados and include such dishes as mole poblano, chorizo and egg, picadillo, and moronga (blood sausage). At some taquerias, rice can be added to the fillings, which is where boudin comes into play. The boudin taco with servings of the pork sausage bound with rice is another delectable example of this niche Southern cookery finding a fitting home in a taco and coming in a close second to the gumbo as EaDeaux's best taco.

EaDeaux's Cajun Cocina at EaDo Hand Car Wash

2919 Leeland St.
Houston, TX 77003
713-818-6897
www.eadeauxs.com

Cajun tacos at EaDeaux's Cajun Cocina.

PHOTOGRAPH © ROBERT STRICKLAND.

Three thousand people showed up for the inaugural happening. I was one of them. The variety of vendors—traditional taquerias were next to fancy restaurants like Johnny Sánchez and Cochon—is what impressed me.

The following year, Top Taco NOLA was an even bigger success, with forty-five hundred attendees, more than fifty restaurants represented, and nearly as many spirits companies. The winner for Most Creative Taco was the cauliflower taco from Johnny Sánchez, a fascinating choice considering that the cauliflower taco is the lynchpin of so many "chef-driven" or specialty taquerias.

Elsewhere in Louisiana, Somos Bandidos, out of Baton Rouge, hits plenty of correct notes with prickly fillings like an Andouille-chorizo blend and a jerk chicken. Gov't Taco runs with historical and legal motifs in its taco names. For example, Clucks and Balances tosses pimento macaroni and cheese and smoked chicken thigh meat with Nashville hot chicken skins and Alabama white barbecue sauce. The Catfish Are Coming! tucks in with mustard-molasses fried namesake fish and crispy greens. The Magna Carrot is founded on glazed carrots. Parish Taceaux in Shreveport has a solid array of Sur-Mex options. The Alabama BBQ Chicken arrives concealed under a wet and thick buttermilk bacon slaw with a peppy white barbecue sauce. The Nashville Hot! Chicken taco slides to the medium end of the heat spectrum, although the pebbled Cotija cheese and pickles add salty and puckering contrasts. The fried oysters are plump, blitzed with bands of lettuce.

Yet, there is reason to be cautious. There is much eyebrow-raising corporate cultural appropriation and cheffy dreams masquerading as innovation.

Take Sean Brock and Minero.

When Brock—noted for his dedication to local and seasonal ingredients at his restaurants, McCrady's and Husk—announced that he and his partners at the Neighborhood Dining Group would open their own taqueria in Charleston, South Carolina, a Sur-Mex regional hybridization was inevitable. The taqueria would take the name Minero, a name that takes, I think, a white man a whole bunch of cojones to use. The name translates to "miner" and evokes the silver miners who are said to have consumed the first tortilla-based food to carry the name "taco." "Taco" also refers to the explosive charges used to clear rock in the mines. These rolled foods were called "tacos de minero." Whether Brock's decision to christen his newest venture after the earliest tacos was deliberate, I don't know. But it raises suspicions of cultural appropriation. According to his handlers, Brock was unavailable for an interview. I was however given the opportunity to speak with Wesley Grubbs, Minero's chef de cuisine, the individual in charge of daily kitchen operations from the beginning. He was gracious and forthcoming.

Brock's impetus in establishing Minero was his opinion that there were no good tacos in Charleston, and he wanted to eat good tacos while in Charleston. His motivation was selfish, he admitted in the *Charleston City Paper*. "It was really that simple," Grubbs told me. Could there really not have been more for a chef dedicated to the roots of his own Southern culinary heritage? It is no secret that Brock is as enamored with corn as he is with rice. So, after several research trips to Mexico and going through close to thirty varieties of corn and corn tortillas, he and Grubbs settled on Oaxacan white olotillo corn for Minero's tortillas. Then came the hard part: nixtamalization. Brock and the Minero crew worked for three months before they were comfortable with their grasp of nixtamalization. Grubbs led the project. For the first two months, it was Grubbs inside McCrady's dry storage, using two induction burners, a small Nixtamatic mill grinder, bags of corn, cal, and a computer. "It was a learning process, for sure, and a lot of fun," the chef told me, adding that the team jokingly refers to that time as the "Summer of Wes."

Three months is an incredibly short time to claim that you've mastered something as nuanced and difficult as nixtamalization. (Cultural appropriation claims are made of such stuff, a subject we'll delve into more thoroughly in chapter 8.) Tweaks occurred over time and after discussions with the Mexican women who make Minero's tortillas. "It'd be silly for us to think that we nailed in three months what an entire culture has been doing

Indo-Mex tacos

Indo-Mex, or Desi-Tex, is the tortilla-based patchwork of subcontinental India-inspired tacos available in cities like New York, Los Angeles, and Austin, but its birthplace might just be Houston, home to a sizeable population of Indian immigrants and Indian Americans. The tacos are usually composed of an Indian dish (e.g., aloo tikki, sag paneer, curries) in a flour tortilla. In some cases, the tortilla is replaced by a similar flatbread, including roti and the paratha used at Goa Taco locations in Los Angeles and Santa Barbara, California, and Kurry Takos in Austin, Texas. Chutneys can be added to the condiment options or substituted for salsa.

The filling receives greater emphasis than the base (the tortilla) in Indo-Mex. Roxie's Tacos has been offering what co-founders Fletcher Starkey and Roshani Patel describe as "the harmonious dance of Latin and Indian flavors," rolled up in a soft handmade tortilla since 2017. One of my favorites is Halal Mother Truckers' tikka taco, a chicken tikka masala with creamy raita and chile chutney over basmati rice in a commodity tortilla toasted cracker crisp. Lotus Joint Tacos Con Chutney, on the other hand, produces its tortillas with adjuncts like turmeric and spent grain. It's not surprising to see Indo-Mex taquerias certified halal, as is the case with Tacos 'N' Frankies and Halal Mother Truckers, both in Texas.

Tandoory Taco in the Houston area, which opened June 2013, with a Dallas outpost opening in August of the same year, seemed to presage the developing taco category. The aspiring chain closed the next year. It was a rough start, but Indo-Mex seems to have recovered in Texas and beyond, including New York, California, and Colorado.

Among the best of the new batch is Twisted Turban. The Houston taco shop subs paratha for tortillas. The switched-out wrap is flaky like phyllo dough and as fluffy as a San Antonio–style flour tortilla. The fillings include juicy, well-cooked chicken and runners of beef spiced up with sauces.

Goa Taco

718 State St.
Santa Barbara, CA 93101
805-770-7079

785 Bay St.
Los Angeles, CA 90021

goataco.com

Halal Mother Truckers food truck

Dallas–Fort Worth, TX
214-732-5959
halalmt.com

Kurry Takos

2730 E. Cesar Chavez St.
Austin, TX 78702
512-779-6964

Lotus Joint Tacos Con Chutney food truck

Austin, TX
facebook.com
    /lotusjointtacosconchutney

Roxie's Tacos

1135 Broadway St.
Boulder, CO
303-444-4465
roxiestacos.com/locations.html

Tacos 'N' Frankies

1460 Eldridge Pkwy, Ste. 110
Houston, TX 77077
281-809-5050
tacosnfrankies.com

Twisted Turban

2838 S. Texas 6, Ste. B,
Houston, TX 77082
281-372-8184
twistedturban.co

for thousands of years," Grubbs acknowledges. "It's different from family to family and everyone has their own secret recipe. 'My grandmother does it like this' or 'My mom taught me like this.' But, we didn't have those grandparents cooking these things." These women, whether kitchen workers or grandmothers, aren't named as individuals; rather, they are described as "labor" or "archetypes." This does come off as exploitation. The Abuelita Principle is rooted in exploitation. However, Grubbs does have enough self-awareness and humility to understand the reality of the situation.

When the restaurant opened, the taco menu included options with green chorizo, a specialty of Toluca, Mexico, and the iconic taco al pastor. My favorite Minero taco is the striking fried masa-mixed tempura catfish, given a shot of cabbage bound by pickled green tomato tartar with a Duke's Mayo base and a bramble of ruby-colored, pepper-dusted red onions resting on a coarse corn tortilla with frayed edges. A small nosh, the catfish, akin to a mudfish, connects West African foodways to the American South, as Adrian Miller notes in his seminal book, *Soul Food: The Surprising Story of an American Cuisine One Plate at a Time*. When taken as slaves to the Americas, West Africans brought with them an affinity for mudfish and adapted their preparation methods to catfish. Now, firmly set into Southern food, the catfish is given a Mexican base, creating a racially and culturally complex culinary link that includes the often-overlooked (read: whitewashed) African foundations of Southern food.

The catfish taco demonstrates that when Brock and Grubbs allow Southern instincts to drive menu development, they're creating exceptional tacos. "Realizing that we are in the Low Country and how much we love those flavors and how much they're ingrained in us. Bringing the two together because there are many similarities—whether it be the climate or the agriculture or the geographic landscape of the areas—they just kind of go hand in hand," Grubbs says. Indeed, Minero lets loose now and again. Grubbs calls it "having fun." He is communing with sense memories, bonding kin with food. Both Mexican and Southern cultures prize family and grandmothers. It's the smell of cookies and of corn bread. It's having an opportunity to roll biscuit dough or tortilla masa. It's family. Plugging into place and family means okra tacos, fried green tomato tacos, and, with the popularity of charcuterie in Charleston, a pork rillettes taco.

But problems arise when a chef attempts to exhibit control of Mexican food or claim legitimacy with upmarket renditions of classic tacos. At Minero, the carnitas with confit pork jowl and chicharrones, with a tart salsa verde and a dark chilmole sauce, on another coarse tortilla, quickly turn to mush with little flavor. The chicken, given support from pickled onions, citrus fruit in the form of papaya, and cheese, was, in short, dry.

Ultimately, the food falls short of expectation and taste. Wanting "to eat good tacos" isn't enough. Minero should be at the forefront of Sur-Mex development. They have the foundation of the tortilla and understand its significance. They have their innate knowledge of Southern food. Most importantly, they have a semblance of humility about cooking and Mexican food. I wish they would dive into the blank-canvas arena, shake up Minero's menu, and see what shakes out. Perhaps then they would be able to live up to the word "minero."

There is a possibility of such a thing. In summer 2018, Brock parted ways with the Neighborhood Dining Group hospitality company that owns the Charleston restaurants and his Charleston eating establishments, including McCrady's and McCrady's Tavern, to focus on his Nashville restaurants. He shifted to an advisory role regarding Husk operations. (Maybe Minero was a whim, after all.) Grubbs would take on the mantle of Minero's executive chef and would oversee more of the "fun" he mentioned in our conversation. Yes, the regular tacos would stay, but there would be more okra tacos and, hopefully, more channeling of Southernness.

Nevertheless, as long as Anglos drive the narrative, the majority of Southern tacos will remain subpar tortilla parcels employing desiccated flour discs easily pulled from any supermarket's ethnic aisle and filled with heaps of misunderstanding. Even the name Sur-Mex is problematic, as Perla M. Guerrero points out in *Nuevo South: Latinas/os, Asians, and the Remaking of Place*. It is an attempt to refashion and better describe the American South's

West Indian tacos

This subset of Sur-Mex tacos is characterized by such fillings as jerk chicken, rubbed with the chile pepper seasoning of the same name and committed to lighting up your eyelashes. The name is derived from the same origin word for beef jerky: the Quechua word "ch'arki," meaning "dried meat." Jerk seasoning is a Jamaican dry rub made so intense with chile, allspice, and other earthy spices that some describe it as "painful." I call it life-affirming.

While most of the American South has a small population of West Indian immigrants or West Indian Americans—among them, Jamaican immigrants or Jamaican Americans—it is the South where West Indian tacos are gaining momentum. Cities of interest include New Orleans and Baton Rouge, home of The Rum House taco shop locations, and San Antonio, home of The Jerk Shack. Both establishments specialize in Caribbean cuisine. New York City, home to the largest Jamaican community in the United States, is the location of two Miss Lilly's restaurants. Although the taco on the Miss Lilly's menu isn't jerk, it is a classic fried fish with intense Jamaican escovitch sauce.

The Rum House

3128 Magazine St.
New Orleans, LA 70115
504-941-7560

2112 Perkins Palm Ave.
Baton Rouge, LA 70808
225-930-4480

therumhouse.com

The Jerk Shack

117 Matyear St.
San Antonio, TX 7832
210-776-7780

Miss Lilly's

multiple locations
misslilys.com

dynamic evolution. Yet, Sur-Mex as a categorization—and with it "Nuevo South," "Nuevo Sur," and "El Sur Latino"—further exoticizes the concept of a South with an increasing Latino immigrant population. "Latinas/os are moving to the South and they speak Spanish, so we can now refer to the South as the 'Nuevo South,'" Guerrero writes. "In these cases, the term is vapid because the authors never define it or explain how using it will help reveal how ideas of race, labor, and belonging are reshuffled and rearticulated in the region."

What do Mexican immigrants and Mexican Americans have to say about this? Their voices are critical. It is, after all, their food that is being manipulated. These individuals should be given the agency to define their experience in the South. In attempting to embrace a diverse South, we are further exoticizing this contemporary South by often excluding Mexicans and Mexican Americans in favor of Anglo expressions. Sur-Mex at least bridges to something familiar, evoking Tex-Mex, the regional cuisine of Texas founded on the blending of Mexican, American, and European ingredients. Still, Tex-Mex continues to be maligned for its chile con queso (a Velveeta and Ro-Tel canned chile and tomato cheese dip), for its heavy enchiladas, and for its fried tacos.

Sur-Mex as a category of taco continues to fascinate me—not just because the cultures of Mexico and the Southern United States emphasize the role of corn in the evolution of their respective gastronomy, but also because of increased settlement of Mexican immigrants in Southern cities and how that development plays with local foodways. An increase in population alongside the interplay of ingredients is creating a true American taco, one that is redefining the taco in this country.

When I began writing *American Tacos*, Louisville, Kentucky, was home to The Ville Taqueria, where Fabian Leon Garcia and family served orange-bourbon carnitas. The restaurant is now closed, but Garcia's story and his thoughts on Sur-Mex remain important to the taco style and an inclusive understanding of it. "It was time to do something different," says Garcia, who has been in the restaurant industry since the age of eleven. The carnitas were on the menu from the start, with multiple test batches prepared before tweaking the original test recipe, which would ultimately be the one that hit the plate in fresh, handmade tortillas. For Garcia, the carnitas were a way to connect with Louisville while offering the community a taste of Mexican food. "I just wanted to do something that was from Louisville, something that people could relate to. And bourbon was one of them. So I decided to marinate the carnitas in a little bit of bourbon and it came out really nice. We stuck with it." Made with pork butt and marinating for twelve hours before getting its bubbling lard bath, this was the Southern taco—a sweet and vibrant combination of corn and pork. It wasn't the only Southern-inspired taco on the menu. The masa-crusted catfish—seasoned in a secret dry rub, of course—was yet another joyous bond between cultures.

Jose and Sons is repping Sur-Mex and its tacos with humor and honesty. Opened in 2014 in Raleigh, North Carolina, as a reconceptualization of Jibarra, a fine-dining Mexican restaurant from the Ibarra family, Jose and Sons started with a word that chef Oscar Diaz wouldn't let go of: Confederxican. "I kept pitching the idea to them about doing Southern-Mexican," Diaz says, "and I used to actually joke around and say I have the perfect name for it. Which I thought was kind of funny."

At the time Diaz and I were talking, he didn't know that South Carolina Jewish businessman Alan Schafer, owner of the tacky Mexican-inspired South of the Border theme park, ran newspaper ads in the 1960s for a fictional "Confederate Kosher Mexican motel and restaurant in the country." Schafer also sold "almost-Kosher" Virginia ham. (We'll revisit South of the Border in the next chapter.) "Yeah, those billboards are slightly racist stuff," Diaz remarked once I told him about that. "I could see how people would get offended by them."

A first-generation, Chicago-born Mexican American, Diaz grew up visiting family in Mexico three months out of the year. So when he got to North Carolina, working as the chef at Jibarra's, and the Ibarra family wanted to take their restaurant in a new direction, Diaz had just the thing. "I started eating, you know, their style of barbecue here in North Carolina, which is a pulled pork, and all that, with the vinegar. It kind of reminded me of cochinita pibil. And so I started seeing a lot of similarities." Collard greens would make a great, edible wrap for tamales along with the green of the hoja de platano. Chicken and waffles would be chicharron and corn-masa waffles; frijoles charros, a bean soup with black-eyed peas. But not everything needed a recognizable Mexican component or an overtly Southern ingredient. The menu is first and foremost dependent on what's available at the farmers' market or from local producers. That manifests in the local beet salad getting a sweet kick from piloncillo in the accompanying vinaigrette. North Carolina kale is in the Gouda macaroni and cheese. Beer from a craft brewery down the road gets poured into the barbacoa preparation. It's also mixed in with the batter for the fish tacos with a serrano chile tartar sauce.

It is such a bridge, built from the work of The Ville Taqueria, El Mero Taco, Jose and Sons, and Taqueria del Sol, that will carry Sur-Mex into a brighter future. As Diaz puts it: "We're Latinos born and living in America. This is our food, not foreigners' food. And we're not done with it yet."

Where to Find Them

Del Fuego Taqueria

4518 Magazine St.
New Orleans, LA 70115
504-309-5797
delfuegotaqueria.com

Gov't Taco

4624 Government St.
Baton Rouge, LA 70806
225-999-3311
govttaco.com

Johnny Sánchez

930 Poydras St.
New Orleans, LA 70112
504-304-6615
https://www.johnnysancheznola.com

Jose and Sons

327 W. Davie St., Ste. 102
Raleigh, NC 27601
919-755-0556
joseandsons.com

El Mero Taco

Memphis, TN
901-832-4074
elmerotaco.com

Minero

153B East Bay St.
Charleston, SC 29401
843-789-2241
minerorestaurant.com

Ponce City Market
675 Ponce De Leon Ave. NE, Ste. 136
Atlanta, GA 30308
404-532-1580

mineroatlanta.com

Parish Taceaux

708 Texas St.
Shreveport, LA 71101
318-626-5999
jasonbradyrestaurantgroup.com
   /parishtaceaux

Somos Bandidos

303 North Blvd.
Baton Rouge, LA 70801
225-330-4546
somosbandidostacos.com

Taceaux Loceaux

737 Octavia St.
New Orleans, LA 70115
504-307-4747
twitter.com/TLNola

Taqueria del Sol

Georgia and Tennessee
multiple locations
taqueriadelsol.com

Tacos at Delicatessen Taco.

CHAPTER 6

Jewish *and* Kosher Tacos, *or* Deli-Mex

Glatt, good eating, and pastrami tacos

REGION(S): New York, Los Angeles, American Southwest, Miami

CLASSIC EXAMPLES: Pastrami, brisket, duck carnitas

TORTILLA(S): Corn, flour, and crunchy

THE LOWDOWN: There would be no Latinidad without Jewish immigration to the New World, which began during the Inquisition and has been informing Latin American cuisines ever since. Besides, pastrami makes everything better.

The story of Jewish and kosher tacos cannot be told without the stories of Crypto-Jews and conversos. And that tale begins with the Spanish Inquisition and the work of Peter Svarzbein. For years, Svarzbein has documented the stories of Crypto-Jews—more specifically, the Sephardim of the Iberian Peninsula who were forcibly converted to Catholicism during the Spanish Inquisition but secretly continued practicing their faith. Some of these conversos fled to the high desert reaches of New Spain—including what would become the heavily Hispanic Catholic El Paso, Texas-Juárez, Mexico borderplex and then north and east along the Rio Grande—in hopes of finding sanctuary from the Church.

"Being from El Paso forces one to think of space and place differently," says Svarzbein, a multimedia artist, El Paso native, and first-generation Hispanic American Jew. Indeed, El Paso isn't just one city. It's half of a city. The other half is Juárez, Mexico. From most vantage points in El Paso, it's difficult to distinguish where America ends and Mexico begins. The cities are nearly inseparable, living in the fuzzy realm between fraternal and identical bilingual twins. And the narco warfare of the 2000s and early 2010s that turned Juárez into a cartel battle zone notwithstanding, residents have freely crossed back and forth for more than a century, going dancing, to dinner, to school, and to work. And because of Svarzbein, they also eat kosher tacos.

In 2013, with the help of an artist incubator grant through the City of El Paso Museum and Cultural Affairs Department, Svarzbein created the food truck Conversos y Tacos Kosher Gourmet Truck est. 1492. It doesn't keep regular hours at its location in a gas station's parking lot. Taco aficionados don't line up for their late-night drunk taco fix of tortilla-wrapped Yom Kippur dishes. Conversos y Tacos is an art installation rolled out for special occasions. It has served up tacos at local food truck rallies and, in 2014, even made a trip to New York City, where Svarzbein attended the School of Visual Arts.

Svarzbein explains the purpose of the truck this way: "To understand that while there are differences among us, there are more things that we share. I created an art installation about those Crypto-Jewish families returning to Judaism. And I created this through food. Food is something that speaks to many cultures. It is a language of love."

But, Svarzbein is quick to note, food can also be used as an instrument of denigration. During the Spanish Inquisition, Jews who outwardly embraced Christianity were referred to as "marranos" (swine). Indeed, the first instance of kosher Mexican food in Texas that I have found uses the cuisine for a dark chuckle. In the September 9, 1959, installment of the *Brownsville Herald*'s fictional humor column "Don Pedro Says," the city editor asks why the writer came into the newsroom carrying banners, saws, and a small barrel. The editor calls the stuff "a load of junk," to which the writer responds that he needs it for Don Pedro's Kosher Mexican Bar & Grill, a fictitious restaurant. In 1961, the Valparaiso, Indiana, *Vidette-Messenger* described another concocted restaurant in Dillon, South Carolina, as the only "Confederate Kosher Mexican motel and restaurant in the country." This "restaurant" appeared in print again in 1968 in a *Carolina Israelite* newspaper ad for a theme highway pit stop, South of the Border. The words above the fictional destination emulated the mocking Spanish accent of Pedro, the South of the Border mascot: ZE ONLEE CONFEDERATE KOSHER MEXICAN MOTEL—RESTAURANT GIFT SHOP ANYWHERE (PEDRO THEENK!).

A Jewish newspaper might seem an odd medium to advertise a problematically themed roadside attraction. But it was par for the course for the

South of the Border owner, Alan Schafer. Schafer established what would become South of the Border as a beer store in 1949 in South Carolina just south of Robeson County, North Carolina, where alcohol could neither be purchased nor sold. Good businessman that he was, Schafer—one of the few Jews in the area—was also known for welcoming customers regardless of skin color. "We only checked the color of their money, not their skins," he once remarked. He also went out of his way to register black voters ahead of the 1948 primary election, making him a target of the Ku Klux Klan. Schafer said that, in addition to the Klan following his beer delivery trucks on route, boycotts were organized against him, crosses were set on fire in front of his house, and a Kavalcade drove through South of the Border property as a "warning." He ticked off the Anti-Defamation League with his "almost-Kosher" Virginia ham. In the words of a local journalist, Schafer was Jewish when it suited him and Southern when it suited him. His use of Mexican stereotypes was just another aspect of his business acumen. Looping Lost Cause sentiment into that Mexican caricature with the Confederateland, USA attraction at South of the Border allowed him to further mock the Jim Crow mentality of his neighbors.

Kosher tacos and Mexican food were fodder for 1960s talk show humor and TV shows. In 1966, Johnny Carson described Beverly Hills as a city "where AAA uses Jaguar tow-trucks . . . where you can find kosher taco stands." Then there's *Dragnet* and the peculiar lunches consumed by the show's cops. It began when "just the facts" Sgt. Joe Friday was introduced by a fellow detective to a kosher taco joint close to LAPD headquarters. "Something you've never had before," the detective tells Friday. In 1970, KTAR disc jockey Bill Heywood suggested that the station needed an anagrammatic motto. One of his proposals was "Kosher Tacos Aren't Religious."

But for kosher tacos in the twenty-first century, humor and creativity took a turn toward a serious dialogue with a whimsical edge. Cultural exchange and curiosity led the charge, especially when it came to Latino Jews like Svarzbein. "I felt exploring this idea through the concept of a taco truck would not only be educational but would also drive my creative process in terms of pushing the limits of what we consider conceptual art," he says. "The liminal space that is the El Paso-Juárez borderplex continues to fascinate me and drives my questions concerning my own Jewish and Latino identity."

The presence of Crypto-Jews in the El Paso del Norte region began to reveal itself in 1986, days into Rabbi Stephen A. Leon's tenure at Congregation B'Nai Zion. Leon received a call from a gentleman—a devout Catholic—in Juárez who said that while he was growing up, his grandmother would light candles on Friday nights. When she had passed away weeks earlier, the man asked his mother who would continue the family tradition. He was rebuffed. That wasn't a family tradition, he was told, that was grandma's practice. The man asked around regarding the candles and was directed to the local priest. The padre said that, of course, he knew why the man's grandmother lit candles on Friday night—a lot of women in the community did just that. But it was better that he discuss the subject with a rabbi. Enter Rabbi Leon. The two men then put the pieces together, and eventually the gentleman converted to Judaism.

He wasn't the only one. The community grew. (Leon estimates up to 20 percent of El Paso's non-Jewish population has Sephardic Jewish roots.) There were vaqueros and yarmulkes. And now Congregation B'Nai Zion and its approximately three hundred registered families—including the Svarzbeins—host the Anousim Conference, an annual symposium on the subject of the Crypto-Jews, which Conversos y Tacos headlined in 2016.

I use the word "headlined" deliberately. The food was served from the truck, but the food, chefs, and truck were also a performance. The loaner food truck—remember, Conversos y Tacos is an art installation, not a full-time rig—has banners duct-taped to its black body. The logos depict a purple cowboy hat-wearing, brown-skinned gentleman with *peyos* hanging to his shirt collar. He's looking skyward and behind him is the Star of David. The vehicle's interior is covered in aluminum foil in minimum compliance with kosher dietary laws—the mandates outlining how Jews must prepare

Brisket and pollo al pastor tacos from Conversos y Tacos.
PHOTOGRAPH © ROBERT STRICKLAND.

food, what foods are fit to eat, and how that food must be consumed, according to different certifications, of which "glatt" is one—and it's stationed in
front of B'Nai Zion as the Sabbath ends.

The observant mill about outside the hilltop synagogue. Below is the
border city, with an estimated 5,000 Jews as of 2011 and a total population
of 674,433, and Juárez with its 1.32 million inhabitants.

English and Spanish can be heard tonight. But whatever language
those present prefer, they're here for the tacos—kosher, of course. Two are
on the menu: a brisket taco and a shredded chicken taco, pollo al pastor. The
latter is a religiously dictated adaptation of the iconic Mexico City taco al
pastor, chile-marinated pork roasted on a trompo, a vertical rotisserie, then
sliced straight from the spit onto a warm corn tortilla. That preparation is

itself a Mexican interpretation of the cooking practices Lebanese immigrants brought with them to Mexico in the early twentieth century.

Tacos at their most basic represent a time and place. Tonight, in El Paso, that's a kosher taco. According to kosher law, pigs are verboten because they do not chew their cud. (As an aside, one of the methods Inquisitors employed to test an individual's Christian faith was to offer suspected Jews what were called "tacos catolicos." These "Catholic tacos" were filled with pork.)

The chefs Svarzbein enlisted to prepare the tacos—Mario Ochoa-Gurany, himself a returned Crypto-Jewish native of Juárez, and Sergio De La Cruz— quickly and quietly assemble the tacos in the rig's foil-lined interior and pass them through the truck's windows.

The pollo al pastor taco is a sneaky treat. Chiles and achiote haven't come anywhere near the chicken. Chef Ochoa-Gurany has replaced commonly accepted ingredients with components like honey and cumin and lime. Yet, the meat mimics the tangy, bright, spicy profile of sienna-colored pork tacos al pastor. There is no char, but there is cubed pineapple. Ribbons of brisket, cooked for seven hours over two days in the synagogue's kitchen, are stretched across a corn tortilla. Next to the beef are pink-hued tangles of pickled onions. A slice of a traditional kosher pickle seesaws atop the meat. Brisket and pickles, used in Jewish, Mexican, and Texas cooking, here combine to bridge cultures in one nosh. It has all the flavors of home. That home includes Mexico.

Farther down the Rio Grande, a slow jaunt from the border with Mexico, stands Laredo's eighteenth-century beacon to Catholicism: the Cathedral of San Agustin. Outside the church, along the colonial plaza, paving bricks are stamped with names of old families: Zuniga, Perez, so many names that end in -ez and -es. These are documented or suspected family surnames of Crypto-Jews. I trace a path along the bricks until I encounter the name Torres. Translated to "tower" in English, it's a good example of how Jewish names in Spain were based on cities or objects. Torres is also my grandmother's maiden name. A deeply Catholic woman, tiny Abuela Eva Torres bristled when my father and I discussed the converso roots of her branch of the family. "Mami, why do you react like that?" my father responded in Spanish. "It's interesante." I added, "It deepens our family history, and, yes, it is interesante." She waved us off with a frail hand, one that's carried our family's farming history and, according to her, held the curse that she believes was set upon us when the first Ralat in the Americas, a Jesuit priest, forsook his vows to live a secular life.

I imagine she thought something like, *We don't run. We push back. We tackle.* My grandmother's ancestors didn't make it as far as Texas. But there I was in a border town, whispering the names etched into the bricks outside the church on an early March day when temperatures flirted with the century mark. Later, I would share pollo al pastor tacos with Jon Daniel and Robert Strickland, my companions throughout much of the journey that led to this book and especially to this chapter. Jon, himself Jewish, and Robert, not Jewish, were with me in El Paso when we had our first stateside kosher tacos. The pollo al pastor in Laredo, sliced into thin, shimmering medallions, would have been unremarkable if it weren't for the early path through the plaza. In this case, being in Laredo—the experience I had there—was more significant than the taco.

This kosher spin on tacos al pastor began with the first conversos and Crypto-Jews in what is now the United States. The immigrant story of Luis de Carvajal y de la Cueva, a Portugal-born Christian of converso parents, is a familiar one. He couldn't catch a break when it came to business, so, down on his luck, he sailed for New Spain. He made enough money to buy a cattle ranch in Pánuco in the northwestern Mexican state of Sinaloa. Then he joined the Spanish navy, was credited with military victories, including the quelling of an indigenous revolt, and was rewarded in 1579 with a governorship of "forty thousand leagues of territory to subjugate and colonize with Spanish and Portuguese settlers." The grant, which required the settlers to be "Old Christians" (limpio de sangre, or pure blood), was christened el Nuevo Reyno de León (the New Kingdom of León), a large swath of land that included what is now Laredo, other territory north of the Rio Grande, and the modern Mexican state of Nuevo León. Not only was this the first European polity to include part of Texas, but the man in charge was the son of "New Christians." Carvajal founded new settlements and ordered his lieutenant Gaspar Castaño de Sosa to establish Villa de San Luis colony—present-day Monterrey, Mexico, the capital of Nuevo León—offering a link to the Jewish-influenced northern Mexican specialty, cabrito al pastor: butterflied milk-fed kid goat roasted slowly on a spit over mesquite coals.

Whether Carvajal was aware that his status as a New Christian withheld from him the same rights and privileges afforded to a longtime Catholic—and therefore prevented him from owning land—or whether he conveniently left that part out of his story, is unclear. What is recorded, however, is that members of his family, including his wife, his sister and brother-in-law, and eight of their children, were accused of being Crypto-Jews and were burned alive in Mexico City. Many of the colonists on his land grant were also declared Crypto-Jews. (At the time of the trial, a relative of Carvajal who claimed he could count the number of true Catholics he knew on his ten fingers was burned at the stake.) The disgraced governor was sentenced to exile, but died in prison in 1590.

The history of Jewish and kosher Mexican food and tacos in modern America begins in the mid-twentieth century—and it begins along the border, not only in Brownsville, as previously mentioned, but also in Los Angeles, where Jews, Mexicans, and Mexican Americans lived and worked side by side in businesses like Lalo's Tacos of El Sereno. Then there was the iconic Kosher Burrito. The restaurant, originally located in downtown LA, opened in 1964 and specialized in the combination of pastrami and flour tortillas. It is further evidence that eventually everything makes it into a tortilla, and the resulting tacos are a product of population demographic and ingredient accessibility.

More evidence is found outside LA and across the United States. In 1977, Rabbi Herbert Berger of Kansas City, Missouri, convinced one food manufacturer to produce its own kosher taco shells. In the telling of this tale in the *Redlands Daily Facts*, writer Tom Fesperman showed his passion for the food: "There's nothing like kosher Mexican. I was brought up on such exotics as grits, navy beans cooked with fatback, and cornbread and buttermilk, because that's all there was in the kitchen. Now even aesthetes from England go out of their way to find these goodies because, man, it's soul food." Kosher Mexican tacos were served at special events such as women's associations gatherings. For example, in 1997, kosher Mexican was on the menu for the second annual Women's Dinner at the Lubavitch Center of Essex County in West Orange, New Jersey. Although many of these examples are, as "taco shells" would signify, the Americanized version of Mexican food given religious approval for consumption, some show the roots of pastrami and Jewish kosher tacos throughout the twentieth century. The cases also illustrate the popularity of Mexican food across yet another segment of the American population. But then, something happened. Jewish and kosher tacos seem to have fallen out of favor and out of the public eye.

The resurgence of Jewish and kosher tacos also begins in Los Angeles. In 2010, Lowell Bernstein, Moises Baqueiro, and Chris Martin rolled out Takosher. The LA-based kosher taco truck was heralded as the city's first such mobile food vendor, slinging "chosen tacos" with cheeky names like the Latke Taco. Despite critical praise, Takosher left the streets the following year.

Katsuji Tanabe, a half-Mexican, half-Japanese native of Mexico City, stumbled into kosher Mexican cooking after working his way through restaurant kitchens in Los Angeles, including Shiloh's Kosher Steakhouse. He opened Mexikosher in 2011. "If you had told me fifteen years ago, 'You're going to own a kosher restaurant.' I would have said, 'No,'" Tanabe says. "But it wasn't my choice. It just came to me in the worst part of my life. After working in kosher, my life changed for better. I always say that kosher made my life better. So I'm glad kosher found me. I actually enjoy the lack of ingredients because it made me more creative. It worked in my favor."

But it wasn't just about the food for Tanabe: "I actually fell in love with the people. I fell in love with the community."

The menu wasn't difficult for him. "It's what I was eating in Mexico, what I was raised eating," he says. "There was no need for more cheese or pork. And the meats that I like, lamb, carne asada, could be kosher or not kosher." Nevertheless, restaurants are a business and to run a successful business, one needs to know what customers want, regardless of your own feelings. "I didn't want to have burritos. But you can't open a Mexican restaurant in LA without burritos. The clientele and the community was burrito burritos burritos. So it was mainly things that I didn't want to have that I needed to have."

Carnitas are a big seller. Now, before you say "¡Dios mio!" or "Oy vey!" it's important to note that while carnitas are traditionally made by cooking pork in its own fat, they don't have to be. Carnitas, which translates to "little meats," can be made using any protein. Tanabe subs beef and duck for pork.

Five years later, Mexikosher was going gangbusters. "We're probably the only kosher restaurant that gets around 60 percent Orthodox Jewish," Tanabe told me during a phone call. "Then we get 30 percent non-Jewish, nondenominational. They come because they like the food, they like the flavors, they like that I was on TV, and they like that I am always at the restaurant. We get a lot of mixed people. It's still very exciting today." Mexikosher was so successful that in 2016 Tanabe and his partners opened a branch on the Upper West Side of New York City. It was followed by the opening of a Mexikosher restaurant in Queens, New York. The original LA location shuttered in April 2018. The Queens location also closed in 2018.

Before all that, though, I was able to stop into Mexikosher and try it for myself. That first visit to Tanabe's restaurant was a deflating experience. After entering with such anticipation to finally check out Mexikosher, I found a fast-casual, walk-the-line-and-point setup with desiccated duck carnitas and tough birria. The tortillas, crusty and curled at the edges, didn't help. I had hoped that what I experienced at Mexikosher was just a bad day, but my second visit a year-and-a-half later was equally disappointing.

Kosher Mexican restaurants have opened across the country, especially in New Jersey and New York, which Tanabe calls "the mecca of kosher restaurants." Until it closed in 2016, the Kosher Taco in Asbury Park sold tacos with fillings like buffalo chicken, avocado and rice, and turkey. Across the Hudson River is Carlos and Gabby's Glatt Kosher Mexican Grill, which opened in Lawrence, New York, in 2006, and now has several locations across New York and Long Island. At the Riverdale, Bronx, location, the tacos range from brisket to ground beef to the typical grilled chicken and steak options alongside what is called "The Chabibi," chicken seasoned shawarma-style with lettuce, pickles, and tahini sauce in a soft or crispy tortilla.

Jewish-style non-kosher tacos (or at least not noted as kosher) were and are found elsewhere, including New York. Flats Fix Taco y Tequila Bar near Manhattan's Union Square (with a second location in the Flatiron District) serves up house-smoked pastrami and a Thousand Island–style slaw in taco form. While the bar offers burritos, a pastrami option isn't available. There is, however, a pastrami torta with guacamole, slaw, mozzarella, tomatoes, and ancho dressing.

Also in New York, Empellón owner-chef Alex Stupak sells a short-rib pastrami taco. He began his culinary career as a pastry chef in Alinea in Chicago and wd~50 in Manhattan, restaurants with first-class modernist cuisine. He was trained on foams and gels and all the science-y stuff. And then he became obsessed with the cuisines of Mexico. Stupak opened the first of his Empellón restaurants, Empellón Taqueria, in the West Village in 2011. With it, Stupak made it clear that Mexican food in New York would undergo a sea change, albeit under the direction of an Anglo chef from Connecticut. Stupak wasn't interested in following or even honoring the well-established traditions of tacos. He was looking at quality and whim.

Empellón Taqueria is unlike any taco spot I've ever been to. It gleams with white tablecloths and dark woods. The short-rib pastrami and sauerkraut taco with a salsa of pockmarked mustard seeds on an airy flour tortilla is an impressive taco in its manifestation of the heyday of New York's Jewish delis. But, when I visited the West Village original, the taco lacked an essential element: a rye tortilla. The incorporation of rye into a tortilla would give the taco the push over the status quo line that is Stupak's mission as outlined in the restaurant's name: Empellón translates to "shove." Stupak and co-author Jordana Rothman include a rye tortilla recipe in their cookbook, *Tacos: Recipes and Provocations*; wrapped around their pastrami, this tortilla would make the quintessential Gotham City taco.

My favorite brined-meat taco is found at Delicatessen Taco in DeKalb Market Hall in downtown Brooklyn, New York. The peppery barbecue brisket pastrami is enveloped in so much smoke that I wondered if I would be able to shape the smoke cloud that I might exhale at any moment. It's a hefty order with deep charred green salsa and pickled mustard seeds offsetting the beef's dominating flavor. The cap of onion and cilantro offers the taco a bright edge. An offshoot of Macondo—a pan-Latino street food and tapas joint heavy on the Mexican eats in Manhattan's West Village—Delicatessen Taco braids the smoked traditions of the South and Texas that have taken root in New York with the local Jewish deli and taco cultures. A smoked salmon taco packaged in a crispy shell gives customers an extended experience in what could be called the "Deli-Mex" category of tacos. Macondo's tacos, offered under the title "Taqueria Latina," include the brisket pastrami and the lamb barbacoa (another Delicatessen Taco option) alongside tortillas conveying barbecue pork belly, smoked crab, cauliflower, and huevos rancheros.

But it's in Santa Fe, New Mexico, where we find a stellar example of a pastrami taco in appetizer form at Eloisa, a hotel restaurant from native son John Rivera Sedlar. Eloisa is named in honor of Sedlar's Hispanic grandmother, and the restaurant offers a menu inspired by her cooking and the cooking of New Mexicans, informed by elements from Sedlar's time working in Los Angeles. The beef pastrami slices, thin and presented atop tangy sauerkraut, are the briny ribbons to the kick of the pickled serranos bows. And then there's the mustard, a required condiment if ever there was one. All of it in a lightly crisped, classic New Mexico blue corn tortilla.

None of the aforementioned are anything like Conversos y Tacos, that El Paso, Texas-Juárez, Mexico, kosher taco truck that takes the conversation about Jews and Jewish cuisine in Latin American to the realm of art. They do, however, offer us a window into an off-center American taco style that is finally getting its due. And in the case of Sedlar and Stupak, this style is crossing over to contemporary, chef-driven tacos: El Taco Moderno.

Where to Find Them

Carlos and Gabby's Glatt Kosher Mexican Grill

multiple locations

carlosandgabbys.com

Conversos y Tacos Kosher Gourmet Truck est. 1492

El Paso, TX

facebook.com/WhyKosherTacos

Delicatessen Taco

Dekalb Market Hall
445 Albee Square W
Brooklyn, NY 11201
929-397-0110

Eloisa

228 East Palace Ave.
Santa Fe, NM 87501
505-982-0883
eloisasantafe.com

Empellón

510 Madison Ave.
New York, NY 10022
212-858-9365
empellon.com

Empellón Taqueria

230 W. Fourth St.
New York, NY 10014
212-367-0999
empellon.com/taqueria

Flats Fix

28 E. Sixteenth St.
New York, NY 10003
212-633-0071

14 E. Twenty-Third St.
New York, NY 10010
212-353-2400

flatsfix.com

Macondo

2 Bank Street
New York, NY 10014
212-463-0090
macondonyc.com

Mexikosher

100 W. Eighty-Third St.
New York, NY 10024
212-580-6200
mexikoshernyc.com

Blue corn tortillas at Galaxy Taco.

CHAPTER 7

Alta California Tacos

Chicano locavore

REGION(S): Southern California

CLASSIC EXAMPLES: Clam and lardo, sweet potato, Jardineros, Cali Taco

TORTILLA(S): Blue corn and yellow corn

THE LOWDOWN: Put on those ruby red zapatos and say, "There's no place like home. There's no place like home. There's no place like home wrapped in an heirloom corn tortilla."

T he end of Peter Weir's 1981 World War I movie *Gallipoli*, portions of Walt Whitman's "Song of the Open Road," the political and social struggles of my people: These are things that have made me or make me cry. I never thought tacos would make me cry, but there I was in Southern California with my friend and trusted taco traveling companion, Robert, getting misty-eyed over plates of tortillas—in two cities.

The first time began with a frustrating search for a parking spot near Blue Bottle Coffee in the Arts District in Los Angeles. It was at that coffee shop where I would at last get my hands on Wes Avila's blockbuster tacos at his Guerrilla Tacos truck. The sweet potato taco with chunks of the orange-tinted root vegetables punctuated by feta and corn nuts is Guerrilla Tacos' best-selling taco. Its inspiration is found in the mashed potato-packed tacos dorados of Avila's youth. As the chef tells it, when he acquired Guerrilla Tacos' first iteration, a street cart, that was the taco he went back for—"with a few modifications." From the get-go, upon the first bite, I had forgotten that I loathe sweet potato, especially in its common form: the sweet potato fry abomination.

Avila's touch is a golden one. It's seen—and sampled—in the bay scallop taco with cashews, the swordfish taco with cherry tomatoes, and the rib eye taco with spindles of beef. It's in his pocho taco, what he calls the folded meat-and-potato fried tacos he grew up with. Avila's version is imbued with lemon zest-freckled crème fraîche and dispenses with the shredded lettuce. "I like shredded lettuce on other people's tacos. But not on my tacos!" Avila says in his cookbook. Guerrilla Tacos is personal, "all the flavors and food I dream about." Though he calls Guerrilla Tacos "authentically inauthentic," his tacos are as Los Angeles as the Santa Monica Pier, the Hollywood Walk of Fame, Dodgers baseball, and his favorite LA taco, Cielito Lindo's rolled taquitos.

His culinary experience is key. Avila came to cooking while a working teamster, experimenting with cooking at home and during trips with co-workers. Fresh out of the California School of Culinary Arts, he got a job at a tapas restaurant. He was a baker at Whittier College and even worked for a spell in the kitchen at Tortilla Jo's in the Downtown Disney District. (I've been to Tortilla Jo's—not while Avila was there—and, I got to admit, it's decent for amusement park Mexican food.) He went on to work at Walter Manzke's L'Auberge along the California Central Coast. Avila also did time at a country club, which ended up sending him to the prestigious culinary academy La Centre Formation d'Alain Ducasse. After that, he worked under Gary Menes, whom Avila calls a mentor. It's the culmination of this knowledge that is poured into Guerrilla Tacos, which, as previously mentioned, started even smaller than a food truck. Avila began his taco venture with a market-purchased taco cart and hibachi grill—and no vending license. His operation was a real guerrilla taco operation.

By the time you read this, you won't have to sniff around for parking at the Guerrilla Tacos truck. You will have to sniff around for parking near the operation's first brick-and-mortar in the Arts District. You'll gladly do this. I will gladly do this again and again.

I would do the same for B.S. Taqueria, a former downtown restaurant with an airy space that closed its brick-and-mortar location and scaled down to a catering operation. The tall communal table made for an excellent vantage point from which to watch the kitchen staff quietly work to send out the sprightliest churros you've ever had and the spice-charged brine pouch that is the clam and lardo taco. A serape pattern–stylized US flag hung on a nearby wall. The backroom offered a respite from the urban center with walls decorated as the loose, open curtain of a bright forest.

Plants hung from the overhead wood beams. But during my visits to B.S. Taqueria, I always sat in the front room, where I enjoyed the aforementioned clam and lardo taco, but also the cheese-covered chorizo and potato taco, both served on a blue corn tortilla. The latter taco was one of rich swells, showcasing chef-owner Ray Garcia's expertise with classic preparations. Meanwhile, the bologna taco recalled Garcia's upbringing. It was one of the first things he learned to make for himself as a kid. Heating up a tortilla, maybe a little bit burned, warming up bologna ("or not," he says), rolling it up—and that was a snack. With rare exception, Garcia says in regard to the bologna taco, "There are not a whole lot of things that were a replica of a dish that my mother or my grandmother made that are still on the menu."

Garcia didn't grow up in a restaurant family nor did he decide to take up cooking in his youth. After earning his bachelor's degree, he planned to attend law school and considered joining the FBI. To that end, he took an internship at the Department of Justice the summer before his senior year of college. "It was a cool thing with limited access and security clearances, taking an oath, all this kind of a spy-type stuff that you think of as a kid," Garcia explains. However, what he encountered after the youthful excitement was a group of people who were disgruntled and unhappy.

"Almost everybody was advising me not to go to law school and how they wish they would have chosen a different profession," the chef says. But Garcia isn't the kind of person who is easily swayed. He wasn't going to ditch law school because a few people told him not to go. However, he took the experience as reason enough to think more about what he wanted to do with his life and career path. Garcia deferred law school acceptances for a year of self-reflection. Then he enrolled in cooking classes. The decision to take classes grew out of learning to cook for himself and to feed what he calls a newfound curiosity. Suffice it to say, he never made it to law school— and no one attempted to talk him out of going into the food industry.

Garcia went on to be the executive sous chef at the Peninsula Hotel's Belvedere Restaurant. The job included managing the hotel's other food

Ray Garcia of B.S. Taqueria.

operation. He was the opening executive chef at Fig, a high-end restaurant at the Fairmont Miramar Hotel. Again, he also led this hotel's other culinary programs. While competing in a 2013 cooking contest, he realized he wanted to open a Mexican restaurant. B.S. Taqueria and its full-fledged restaurant sibling, Broken Spanish, opened in 2015.

His downtown taqueria showcased a contemporary take on the taco with heirloom, non-GMO Mexican blue conico corn that is nixtamalized and made into tortillas carrying high quality products with the equivalent price point. It was the price, sometimes clocking in at five dollars per taco, that was met with resistance. As Garcia notes, "Some people felt that it challenged the authenticity of the taco." There was a disconnect between what people believed they should pay versus what restaurants actually have to charge to remain in business. "I could take the same taco and remove the tortillas. If I had pork belly and some vegetables in a sauce, that's probably a $17 appetizer at a nice French restaurant, but at the taqueria it has to be six dollars at the most. The addition of the tortilla or assigning a Mexican name somehow devalues the product."

By any account, Garcia is successful. The chef has his own line of salsas at Williams-Sonoma, he is sought after for appearances, and he led a session of the Taco Academy at the Rosewood Mayakoba resort. So he has the opportunity to travel a lot. It's all about place. "For me, it's constantly revisiting other cities and connecting with their food, especially when in Mexico. When you go to Mexico, when you eat Mexican food—not that we can't re-create the flavors, not that we can't re-create a lot of the techniques or look at a recipe and say, 'Oh yeah, I can get all of those ingredients in Los Angeles'—it provides social and cultural context. It provides a framing of the meal. It provides a connection to the people who made it, their motivations or their desires for their resources. It makes a lot more sense."

Neither B.S. Taqueria nor Guerrilla Tacos popped up out of nowhere. Rather, they are the creations of two of a growing number of Mexican American chefs inspired duly by the foods of their Chicano upbringing, by their classical training, and by time spent working restaurant lines, cultivating the genre of Alta California cuisine. Author of *L.A. Mexicano: Recipes, People & Places*, Bill Esparza is also the longtime chronicler of Southern California Mexican food and co-owner of culinary tour company Club Tengo Hambre with guides in Los Angeles, Baja California, and Mexico City. He coined the term "Alta California cuisine" for the style of cooking that grew out of an appearance by Ricardo Diaz, the chef who started his first restaurant job at the age of nine, working every weekend and all summer at his uncle and grandfather's restaurants, including their Mexican seafood chain El 7 Mares. Diaz moved on to busboy and, soon enough, line cook. Eventually, the family got into distribution, imports, and exports, sourcing products not just from Mexico but also from as far as Indonesia. He opened his first restaurant, Dorados, also a seafood establishment, in 1997. Next was Cook's Tortas, a Mexican sandwich spot not stuck on Mexican traditional fillings and using bread made in-house.

Dorados and Cook's Tortas were present at the 2009 AltaMed East LA Meets Napa fund-raising event that brought together Mexican American eating establishments with Latino winemakers or winery owners. It was there that Esparza first noticed something was stirring. "I started to see that there was definitely a cuisine developing here," he says, tagging Diaz as the founder of Alta California cuisine. Like many of us, Esparza had seen food TV personalities concoct fancy tacos on cooking shows, but they reflected neither the Mexican or Mexican American experience nor the culture. But Diaz was doing just that.

Guisados, a follow-up venture, focused on home-style stews and braises, inspired by Mexican home cooking. "I thought instead of just constantly doing all this kind of weekend barbecue food, carne asada and pastor, why don't we try to show people what we normally eat at home?" Diaz tells me. Its first location was in the Mexican American East LA enclave of Boyle Heights. Although Diaz is no longer involved in Guisados, the original spot remains open, joined by several other locations, including restaurants in Burbank and downtown LA.

My favorite of Diaz's restaurants was Colonia Tacos Guisados in his hometown of Whittier, California. The restaurant dished out beef tongue with Sriracha mayo, a taco dorado filled with potato and given a guacamole vinaigrette, shrimp with coconut rice, and the corn masa-thickened mole, tesmole. I use the past tense for Colonia Tacos Guisados because the restaurant is now closed. Diaz has moved into developing and opening his latest project, the Poet Gardens dining hall with his craft brewery, Whittier Brewing Company, and seafood concept, Fish God, also in Whittier. For Diaz, Alta California is local and supporting local; that's why he's sticking close to his hometown. But it's also about applying the cultural diversity of the Los Angeles area to the Mexican American canvas.

The label itself is shared with the Spanish name for the state before the 1848 Treaty of Guadalupe Hidalgo, the deal that transferred Mexican-held lands north of the Rio Grande (i.e., parts or the entirety of present-day Arizona, New Mexico, Colorado, Wyoming, and, yes, California) to US-controlled territory. The cuisine's antecedents were later teased in Encarnación Pinedo's cookbook, *El cocinero español* (*The Spanish Cook*). Published near the end of the nineteenth century, the tome laid out the breadth of California's culinary pickings: chile mulatos, carrot, champagne, parsley, rabbit, pepitas, crab, and on and on. Recipes for beef tongue, salmon with capers, goose stuffing, macarons, mole, and hundreds more are included. Later, at the request of local priests, Pinedo wrote about "those early days that preceded the American occupation of [Santa Clara] valley." In the recollection, she recounted a life of religious ceremonies, Indian conversion, and labor, detailing farming, as well as what once existed in place of the area's streets.

Alta California expresses the connection of a culinary tradition rooted in land and season and the history and legitimacy of growing up Chicano and all the foods that define such an upbringing with classical culinary training and the premise that all foodways are worthy of respect in the realm of fine dining. (A humble beginning is not a permanent exile to poverty.) It is Santa Barbara sea urchin and farmers' markets; it's mole amarillo and citrus. And it is heirloom corn. For most Alta California chefs featured here, that corn is blue conico from Masienda, the American purveyor that connects small, private Mexican farmers growing heirloom native corn with chefs looking for such careful, family-farmed products.

If Anglo California cuisine chefs practice farm-to-table cooking, call Alta California "milpa to mesa." That is, cornfield to table. Esparza calls this "a culinary reconquista afoot in the barrios and kitchens" of the former Alta California. "It's an extension of that tradition of California being Mexican, especially L.A. being very Mexican, but also being so far from the center, the traditional Mexico found in Central and Southern Mexico that most people reference when they crave Mexican cuisine. Still, we have the second largest Mexican city on the planet here and its cuisine is just as valid," he says.

Alta California started at home, which leads us to the other place where the tacos brought me to tears: Taco María in Costa Mesa, California. Named after the women in chef-owner Carlos Salgado's family, Taco María is tucked away in a group of shops called the OC Mix, which is why I got lost. But at last I stumbled upon the restaurant. Ready and eager to try Salgado's tacos, I took a seat at the bar and found myself face to face with the kitchen staff.

To be clear, Taco María is not a taqueria. It's a prix fixe dinner tasting menu establishment with chefs in muted blues and grays and a lunch service with a selection of tacos. The texture of the blue corn tortilla plays against lightly fried black cod brightened further with tart acidic kumquats, with backbone supplied by a charred scallion aioli. Lumpy potato sections are set against chorizo, queso fresco, and shiitake mushrooms with threads of wine-colored onions. This taco is an offering of respect to farmers and laborers who are our Latino family patriarchs and matriarchs, the men and women who, after hours hunched over in the fields, would playfully toss us in the air. They convinced us we could fly, that we could do anything. Repaying such acts is difficult. This taco knows that and attempts to do so.

Carlos Salgado is no mere taquero or even a mere chef. He is America's contemporary philosopher-taquero. When I ask about his compelling astronomy tweets, he tells me that he doesn't separate topics in his brain. Indeed, when asked about corn and agriculture, he discusses commodity farming and economic systems. This is how he looks at food and tacos. It's all in for Salgado, and it began in his parents' hole-in-the-wall Americanized taqueria, the kind of place where combo platters, cheesy enchiladas, and hard-shell tacos were the draw. It's where, Salgado says, "I did my homework, it's where I learned to cook without knowing it, and it's where I learned the logistics of running a restaurant without realizing it." So, when it came time for him to open his own place, he had already acquired the tools needed to operate a restaurant. Taco María came much later, though.

It's important to note that Salgado never considered going into cooking while growing up. "While in high school and as a young adult, I didn't think much of the work my parents did. It seemed very mundane and compromised. There was no romance or creativity. It seemed very proletariat and sort of drab to me," he says. It wasn't until he was in his twenties and working in the technology sector that his outlook changed. "I had a philosophical inversion. I realized that the work my parents were doing was actually quite noble and the work that I had been doing was hollow and self-indulgent." He left the industry and moved to San Francisco to immerse himself in food.

He reencountered chiles and beans and corn. Tapping into his genetic memory, he knew how to make a mole. He knew how to make a tinga and prepare all sorts of Mexican dishes from memory. But he had never considered that food and cooking were complex and multidimensional areas of study. "When I was cooking—contrary to the technology work—I found it was extremely social and allowed me to connect and interact with other people. It allowed me to do things I was never able to do with my technology career," he says. Tech work was lonely and internalized. Cooking was transformative. So he applied his technical and academic mind in the space of food and his career accelerated quickly.

While working at Michelin-starred Coi, under friend and mentor Daniel Patterson, Salgado learned to taste. "I thought I knew food," he says. "It was a very different thing. The prominence of agriculture, seasonality, and the availability of many different varieties of many different products is critical. I remember going to Tartine Bakery to get a loaf of bread. That was revelatory. The wheat was different. It was something someone cared about enough to invest in. It's difficult to grow, but it's better," he says. Salgado describes tasting a contorted heirloom tomato for the first time: "When a Mexican experiences a better tomato, we're just thinking about how to make a better salsa."

When he decided to return home, Salgado wasn't going back with the intention of opening a restaurant. He was returning to work with his aging parents, to support the family business. "I thought I was moving back home to be anonymous and have a little restaurant in my hometown," he tells me. Later, Salgado acquired a food truck, experimented with different foods served from the truck, and decided that operating a truck wasn't the direction he ultimately wanted to take with the family restaurant. Instead, he would open his own restaurant, Taco María. Corn would be its foundation. But Salgado wasn't going to use a commodity agricultural product with muted flavor that did not contain or evoke the elusive aroma of maiz. Industrially produced, bagged discs were fillers, placeholders to Salgado. "They didn't taste like anything, which doesn't make any sense. Why we would eat anything that doesn't taste like something?" The corn is used for animal feed, plastics, fillers, emulsifiers, fat replacers, texture modifiers. It's an unnatural resource. That's the corn used to make tortillas. "It's a species of plant that is no longer alive."

A three-hour phone call with Masienda owner Jorge Gaviria about the global economy and the symbolism of corn was enough to convince the chef to use Masienda corn. The Taco María team tested blue conico corn, the corn ultimately used for the restaurant's tacos. "Even though it was something completely new to me, it felt very much like coming home or becoming centered or grounded."

By using heirloom indigenous corn, restaurants like Taco María, B.S. Taqueria, and, as we'll see below, Galaxy Taco, engage small farmers throughout Mexico in a global economy. This creates opportunities for families that have grown a regionally adapted corn for generations to share it with people who would be willing to pay a fair price for the product. "We were quite proud to be able to create a large market for a number of different places that were not readily available. We're able to pay a fair price and contribute to the agricultural community," Salgado says. Mexicans are the keepers of corn, and corn diversity is culturally significant. This too is part of Alta California cuisine. What's more, Mexican food is the indigenous cuisine of California, says Salgado. California cuisine is not the Mediterranean-inflected dishes of Northern California. Beans, squash, corn, chiles: "That's what the land will revert to if abandoned," he notes.

Chef Christine Rivera also uses blue conico for tortillas at Galaxy Taco in La Jolla, California. The resulting disc is textured, denim-hued in form, and filled with the steak Cali Taco, upon which teeters a loose stack of thin fries. I'm reminded of the French fry–topped tacos of Mexico City, but Rivera says she was inspired by the late-night stops for California burritos—which, you know, makes more sense. The taco reflects the creative freedom she has at Galaxy, which owner and chef Trey Foshee opened in 2015 with Rivera at the helm. Foshee tapped her as Galaxy Taco's chef while she was at George's at the Cove, Foshee's contemporary California restaurant. Considering his dedication to local bounty, it's not surprising that Galaxy Taco is an Alta California taqueria. At the beachside taco spot, mushrooms swirl in red salsa with hoja santa providing a teasing aroma, beans top carnitas, and the grilled fish has an optional topping of uni, sea urchins' roe-producing gonads, orange-hued and buttery in flavor, for three dollars more. The lengua taco, shot with a swatch of avocado-fortified salsa

Chef Christine Rivera at Galaxy Taco.

verde, and diced onion and cilantro, is the beef tongue preparation that Rivera enjoys with her family.

But it always goes back to the blue tortillas, the production of which takes twenty-four hours at Galaxy Taco, from nixtamalization to pressed tortilla. "When you go home and your mom's cooking something, that feels like home. That smell is home. That smell is with us now with this blue corn. It just feels like home," Rivera says. Aside from the blue corn tortillas served at Galaxy, Rivera's crew makes hundreds of white bolita corn tortillas for George's at the Cove. Occasionally, Rivera employs adjuncts, additional ingredients, into tortilla production, although usually for events. She has used kale, chapulines, carrot, and gaujillo chiles, among other components.

Galaxy Taco, Masienda, and blue corn tortillas have proven so popular that, as Rivera tells me, the kitchen is outgrowing the space dedicated to nixtamalization and masa production.

> We literally make masa in this really small corner. We're going to move this production to a bigger area so that we're able to fulfill orders that we're getting. So right now we make tortillas for a few L.A. chefs. We make tortillas for George's at the Cove . . . then we sell our masa and tortillas through our produce company here in San Diego. People order their masa the day or the night before they want it. We get the email, they come in the morning, and pick it up. So, little by little, our orders are getting pretty, pretty, pretty heavy, especially during the summer. . . . It's getting a little too hectic in here. So we're looking into expanding, just having the masa move somewhere else and not having it here at the restaurant.

Rivera, Garcia, and Salgado have helped popularize the use of Mexican blue corn tortillas in Mexican restaurants and taquerias across the country. They're used in tacos served at Taquiza Tacos in Miami, Barrio in Chicago, and Dai Due Taqueria in Austin, Texas, to name a few. That being said, as popular as blue corn tortillas are, they are not the defining element of Alta California.

Unlike other American tacos—say, breakfast tacos and K-Mex—Alta California is tied unequivocally to individuals and physical space. Extracted

Art at Galaxy Taco.
PHOTOGRAPH BY ROBERT
PETRIE, COURTESY GALAXY
TACO.

from Southern California and the Chicanos who developed it and cook it, Alta California is diminished. Ray Garcia could open a restaurant in Miami, but he wouldn't have access to the same ingredients or to the same ingredients at the same frequency. Garcia would have access to Masienda corn, yes, but he wouldn't have Santa Barbara sea urchin dropped off that morning by the diver himself. Put another way, the food of Michoacán can be approximated in the United States, but it can never be wholly replicated. There are components the market can't connect to stateside chefs. Place has a flavor. For Alta California, there is no place like Alta California.

What there is, however, is the future of Mexican cuisine in the United States: Mexican American chefs and cooks are the backbone of restaurant kitchens, whose classical training or time on a kitchen line becomes a toolbox from which they can express themselves as chefs. They are transforming what Americans call Mexican food through higher-quality ingredients; time-intensive techniques, both classical and indigenous; and the consequential higher price point. Uni isn't cheap. Neither is the process of making the foundation of the taco: the tortilla. It's evident in the tempura chile guero and sea urchin taco of the stalwart CaCao Mexicatessen. It's the black trumpet mushroom taco with chapulines on a Hatch green chile tortilla served at the Macheen pop-up. It's shown in the coils of octopus tentacles with an olive tapenade and once more in the pork belly taco that resembles more a segment of brilliant coral reef than what it ultimately is: a finely considered dish, the tortillas for which are sourced from Galaxy Taco.

It's seen again in the low-rider cuisine—also known as "comida chicana"—subset of Alta California cooking spearheaded by the likes of Dia de los Puercos and its Darth Mariachi pork belly-and-pickled-red-onion taco, as well as ¡Salud!, a San Diego taqueria that skews toward dollar tacos of yore. They're deceptive, though. The corn and flour tortillas are hand-pressed and buoy carne guisada, fried catfish, pastor, chile relleno, mesquite-grilled carne asada, and, perhaps in a nod to the style's increasing popularity, a breakfast taco of chorizo, bacon, and an over-easy egg, two cheeses, and avocado on a flour tortilla. The Califas taco with a customizable filling is topped with French fries. These are not the dollar tacos of yore. Those days are long gone. What lies ahead is a new taco, el taco moderno.

Where to Find Them

CaCao Mexicatessen

1576 Colorado Blvd.
Los Angeles, CA 90041
323-478-2791
cacaodeli.com

Dia de los Puercos

117 W. Second St.
Pomona, CA 91766
909-469-6992

73605 Market St.
Riverside, CA 92501
951-595-4511

diadelospuercos.com

Galaxy Taco

2259 Avenida De La Playa
La Jolla, CA 92037
858-228-5655
galaxytaco.com

Guerrilla Tacos

2000 E. Seventh St.
Los Angeles, CA 90021
213-375-3300
guerrillatacos.com

Guisados

multiple locations
guisados.co

Macheen

Los Angeles, CA
instagram.com/_macheen_

¡Salud!

2196 Logan Ave.
San Diego, CA 92113
619-255-3856

2333 Highland Ave.
National City, CA 91950
619-434-6464

saludsd.com

Taco María

3313 Hyland Ave.
Costa Mesa, CA 92626
714-538-8444
tacomaria.com

Duck mole taco.

PHOTOGRAPH BY DEBBY WOLVOS,
COURTESY CRUJIENTE TACOS.

REGION(S): Nationwide

CLASSIC EXAMPLES: A seemingly endless array, including cauliflower, wild boar al pastor, and seasonal ingredients

TORTILLA(S): Corn and flour, but absolutely not lettuce. A lettuce wrap is not a taco. Tacos require tortillas. A lettuce wrap is a sad, wet heresy.

CHAPTER 8

El Taco Moderno

Contemporary, "chef-driven," and nuevo immigrant tacos

THE LOWDOWN: Everyone notices the best-dressed person in the room, but not everyone can pull off a double-breasted pinstripe suit. Modern tacos are often dismissed as fancy—"muy fancy"—"hipster tacos" or, in the same manner as crispy tacos, labeled "white people tacos," lobbing charges of cultural appropriation. Here's the thing: Those elements exist, but the category of "el taco moderno," sometimes also described as "chef-driven tacos," includes the aforementioned styles like K-Mex, Sur-Mex, and Alta California. The category also refers to Mexican immigrant and Mexican American chefs employing high-quality and locally grown ingredients in the construction of traditional Mexican tacos. It's where the boundaries of the taco are pushed, at times to consumers' displeasure and without a rudimentary knowledge of taco traditions. The arena of el taco moderno is where the narrow, rigid view of tacos comes to die a cauliflower-riddled death.

I think the taco is underplayed," says Oscar Diaz, executive chef of Jose and Sons, a Sur-Mex restaurant in Raleigh, North Carolina. "One thing I always want to tell people is how difficult it is to actually make tacos. I feel like tacos should be served like sushi."

For Diaz and many other chefs, the taco should be treated as seriously as any other dish or cuisine. I agree. Tacos are hard work, beginning with the tortilla, whether corn or flour. If it's corn, though, there is the hours-long process of nixtamalization. The ancient method is experiencing a renaissance. The process attracts chefs driven by the idea of handmade, artisanal products rather than the industrialized, processed forms of food. In the case of tortillas, an example of the latter would be the commodity-grade discs made from dehydrated corn flour commonly referred to as "masa harina," the most famous brand of which is Maseca. Tortillas made from masa harina possess a chemical, bitter taste—if they have a taste at all—that seems to deaden any flavor that's not corn. Unfortunately, it kills the corn's aroma, too. Handmade, hand-pressed tortillas are very much like sushi rice, both the result of a serious craft that takes years, if not decades, to understand and master. It's as much science as it is art. Sushi is taken with utmost seriousness, so why not tacos? It's time the taco sloughed off the qualifier "humble" and took its place among the other working-class foods granted high regard.

Chefs like Diaz, the practitioners of Alta California tacos, and many others who appear in this book see the taco, beginning with the tortilla, as the nuanced object it is. "There's a window of perfect flavor," Diaz continues. "In a restaurant, it is really hard to make that happen because you're preparing ten people's tacos, and they all sit in the window for a little bit until everyone's tacos are finished. They then get run out and set in front of the guests and the salsa starts to seep into the tortilla. I feel like it misses its window."

The best modern tacos straddle the line between boundless creativity and respect for tradition and history. This begins with ridding ourselves of the idea of the tortilla as a blank canvas. It's not. Rather, the tortilla is the foundation of Mexican culture, and many American tacos are built on that foundation—be they of the K-Mex style made famous by Roy Choi of Kogi BBQ, the Sur-Mex developing in the American South, the astonishing work of Anglo and Mexican American chefs, or the Nuevo Immigrant tacos developing wherever Mexican restaurants dedicate themselves to using high-quality, fresh ingredients that counter the stereotype of greasy, cheap eats. These tacos can be equally highfalutin or classical and get bonus points for focusing on locally, seasonally available products. But the tortilla must be taken seriously.

The modern taco is sometimes referred to as the gourmet taco, the specialty taco, the chef-driven taco, or, mistakenly, as the hipster taco or the white people taco. This version began its journey with reports and advertisements declaring crispy tacos as gourmet tacos. Some of those crispy tacos were called "cocktail tacos," evoking images of little black dresses and cigarette holders and civilized dinner parties, and were available in the supermarket freezer case. Modernity and convenience often go hand in hand.

History took another step forward with the formation of the New Southwestern cuisine pioneered by classically trained chefs passionate about exploring the region's indigenous ingredients and dishes. Among the figures driving the development of this cuisine were Stephan Pyles, Dean Fearing, and John Rivera Sedlar. Although he is from Santa Fe, New Mexico, Sedlar made his name in Los Angeles. In 2011, he went from working for other chefs and restaurateurs to being the chef and restaurateur when he opened

Rivera Restaurant in LA. After decades of pushing the boundaries of fine dining and Southwestern and Californian cuisine, Sedlar returned home to open Eloisa, an homage to the food and culture of his native New Mexico, framed by warm high desert colors and light bricks. The pastrami tacos (see chapter 6) connect the historical threads of Jewish immigration to the New World, Mexican immigration to the United States, and the synthesis that breeds life along borders. The lunch menu prepared in the exhibition kitchen includes more tacos than the iconic pastrami selection. Barbacoa tacos are made from brisket, garnished with grilled red peppers, and dressed with a sweet and peppy Turkish apricot barbecue salsa.

While names like Alex Stupak of Empellón (Empellón Taqueria, Empellón Al Pastor, and Empellón) might be better known in connection with modern tacos, others who have been at it much longer continue to thrive. For example, Richard Sandoval owns more than forty restaurants across the country and globe, including Mexico, Qatar, Japan, and Serbia. Tamayo, one of his restaurants in Denver, Colorado, is a contemporary, upscale eatery where cocktails like the namesake Tamarind Margarita Tamayo accompany taco fillings as iconic as the taco al pastor or as nouveau and imaginative as the Chef's Artisanal Tacos. Some, like Taqueria Nueve in Portland, Oregon, tweak traditional ingredients in fashionable dining spaces with or without an Anglo chef or restaurant owner, earning them miscategorization as purveyors of hipster or white people tacos. It's not out of place to find a good old-fashioned crunchy taco on the menu of such restaurants. ¿Por Que No? and Stella Taco, also in Portland, Oregon, are two more examples, although only Stella Taco offers hard-shell options.

Other chefs see the tortilla and the taco as inspirations. They embrace the narrative of tortilla as blank canvas and describe their dishes as "chef-driven." This isn't a white people thing. Alta California pioneer Wes Avila of Guerrilla Tacos, known for wrapping the flavors of his Chicano upbringing with his fine-dining expertise, has gone on record as calling a tortilla a blank canvas, but he's spurring taco development in a clear, well-informed manner. Avila gets tacos. Others find clarity in reducing entrees to a taco portion. Although some chefs warrant the high price point by using expensive ingredients in a preparation that is first a dinner plate, there is little life to their tacos. What's compelling about a fish-and-chips taco? A falafel taco is a cheap gimmick exposing a lack of imagination. Worse yet, a "seasonal vegetable taco" composed of locally sourced greens and veggies in a hand-made corn tortilla is a modest taco salad, not a taco.

From Trejo's Tacos in Los Angeles and Resident Taqueria in Dallas to The Funky Taco in Boise, Idaho, and Minero in Charleston, every seemingly self-aware modern, chef-driven taqueria (franchise or not) slaps a cauliflower taco on menu boards. I first encountered this taco at Resident Taqueria, one of my favorite taco spots in the United States. The lightly roasted crucifer is tight with dark islands of caramelization. It's topped with shreds of kale and a scarf of lime-epazote cream salsa before being presented on a metal plate. The firmness of the cauliflower and crunch of the pepitas play against the citrus-piercing salsa. Chef-owner Andrew Savoie says the idea for his cauliflower taco "starts with my experience at Jean-Georges and his caramelized cauliflower with caper raisin sauce and nutmeg. Tasting endless amounts of caramelized cauliflower, I became addicted to the flavor." He wanted to revive the experience of that dish while creating his own cauliflower dish, enhanced with the texture of kale, pepita, and the robust characteristic of epazote. It now outsells every other Resident Taqueria taco by 25 percent.

The cauliflower taco is also a staple at Trejo's Tacos. The tacos at this small chain bearing the name and likeness of actor Danny Trejo, perhaps best known for his Machete character in the *Spy Kids* movies, *Grindhouse*, and the *Machete* flicks, are a vegetarian and vegan magnet. At Trejo's, the jackfruit taco evokes migas with the inclusion of tortilla strips. Mushroom tacos are another generic sort of filling, sautéed with "seasonal ingredients" and tucked into a tortilla. The dependence on these tacos as anchor items has transformed what could have been a whimsical vegetarian option into a fundamental building block.

The excellent restaurants of Alta California cuisine aren't immune to the tyranny of the cauliflower. B.S. Taqueria has served one done up in an al pastor marinade. A cauliflower taco was also available at Ricardo Diaz's Colonia Tacos Guisados before the taqueria closed.

Alongside these cauliflower creations are other nouveau-stereotype tacos commonly found at modern taquerias. These include the fried avocado prepared with alchemy that allows an oil-bath crisped shell to conceal a cold interior; a fish taco (mahi mahi! salmon! tilapia! by-catch! seasonal!) lathered in an excessive amount of "spicy mayo" or "aioli"; brisket (smoked or not) with damp, crumbled cheese; and chicken tenders whose fried batter deteriorates into a steamed mess in a warm tortilla. Forays into K-Mex and Sur-Mex are spied now and then.

Not every modern, chef-driven taco shop falls into this mold. Nor are the aforementioned examples uniformly disappointing. However, taking a cynical stance, I think that tacos like the cauliflower, jackfruit, and mushroom offerings can, at their worst, be little more than talking points at menu-development meetings that begin with the brainstorming premise that tortillas are blank canvases. Like all businesses, restaurants take pains to reduce risks in favor of an increased chance of success. That's sensible. What experiments do materialize are usually seasonal or couched as specials. Take Mexicue's grilled chipotle pineapple and bacon taco garnished with ramps. Then there are the lettuce "tacos," which swap tortillas in favor of healthier lettuce wraps. Tacos without a tortilla or an approximating flatbread are not tacos.

Few taquerias take their own cues from regional Mexican cuisine and its myriad vegetarian-friendly dishes, among them some tacos de guisados. They're plentiful at the taqueria chain of the same name, Guisados, in the Los Angeles area. Go for the sampler platter, although it's best not to share. The sampler tacos are one-bite noshes. My favorite stateside guisado joint is Mi Mero Mole in Portland, Oregon, where the rajas con crema (poblano strips in a creamy cheese sauce) are delectably gloopy.

That's not to say cauliflower tacos can't excite or that the category of tacos they help define doesn't have the capacity for creativity. Resident Taqueria's cauliflower is excellent. And modern tacos shine across the country. Two contemporary taquerias that serve as examples are Crujiente Tacos in Phoenix, Arizona, and Boca Tacos y Tequila in Tucson, Arizona. Sitting along the city's Fourth Avenue, Boca Tacos is chef Maria J. Mazon's misperception-busting tortilla platform. The Tucson-born, Sonora-raised Mazon sees tacos as more than quick curbside noshes. They are refined eats presented in tortillas. Mazon and crew do a superlative job of balancing renderings of traditional tacos, especially the regional sort, with interpretations of favorite foods and ingredients applied differently, beginning with house-made corn and flour tortillas. My number one out of the twenty-four options is the Taco Dog. This take on the beloved Sonoran hotdog includes a bench of bacon-wrapped hotdog upon which rests a union of onion twists, tomato-dominated pico de gallo, and whole beans. Vegetarians are sated with grilled tofu lathered in honey mustard, a breakfast taco of sorts in the hash browns and fried egg taco, and my preferred choice, a ladle of poblano and Anaheim rajas and corn enveloped in cream. Don't sleep on the northern Mexican–style discada with a beef-chorizo base or specials like the sliced rib eye with a peanut sesame-basil salsa. My only quibble is the heavy hand of cabbage obscuring the fillings. Next time I visit, I'll ask them to go easy on the leafy vegetables.

To the north in Arizona's capital is Crujiente Tacos ("crujiente" is Spanish for "crunchy"). There are beef and green chile pork crunchy tacos, and a birria-style lamb replaces the standard chicken, both options juicy and topped with cheeses. Beef gets a Tex-Mex-leaning cheddar/Monterey Jack blend; pork is matched with spice-prickling pepper jack; and the lamb is paired with a classic Mexican crumbled cotija. Executive chef Richard Hinojosa's versions of street tacos are served on blue and white corn tortillas and represent a worldly experience that hints at his well-traveled fine-dining background at resorts in Hawaii, San Diego, Colorado, and Arizona.

"I was thinking, I've got twenty years of cooking and all these different styles of food and all these techniques from working at all these four- and five-star-type places. To incorporate that into tacos could be really cool," Hinojosa explains. There's also a toe dip into the codified category of

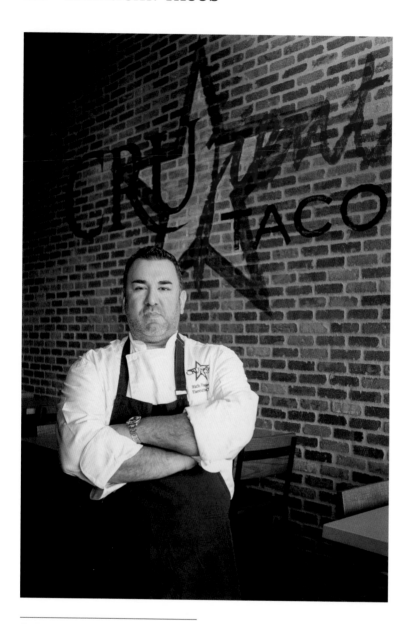

Crujiente Tacos Chef Rich Hinojosa.

PHOTOGRAPH BY KARLIE COLLEEN
PHOTOGRAPHY, COURTESY CRUJIENTE TACOS.

Texas Wagyu cap steak taco.
PHOTOGRAPH BY CHRISTIAN BRABEC,
COURTESY CRUJIENTE TACOS.

modern, chef-driven tacos. His Korean fried chicken emits a steady heat from chili paste paired against an onion sauce. A mellow yet constant burn in the form of an ancho tartar sauce dresses the fried fish. The tempura avocado bears a touch of black bean sauce, while pink-tinged duck breast rests on a spoonful of mole and a sprinkle of sesame seeds.

Hinojosa's culinary foundation is also visible in the Crujiente Tacos weekly specials, which at the time of this writing have not been repeated. (An abbreviated sampling, provided by Hinojosa, is available in the list on page 201.) There is one exception. The Wagyu steak taco with pickled shimeji mushrooms, fresh horseradish (not the sticky green stuff in your

Charred carrot taco.

supermarket sushi), and potent Japanese karashi mustard began as a weekly special, but its popularity warranted it a spot on the permanent menu.

"I want people to look at it more the way you would look at sushi or tapas. You can take a journey. You can take a trip. You can tell the story of Mexico through different techniques." Hinojosa's tacos, and modern tacos in general, are not beholden to the conviction that tacos should cost two or three dollars and be built on a framework of two corn tortillas stuffed full of chopped meat with a salsa bar and free chips. "That's not what I wanted to do," Hinojosa says. Indeed, it's not what he's doing.

Crujiente Taco weekly specials

Crispy Ipswich Clam Belly with Heirloom Tomato-Basil Aioli-Citrus Habanero Reduction-Pickled Red Onion-Tomatillo

Duck Confit with Soy-Balsamic Glaze-Pickled Rhubarb-Jalapeño-Scallion

Crispy Veal Sweetbreads with Jalapeño Apple Soubise-Cucumber-Pickled Carrot-Jalapeños and Cilantro

Elk Carne Asada with Blueberry Habanero Hot Sauce-Avocado Mousse-Charred Onion-Cilantro

Seared Sea Scallop with Avocado Spring Pea Puree-Serrano Cilantro Mojo-Heirloom Tomato-Pea Tendril

Cabeza Mezcal Sichuan Pepper Braised Beef Cheek with Doubanjiang-Pickled Onion-Charred Scallion-Cilantro

Fried Green Tomato with Candied Bacon Jam-Cilantro Aioli-Arugula-Shaved Sweet Peppers-Citrus Habanero Vinaigrette

Blackened Shrimp Étouffée with Organic White Rice, Lemon, and Scallion on Flour Tortilla

Charred Spanish Octopus with Chorizo-White Beans-Citrus Reduction-Avocado-Red Onion-Fresno-Cilantro on White Corn Tortilla

Indian Spiced Lamb with Vindaloo Sauce-Chermoula-Pickled Onion-Fresno-Puffed Basmati-Cilantro

Tempura Oyster "Rockefeller" with Candied Bacon Jam-Spinach Puree-Cabbage-Toasted Bread Sauce

Roasted Maitake and Shimeji Mushrooms with Gold Potato-Lemon-Yeast-Soy-Arugula-Cotija on Flour Tortilla

Also in Phoenix is Barrio Café, a Mexican restaurant from chef Silvana Salcido Esparza that very much gussies up traditional tacos. The chef is an unrepentant defender of Mexican food and tacos, especially in the face of cultural appropriation.

"What is a taco?" she asks rhetorically during our phone conversation. "A taco is anything you want it to be as long as you're Mexican and serving your *cultura*. . . . Look, I can be a warrior all I want, but the truth is that tacos are being served everywhere." She goes on to mention a Facebook-sponsored ad for an Irish pub serving pastrami tacos with Guinness. "Now there's not a menu that doesn't have a category of tacos, anywhere, any kind of restaurant." Esparza sees this as exploitation and contends that Mexicans and Mexican Americans are being left out of the enterprise. It's happening as Mexican food is more popular than ever, but Mexicans are being denigrated by the dominant culture.

That being said, she allows for the regionality of tacos. For example, an Anglo-owned Texas breakfast diner—let's call it Jim's Breakfast Joint—that serves a smattering of breakfast tacos isn't cultural appropriation. It's a regional breakfast, Esparza argues. "Jim could make all the tacos he wants at home. Cultural appreciation versus appropriation is a fine line," she says. "Here's the problem: Maria, Doña Lupe, Don José make better breakfast tacos than Jim. But Jim's a rich guy who got the loan and the financing to open up that place. Of course, the restaurant is going to be successful—it's Mexican food. He might even hire Maria," she says. "I have a responsibility to serve the highest quality food that I possibly can get at a good price. Those are my responsibilities. It's also my responsibility to protect the food and the culture."

Esparza's prime target in the protection of her culture is Rick Bayless, the Chicago-based chef whose perceived definition of traditional Mexican food, served at his restaurants and via his television programs, is said to have given Mexican food the national spotlight on the backs of Mexicans. I have only been to one Bayless restaurant, Cruz Blanca, a beer hall and taco place that does a great job of messing up preparations like pork in a tomatillo salsa, which carries an aftertaste of turned milk, and the cauliflower taco with crema and queso añejo that, unfortunately, coat the tongue. But other writers have better made the argument against his "contribution" to Mexican food in the United States.

Mexicans and Mexican Americans deserve to have control over their culinary heritage. Esparza is a steadfast advocate. For that, I admire her. My admiration is deepened by the tacos on her Barrio Café menu. My favorite is the Baja-style shrimp, lightly encased in a Tecate-buoyed batter, offset in texture by fans of avocado and knots of cabbage. The taco is finished with a classic chipotle cream sauce that gives the pocket zing. The restaurant's signature cochinita pibil, pork bathed in achiote and sour orange juice and roasted in banana leaves, is as close as one gets to the traditional in-ground preparation. The finished meat is pleasantly puckering and topped with cuts of pickled red onions.

Although Bayless's specter looms large both over popular Mexican food in Chicago and the United States and over the ongoing, knotty conversation of cultural appropriation, Esparza knows that he doesn't define Chicago Mexican food. Chicago is home to a vibrant Mexican restaurant community that thrives with a diverse range of eating businesses. I'm talking carne asada places; birria counter spots, where the bone is fought over as a Christmas treat; tacos al pastor joints where the Virgen de Guadalupe stands sentinel; and cafeteria-style eateries where hearty stews find dreamy cradles in double-ply corn tortillas and where modern tacos are prepared by Chicanos, Mexicanos, and gringos alike. These places include Antique Taco, opened in 2012 by husband and wife Rick and Ashley Ortiz. Their talents as chef (Rick) and designer (Ashley) have created a fanciful space that could be described as cute or brunch-perfect, replete as it is with reclaimed materials, Mason jars, distressed wood, and flea-market tchotchkes. The headliners, though, are the tacos built around farmers' market produce. A refreshing aroma of curry and raita permeated the space when I visited the taqueria. A bright mural decorates an exterior Antique Taco wall, where a pink llama stands proud. All that aside, the fish taco, Antique Taco's signature offering, is a fantastic nosh. My fish taco began with a fair tortilla, and the fish was dense but flaky underneath an airy tempura batter. (A miniaturized person could run fun laps in the space between the batter and the fish.) Atop the protein are layered Sriracha and fish sauce–infused tartar sauce and a cap of rice wine vinegar-tossed cabbage.

Big Star is arguably the most famous of Chicago's first wave of modern taco joints. Opened in 2009 by James Beard Award–winning chef-restaurateur Paul Kahn of The Publican Restaurant, with its menu of rustic eats and seafood dishes, and The Violet Hour, a renowned cocktail lounge, Big Star is a fine taco spot, though it is more party venue than taqueria. To better experience Big Star's tacos, order them at the walk-up window across the restaurant's patio. The window is meant for takeout, but in cold weather, when the space is protected from the biting Chicago winter, it's best to open the to-go containers and scarf the tacos there. The ones to get, if you are so inclined, are the crisped pork belly taco with a dusting of queso fresco and a tangle of onions and the chopped, earthy-seasoned carrots drenched in a yogurt darkened with chipotle. What Big Star delivers most is the impression many Americans have of Mexican food in Chicago: all flash, no substance. Of course, that's wrong.

Also in Chicago, Carnitas Uruapan, which sees lines forming early for their subtle carnitas sprinkled with salty, snappy chicharrones, is but one of many carnitas restaurants opened by Mexican immigrants from the state of Michoacán and their families. Cantón Regio Mexican Steakhouse, successor to the Nuevo Leon restaurant that burned down in 2015 after more than fifty years in business, serves northern Mexican food in a rancho hacienda-style dining room. Grab a taco de Sabinas, a collection of refried beans, chunks of beef, tomatoes, and jalapeños under a cheese netting. This spicy taco is a piece of the Texas-Mexico border, reminiscent of the norteño stew known as carne guisada, popular as a breakfast taco in South Texas and the Rio Grande Valley. Goat birria is also popular in Chicago. No restaurant is more closely associated with the preparation than Birrieria Zaragoza. The roasted and stewed dish is best ordered as the large platter, a mix of chopped meat and bone-in meat, burnt umber in color, with a ladle of goat consommé atop the dish and a stack of fresh corn tortillas on the side. It's rich in flavor, yes, but it reflects also the richness of Chicago's Mexican food and tacos.

But back to the Windy City's fancy places: Mi Tocaya Antojería might just top the list of Chicago's modern Mexican and taco joints. Chef Diana Davila adds a contemporary touch to the city's Mexican cuisines—and that's without considering Bayless. Mi Tocaya is more than a taco shop. It's a full restaurant where moles are just as likely to adorn a plate of fish as they are a medley of vegetables, which, in this case, are cauliflower (harrumph) and fiddlehead ferns. There is whimsy, too. A steak burrito makes an appearance and an appetizer playfully announces itself with the name "Peanut Butter & Lengua," a flourish of mole strikes with light blocks of beef tongue. Meanwhile, the tacos riff on the diversity with a wink. The smoked beer can chicken with xoconostle (a sour prickly pear) is joined by a riff on the Three Sisters of agriculture with squash, beans, chiles, and a corn cream sauce. Both get a sprinkle of cheese. The campechano (a traditional taco of steak, chorizo, and chicharrones) subs cochinita pibil for the usual fried pork skin. Other times, al pastor might be the pork component. The list is closed out with a fried oyster taco.

Dai Due Taqueria, a counter-service stall at the Austin, Texas, food hall Fareground at One Eleven, takes the idea of modern, regional tacos to dangerous and exciting lengths. Until late 2018, Gabe Erales led the kitchen of the taco spin-off of the popular Dai Due restaurant and butcher shop specializing in local wild game and doing things the hard way. Born in the state of Quintana Roo, Mexico, and raised in El Paso, Texas—by now, you've doubtlessly realized how important El Paso is to American tacos and Mexican food in the United States—Erales previously spent time staging at Noma, long considered among the best restaurants in the world, in Copenhagen, Denmark, and worked in the test kitchen of Noma's Mexico pop-up in the tropical forest resort town of Tulum, before taking the helm at Dai Due Taqueria.

That "doing things the hard way" aesthetic takes form in the nixtamalization of landrace corn sourced from family farms in Mexico through maize purveyor Tamoa. One week, Erales could use blue corn. The next, he could have conica morada, which has chocolate notes and a soft texture. It's almost like there's cake flour in the masa. The crimson-edged meat on the trompo isn't pork, per se; rather, it's wild boar hunted right here in the Lone Star State. Everything from the chile chihuacle that goes into the mole negro to the limes garnishing plates are acquired and used on a seasonal basis. When limes aren't in season, they're not available fresh at Dai Due Taqueria, if they're available at all. That can cause some confusion on the part of customers accustomed to having tacos and taco components accessible year-round. And it was an issue for Erales and owners Jesse Griffith and Tamara Mayfield. Self-handicapping aside, under Erales, Dai Due offered taco humdingers, including a vegetarian longaniza sausage that replaced the seasoned pork with beets. The earthiness from the seasoning remained, as do enough elements of the original texture of the filling to confuse and please your palate. Mole gets a venison and sweet potato combination. Shrimp gets ground, shells and all, into a filling. This craft and labor, from the tortillas to the salsas, and the seasonality of ingredients like limes, makes for a high-price taco. The wild boar pastor clocks in at six dollars. But that's the price of quality and thoughtful cooking, whether it's in the fine-dining arena or the fast-casual lane.

"I love the idea behind a taqueria that seems counter-service-casual on the surface," Erales says of Dai Due Taqueria. "But you get behind the counter and you see there is a ton of effort going into making tortillas." His love of food comes from growing up watching his mother cook. But he didn't immediately set out to tie on an apron and perfect his knife skills. First he got a mechanical engineering degree from the University of Texas at Austin and went on to work in automotive design at General Motors in Detroit, Michigan. Eventually, he made it back to Austin, attended the same culinary school as Jacob and Clarissa Dries of El Mero Taco in Memphis, and got a job at Steak & Ale. Between the stint at the steakhouse chain and Dai Due Taqueria, he worked at a series of Austin's best restaurants, including Fonda San Miguel, Odd Duck, and La Condesa. From its debut, Dai Due Taqueria was one of the best taco shops in Texas.

The most important component wasn't the Tamoa-sourced corn, though. It was Erales, whose thoughtfulness led to the kitchen's honorable execution of a modern Mexican food that was pinned to Texas but wasn't Tex-Mex. Rather, it is a contemporary form of the taco using prime ingredients and prepared with an understanding of Mexican cuisine and the physical location of Texas within what was once Mexico. Unfortunately, Erales left Dai Due Taqueria in October 2018. Creative differences led to the split, he tells me. Since the chef's departure, Dai Due Taqueria has foundered in silence while Erales has gone on to travel across the United States, cooking special dinners at the James Beard House in New York and at events such as Chef's Indie Week in Denver. His follow-up project, Comedor, takes its name from the Spanish for "dining room." The restaurant, a high-end establishment focused on unique regional Mexican cuisine centered on nixtamalization and native landrace Mexican corn, opened in Austin in April 2019. There is only one taco on the menu, a rich bone marrow taco. The bone, opened lengthwise to reveal the dark marrow, is served atop quelites greens and accompanied by tortillas for assembly at the table.

At about the same time that Dai Due Taqueria debuted in the downtown food hall, East Austin–based Suerte (English for "luck") began serving its own interpretations of Mexican food, one fixated on corn masa. The restaurant, owned by Sam Hellman-Mass with Fermín Núñez in the role of executive chef, offers plenty of classical masa presentations—crispy tlayudas and doughy tamales, for starters. The masa also manifests as dumplings in the duck breast and mole negro and the triangular tetela made from green corn. Tacos have a niche, of course. At dinner there are two options: the suadero, a smooth confited brisket cut endemic to Mexico City, and the Governator Taquitos, rolled and fried red chile–infused tortillas filled with snapper and white cheese, an homage to the Sinaloan taco gobernador. Tacos have a more prominent place on the brunch menu. The lengua taco gets bacon-laced refried beans. A taco of butternut squash is topped with pumpkinseed and sweet corn salsas. Potato and cheese are folded into a red corn tortilla and finished on a grill.

El Naranjo, another modern Mexican restaurant—this one on the edge of downtown Austin—has continued to thrive. The operation started life as a trailer parked in front of its eventual brick-and-mortar space while the building was undergoing construction. During the trailer days, I marveled at co-owners Iliana de la Vega and Ernesto Torrealba's rolled tacos dorados, and now everyone gets to enjoy light tacos of fresh, aromatic corn tortillas loosely cradling a mixture of hibiscus blossoms and carrots. It should be noted, though, that El Naranjo, which specializes in the cuisine of Oaxaca through the prism of classical dining, isn't a taqueria. Rather, the restaurant focuses on platters and other corn-based dishes, some of which are accompanied with fresh tortillas, goading you into making your own tacos. That being said, El Naranjo and Dai Due Taqueria, alongside the newer Suerte, offer the Tex-Mex-saturated town of Austin some of the best modern tacos in Texas. Most importantly, all three take corn and tortillas with the seriousness at the foundation of the Mexican adage: Sin maiz no hay pais, a phrase that cannot be repeated enough in the context of this book or any discussion of Mexican food on either side of the border.

Given the choice between sitting at home or carving a covered wagon into the butt of a Winchester rifle in his Castelan Designs workshop (blocks away from the Fort Worth Stockyards National Historic District), Arturo "El Gorupo" Rojas would choose the latter. "I prefer working," says the mustachioed septuagenarian native of Yurécuaro, Mexico, in the state of Michoacán. "There is always something to do and learn."

El Gorupo, who earned his nickname at birth because he was born small and white like a bird mite, a gorupo, began engraving guns in the Mexican scrollwork style at the age of twelve, taught by his brother Regino. A photocopied cutout portrait of Regino is taped to a white prayer candle on Gorupo's workbench in the gun shop opened by his son, Regino "Gino" Rojas, in 2011, shortly after the family moved to Texas. Castelan Designs allows Gorupo to practice his art his way, and the work has earned him customers from as far away as Australia and walk-ins who say his reputation for precise, florid artistry with antique pieces attracted them to him. Members of a biker gang

The Instataco

The modern taco's development and dissemination is driven in part by social media, namely, Instagram and Twitter. The use of Twitter was instrumental in the early, almost instant success of Kogi BBQ's K-Mex tacos. Twitter and Instagram have also allowed for restaurants to advertise their tacos, the more gimmicky the better. Take the $25,000 taco at the Grand Velas Los Cabos resort in Mexico: a gold-and-corn tortilla filled with Kobe beef and lobster topped with black truffle Brie cheese and beluga caviar and finished with rumpled ribbons of gold. The flashier or the more photogenic the taco, the better for chefs and Instagram users. Instagram accounts like @tacos (with more than one hundred thousand followers) aggregate images for wider social media consumption. Hashtags batch images. The most popular taco-focused hashtag is #tacos, unsurprisingly, and it includes millions of images. Other popular hashtags are #tacosofinstagram and #tacolife. (I use #tacotrail for my account, which, of course, I recommend you follow.) Users with business accounts leverage their chosen focus with access to metrics related to images and to their reach, allowing the account holders to monitor who is seeing what when and what images are more popular than others. My photos of trompos perform crazily well. Photos of gold foil-garnished tacos, not so much.

Social media has also been key to disseminating knowledge and understanding of the taco through higher education. Students taking the Taco Literacy course at St. John's University in Queens, New York, and previously at the University of Kentucky in Lexington, are required to post images to Instagram and include the hashtag #tacoliteracy with each photo. Uploaded images are of more than tacos, though. Students share photos of books, guest speakers, restaurant interiors, whatever informs the course requirement of investigating the link between food and culture and writing in a different medium. It's a form of analysis and contextualization best described as "reading a taco."

wearing 1%er patches, marking them as outlaws, commissioned Gorupo to engrave their leader's pistol. "They were the nicest guys. Very respectful," says Gino. A project can take up to two weeks to complete, but the hours are erratic. "I work whenever inspiration strikes me," Gorupo says. The results of that inspiration fetch as much as $2,600 for single-action Colt Army grips featuring a Texas longhorn steer and Burma rubies or $60,000 for a custom job. On the day I visited the store, Gorupo was working on an AK-47 repurposed into a sniper rifle.

Behind parallel display cases, his cluttered workbench bears gold plating, tangles of wires, gun grips, rifles, and the weighted chisels and hammers that El Gorupo made himself. In a corner is a double-burner electric stove with an ashy hot plate, which turns out to be the engraver's makeshift kitchen. "I cook everything. Bistec, caldo de pollo, carnitas," Gorupo explains. "Everything." Gino adds, "He'd sleep here if he could." El Gorupo nods silently then changes the conversation.

"Are you married?" the elder Rojas asks me. "Yes," I replied, showing him a picture of my wife. Gorupo smiles and hands me a thumbnail-sized parcel held together by blue painter's tape. "For your wife," he says in measured, tightly mouthed English despite the fact that we have been conversing in Spanish all morning. Inside was a pair of gold-plated dime-coin earrings he had crafted while we were chatting. No one had noticed. Gorupo tinkers constantly. His hands are always creating, whether it be engraving a ram's head into a gun or testing new designs on a belt buckle. It might come as a surprise, then, that the elderly engraver is also the dishwasher at what is perhaps the greatest taqueria in Texas, Revolver Taco Lounge, owned by his son Gino.

Revolver initially opened in 2012 in Fort Worth, Texas. It was a mod joint with folk touches. Mexican devil masks hung next to a collage that includes the sentence, "Aqui no tenemos pinche nachos." ("We don't have fucking nachos here.") Floral print oilcloths were placed over fine white tablecloths. An electro soundtrack supported the presentation of ceviche

swirling with smoke under a glass dome and practically barnyard goat birria at the table.

Then there are the seconds-old corn tortillas so hot that if you dare to
lift the monogrammed towel and the warmer's lid under it as soon as the
stack hits the table, you'll be burned. Wait. Wait like you waited for relleno,
a blood pudding prepared with bovine offal and pig's blood. Wait like you
waited for the tacos de huitlacoche, delicate parcels bearing nutty-scented
clusters of the bluish-black corn fungus known as corn smut or corn truf-
fles in English. This food, it takes time.

Behind the partial wall separating the kitchen from the dining room
at the Fort Worth restaurant, time runs differently. Gino's aunt, Tia Tere,
is responsible for the scorchingly fresh tortillas. Juanita, Gino's mother, is
the head cook, with significant assists from her daughters Maria and Chelo.
Juanita is behind the restaurant's signature platters, including the birria,
mole, and a runny egg folded into one of Tere's tortillas, the stickiest, most
world-silencing taco special I've ever been served. The duck, a medium-rare
slice of breast with a band of fat augmented with sautéed onion and a slice
of roasted poblano alongside deep tomatillo-chile de árbol salsa, is stun-
ning. Farther in the back is Gino's dad in a beret and apron, quietly scrub-
bing away at dishes that once held his wife's mole or adobo-rubbed grilled
Japanese red snapper. Occasionally, he'll look up when someone barks an
order or to give a quick scan of the action in the small dining room.

At the first location in Fort Worth, a Colt 1863 Navy .44 caliber revolver
Gorupo engraved, using a melted gold inlay technique, stands framed by
bottles of agave spirits above the bar. The bar itself has inlaid pistols. From
the restaurant's name to the décor, there are hints of the family business.

El Gorupo doesn't like to make a big deal about his profession. "Tell
him about your trip to Tijuana," Gino asks his father in Spanish.

"I don't know. It was nothing. Just something that happens when
you're a gun engraver." Gino won't let his dad off easy, and Gorupo relents.
"I got on the wrong bus," he says. "The police inspected my bag, confiscated

the guns, and threw me into a jail cell. I tried telling them the guns were for their boss. So when they let me make one phone call, I chose to call their superior officer. He came into the police station and fired them on the spot."

It was police harassment that ultimately led to the Rojas's stateside relocation. "It wasn't the cartels that were the criminals. It was the cops," Gino says. "They would steal our guns, plant stuff. The cops can make you look like criminals." In 2010, when the police took his sister and her six-month-old daughter hostage, demanding El Gorupo hand over his inventory of firearms and gold, Gino decided it was time to get his family out of Mexico. "I paid twice the amount the cops wanted for a lawyer, but it was worth it. The cops weren't going to get our money, and my sister and her baby would be released."

The family settled in Fort Worth in 2011 after short stints in Guadalajara, Mexico, and Chicago. Texas, unsurprisingly, is home to the majority of Castelan Designs customers.

The restaurants came later. "My mom was bored sitting around the house with nothing to do," Gino tells me. "And we also realized that if we wanted to eat, we'd have to cook the food ourselves. Everyone pitched in."

Gorupo didn't want to move to the Lone Star State, but when asked if he prefers working in Mexico or in the United States, he admits it doesn't matter where he works. "It's not important," he says as he grabs a dirty platter in Revolver's small kitchen. "Art doesn't have borders. As long as I get to keep my hands busy, and keep practicing, I'm happy."

Happiness and joy exude from everything that is Revolver and pours back into the critically acclaimed and beloved restaurant. When the news hit that Revolver Taco Lounge was closing its Fort Worth location at the end of June 2015 when the lease was up, the local blogs lit up. The building had been sold to a new owner who wanted to increase the rent, but denied Gino's request for expanded parking. "I'm sick and tired of having my customers' cars towed because of the parking situation around here," he told me.

The popular response was loud enough that Gino was able to negotiate an extension through the end of the year, giving him time to build out a location in the Deep Ellum neighborhood, hold pop-ups across the area, and participate in festivals like Taco Libre, where he sold one-dollar market-style potato-filled tacos dorados sealed with toothpicks. The dish was served in zip-top bags that also contained cabbage doused in Valentina hot sauce before being shaken. It made for a messy snack, one that should have come with a warning not to rub your eyes after consumption.

Eventually, the original Revolver Taco Lounge shuttered but was revived in the Dallas nightlife district of Deep Ellum as a small front room dominated by a long, raised communal table and a private, reservation-only dining space in the rear of the restaurant. That space, known as the Purepecha Room, is appointed to resemble Doña Juanita's kitchen in her native Michoacán. Earthenware pots hanging from the back wall, a beverage cart here, utensils there, and the kitchen as the centerpiece. And since the Rojases closed Castelan Designs in Fort Worth, the Purepecha Room, or at least a corner of it, has become Gorupo's workshop. He chips away at handles and barrels while customers revel in the prix fixe eight-course dinners featuring octopus in a pipian rojo mole, a cucumber-poblano gazpacho with a tiny archipelago of Agrumato Orange olive oil pressing against diced vegetables, and roasted corn topped with a dusting of cotija cheese and a punctuation of an edible blossom—yes, that was one dish—and any number of rotating, seasonal platters. The menu is bolstered by ingredients carted from Mexico during Gino Rojas's trips home. But it's the tacos, both in the Purepecha Room and in the front taqueria, that keep me returning. If I lived close, I might just be a weekly regular.

The Rojases' penchant for taco creation seems boundless. It defies rigidity and staid definitions while clearly riffing on traditional flavors and ingredients. I have sat at the front bar when Gino was dishing out heat-prickling lobster tacos that double as a dance floor for undulating bonito flakes; frogs' legs propped up with a house-made yellow curry, a dose of almonds, and Thai basil; a saucy cabrito; and an on-the-fly, ounces-light, and delicate un-chopped Wagyu A5 filet dressed with a couple of chanterelles. What glorious tacos those were.

As driven by creativity as Revolver is, Hugo Ortega's Houston restaurants, Hugo's and Xochi, have been catapulted forward by thoughtfulness. Both restaurants emphasize platters, but both also feature several delightful tacos and tortilla-based dishes. At Xochi, pressed, rectangular cuts of cabrito sit matter of factly on three blue corn tortillas. Between the meat and the tortilla, a hefty but bright salsa verde keeps the kid goat in place. A thin wheel of radish leans against the meat. Connecting to its predecessor in Mexico, the infladita de conejo, the Tex-Mex salad-bowl puffed taco, is large and made from an inflated blue corn tortilla tinctured with squid ink and perforated and brimming with luscious ropes of rabbit. Perched atop the meat, which, like the goat, lacked gaminess, were ribbons of carrots and a loose collection of greens. Raisins and almonds were sneaky, joyous treats. A bundle of taquitos dorados, fried tacos rolled with nearly translucent, wonton-wrapper thin tortillas, had juicy chicken tucked inside. The assemblage rested on swathes of crema studded with queso fresco and a dark mole shimmering under the restaurant's pre-dimmed lighting. Tacos dorados are also available at Hugo's. However, instead of being filled with the classic potato stuffing, the potatoes were used to form tiny taco shells.

Although the street-style, classic taco fillings and crunchy tacos will always be with us, modern tacos continue to evolve and press ahead, always reaching for a horizon defined by quality and availability. Taquerias and restaurants like the aforementioned are continually tweaking and fiddling with tortillas and their potential fillings, hopefully surprising and delighting customers without pompous disregard for history and flavor profiles. Revolver Taco Lounge, Xochi and Hugo's, Crujiente Tacos and Boca Tacos and Barrio Café, Dai Due Taqueria and El Naranjo, and all the taquerias bound only by the excellent canvases are the future. As are establishments such as Jose & Sons, Macheen, and Guerrilla Tacos. Here's the thing, though: The future of the taco is now.

Where to Find Them

Antique Taco
1360 N. Milwaukee Ave.
Chicago, IL 60622
773-687-8697
antiquetaco.com

Barrio Café
2814 N. 16th St.
Phoenix, AZ 85006
602-636-0240
barriocafe.com

Big Star
1531 N. Damen Ave.
Chicago, IL 60622
773-235-4039
bigstarchicago.com

Birrieria Zaragoza
4852 S. Pulaski Rd.
Chicago, IL 60632
773-523-3700
birrieriazaragoza.com

Boca Tacos y Tequila
533 N. Fourth Ave.
Tucson, AZ 85705
520-777-8134
bocatacos.com

Cantón Regio Mexican Steakhouse
1510 W. 18th St.
Chicago, IL 60608
312-733-3045
cantonregio.business.site

Carnitas Uruapan
1725 W. 18th St.
Chicago, IL 60608
312-226-2654
carnitasuruapanchi.com

Comedor
501 Colorado St.
Austin, TX 78701
512-499-0977
comedortx.com

Crujiente Tacos

3961 E. Camelback Rd.
Phoenix, AZ 85018
602-687-7777
crutacos.com

Dai Due Taqueria

111 Congress Ave.
Austin, TX 78701
512-284-7083
daiduetaqueria.com

El Naranjo

85 Rainey St.
Austin, TX 78701
512-474-2776
elnaranjorestaurant.com

Guisados

multiple locations
guisados.co

Hugo's

1600 Westheimer Rd.
Houston, TX 77006
713-524-7744
hugosrestaurant.net

Mexicue

New York, NY
several locations
mexicue.com

Mi Mero Mole

32 NW Fifth Ave.
Portland, OR 97209
971-266-8575
mmmtacospdx.com

Mi Tocaya Antojería

2800 W. Logan Blvd.
Chicago, IL 60647
872-315-3947
mitocaya.com

Revolver Taco Lounge

2701 Main St.
Dallas, TX 75226
214-272-7163
revolvertacolounge.com

Stella Taco

2940 NE Alberta St.
Portland, OR 97211
971-407-3705

3060 SE Division St.
Portland, OR 97202
503-206-5446

stellatacopdx.com

Suerte

1800 E. Sixth St.
Austin, TX 78702
512-953-0092
suerteatx.com

Tamayo

1400 Larimer St.
Denver, CO 80202
720-946-1433
eattamayo.com

Taqueria Nueve

727 SE Washington St.
Portland, OR 97214
503-954-1987
taquerianueve.com

Xochi

1777 Walker St.
Houston, TX 77010
713-400-3330
xochihouston.com

Obregon's Restaurant #2 exterior.

Signs *of a* Truly Outstanding Taco Joint

"WHERE ARE THE BEST TACOS?" "WHERE CAN I FIND LEGIT tacos?" As a writer who spends his time traveling across the country in search of tacos near and far—and I'm based in Texas, meaning I've got easier, faster access than most folks—I get those questions all the time, and the response is trickier than you might think. My answer is always, "What kind of tacos are you looking for? Cheap ones? Fancy ones? Blue ones? Regional ones?"

Such particularity is usually met with a mix of blank stares and slumped shoulders from people looking for some simple instruction on where to get an inexpensive meal. But, alas, tacos are no simple subject. There's a variety of things that need to go right in order to execute a truly transcendent taco—and really, when it comes down to it, isn't that the kind of taco you should be after?

While there's no fail-safe formula, I've developed a list of questions and criteria you can use to quickly evaluate a taqueria to determine whether it's worth your time and whether you're likely to find it worthy of a second, third, and fourth trip. Whether or not they're cash-only is irrelevant. And free chips—or the quality of the free chips—have nothing to do with it. The following items, however, do.

The place is packed

Say you put together a short list of taco joints to hit up during a weekend. While you're cruising around town, checking off taquerias, you come across a joint that's not on your itinerary, but it does have a full parking lot. Or a line that's starting to creep out the door. Stop. Take a break from the list and wait in that line for a table.

While a crowd isn't a 100 percent guarantee of quality, a jammed taqueria strongly suggests something worth enduring the madness of a busy eating establishment. This is the first sign things are looking up for your taco experience. Throw in any or all of the criteria below, and you just might have a sure thing on your hands.

They're repping a particular regional cuisine

Any indication that taqueria owners are slinging tacos and other dishes from their home state or other regional specialties is a promising sign. Are the words "Barbacoa Roja estilo Sinaloa" splashed across a taqueria window? If so, odds are the makers of the pork-and-beef barbacoa are from the northwestern state of Sinaloa. (Estilo means "in the style of.") They might also have goat birria, red and earthy from chiles, cinnamon, and cloves. Is that birria de res (beef)? You might have stumbled upon a Zacatecas-style joint. What's up with that taco dorado de camaron? It's a shrimp-stuffed fried taco specialty out of San Juan de los Lagos in the state of Jalisco.

However, scarf enough tacos in enough places and you'll notice a glut of Mexican restaurants and taquerias with names that include the word "Jalisco." Not all of them serve Jalisco cuisine. Rather, the frequent use of the name has to do with the state of Jalisco being considered the soul of Mexican culture. It's from Jalisco we get mariachi, pozole, and tequila. Be wary.

That goes double for "DF-style" spots. DF, or Distrito Federal, or Cuidad de Mexico (CDMX), the Mexican analog to Washington, DC, is shorthand for Mexico City, whether used in conversation to refer to one's home or to refer to the cuisine. In cases of the latter, DF is usually code for generic tacos—the kinds found in taquerias across the world: carne asada, pastor, pollo, lengua, and chorizo—or, as I like to call them, pork-beef-chicken (PBC). (More on that later.) As the capital, Mexico City draws people from across the country who in turn serve their own regional specialties. For example, burritos and hotdogs from Sonora are super popular in the capital at this writing.

So again, look for words or phrases beyond "estilo PLACE NAME." Search for specific dishes. If you see "suadero" (a brisket-like beef cut) or "cabeza al vapor" (steamed beef head meat tacos), two dishes that can claim actual DF provenance, you might just have a true Mexico City spot before you. Does the taqueria claim to trade in food from Puebla? Look for tacos arabes, which are credited to Lebanese or Iraqi immigrants to early twentieth-century Mexico.

You can check for regional clues even before entering the taqueria. Just look for the art—what I call "tacos illustrated"—on the exterior of the building. For example, the neighborhood I call home has a large Mexican immigrant population from the northern city of Monterrey, in the border state of Nuevo León. Gastronomically, Monterrey is known for its cabrito (milk-fed kid goat) and tacos de trompo (a regional cousin to tacos al pastor). Like al pastor, tacos de trompo are roasted on the vertical spit known as a trompo (Spanish for "spinning top," which the pork-stacked spit resembles). Unlike al pastor, tacos de trompo come lacquered in a sticky, lightly smoky paprika-dominated marinade. Representations of these rotisseries are painted on the brightly colored signs or exterior walls of taquerias.

Monterrey is also famous for la Cerro de la Silla, a saddle-shaped mountain towering over the city. It too is often painted on the taquerias specializing in trompo. Combined, the trompo and the landmark signal the potential for sliced and chopped pork served on shimmering tortillas.

They're paying serious attention to their tortilla game

The tortilla being the foundation of the taco means that without a great tortilla, there is no great taco. Repeat that. Seems simple enough, right? Wrong.

There is nothing like a freshly made corn tortilla if it's actually done right, redolent of a cornfield with an aroma that lingers on your fingers. Same goes for fresh flour tortillas. Handmade versions come in several regional variations, including nearly translucent, oversized discs on the border to the fat, squishy kind found in Central Texas and the surrounding areas. These tortillas are exceptional, but they will cost you. Handmade anything commands a higher price point. If you encounter an unforgivable supermarket-grade tortilla that chews like worn rubber, skedaddle.

They have fillings beyond the typical PBC

Now that we've covered tortillas, let's hit the second component of tacos: the filling. The majority of taco operations trade in the MVPs (most viable products) of PBC. Inoffensive and approachable, the meats come grilled or simmered. This isn't to dismiss these more common proteins, which can be magnificent—simple, elegant, hit-the-spot munchies dotted with char— when prepared by master taqueros (taco chefs).

However, these fillings are but a few checkpoints on a potentially limitless lifelong taco bucket list. There are home-style south-of-the-border classics like weenie and eggs, chile relleno, cauliflower fritters, all manner of lamb and goat preparations, roasted grasshoppers, and ant larvae. If you can ingest it, the stuff has likely already been put in a tortilla in Mexico. Less familiar fillings are a solid indication that the establishment in question has more up its sleeve than your average taqueria. When in doubt, pull out your phone, fire up Google, and search for information on the ingredients. Don't be the fool who declares something "inauthentic" or "novelty" because you're unfamiliar with the fillings.

They go beyond the standard salsa options

When it comes to salsa, the final component of a taco, the more options, the better the chances of a superlative, personalized experience. In an ideal world, you have a colorful cornucopia of salsa excellence at your fingertips, well beyond the usual suspects of roja, verde, and pico de gallo. Whether they're in refrigerated squeeze bottles, brought to the table in little plastic bowls, or stocked in a sneeze-guarded salsa bar, you're looking for something a little less common. Maybe they have a dark and piquant salsa de chile morita or some elusive throat-melting habanero-peanut salsa. Maybe there's an off-menu topper for those in-the-know. So always ask, or you'll never know.

A Brief History *of the* Taco Holder

Ingenuity

OLD EL PASO WANTS YOU TO BELIEVE THAT THE WISDOM OF BABES, specifically Spanish-speaking Mexican children, spurs innovation. In a 2004 commercial advertising the Tex-Mex foodstuffs manufacturer's newest product, a young boy is saddened by his father's failed attempts at getting their crunchy tacos to remain upright. We see him go so far as to hammer nails into the family dining table, hence creating a workshop-style taco slot. His son bemoans the lack of flat-bottom shells. And then: Eureka! The Stand 'N Stuff Taco is born. The boy is feted as a hero by the entire village framed by cacti and adobe. A voice-over declares "True genius. Mexican style."

However ingenious it might be, the flat-bottom taco shell is not Mexican style. Instead, these prefabricated crunchy tacos exist somewhere between contempt and respect for their place in history. They were developed from the first tacos in the United States (not Mexico) and are considered tasteless bastardizations of their progenitors. Still, they allow for safe entry into the wider world of tacos and carry nostalgia for those who grew up eating them on taco night or at Taco Bell. They're also extremely fragile.

Appearing in the United States in the early twentieth century, these hard-shell vittles were created by Mexican immigrants, embraced by Anglo Americans,

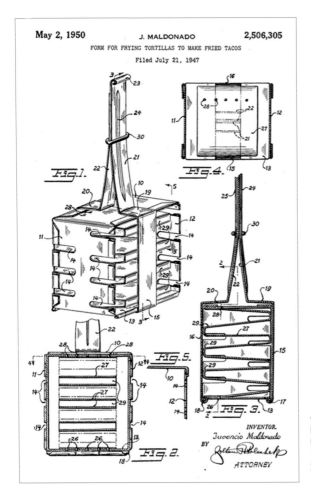

May 2, 1950   J. MALDONADO   2,506,305

FORM FOR FRYING TORTILLAS TO MAKE FRIED TACOS

Filed July 21, 1947

INVENTOR.
Juvencio Maldonado
BY
ATTORNEY

Illustration from Juvencio
Maldonado's patent application.
UNITED STATES PATENT OFFICE, NO.
2,506,305, JUVENCIO MALDONADO,
"FORM FOR FRYING TORTILLAS TO
MAKE FRIED TACOS," MAY 2, 1950.

and reviled by Mexicans as aberrations of their traditional tacos dorados.
Recipes published in newspapers and cookbooks—among them, Myrtle
Richardson's 1934 *Genuine Mexican and Spanish Cookery for American
Homes*—touted the taco as acceptable and safe for Anglo American con-
sumption. Frying, baking, or heating hard taco shells in the home kitchen
took off in the United States.

There was the issue of bodily harm caused by burns from frying the corn tortillas by hand. To solve that dilemma and perhaps to save his restaurant, Xochitl, in New York City, Juvencio Maldonado conceived the first device for frying multiple corn tortillas into the familiar U shape. He filed a US Patent and Trademark Office (USPTO) patent application in 1947 and was awarded the patent in 1950.

Myriad, similar devices followed, including Santiago M. Luna's "utensil for cooking tacos" and Victor Torres's "frying utensil," both in 1953. In his application, Torres outlined the concerns in the production of taco shells:

> The preparation of tacos involves frying . . . tortillas while held in a folded or U-shaped formation and when the tortillas are fried crisp they are removed from the oil or liquid in which they are fried and are supplied with a suitable filling. The frying operation just referred to is deep frying and with methods heretofore employed this operation has been somewhat difficult and tedious as it requires manual holding of the tortilla in the desired shape while frying, or the use of rather makeshift pans to hold the tortilla in proper shape. The fragile nature of the tortilla when fried crisp, and because of this, ordinary methods of preparation have resulted in much breakage.
>
> A general object of this invention is to provide a frying utensil that can be easily and conveniently used to handle one or more tortillas in a bath of oil or fat so that the tortillas are properly fried without constant holding or attention on the part of the cook and without danger of loss or breakage such as ordinarily attends the frying of tortillas.

In a later patent application, Joseph P. Veach described his contraption as:

> A device for frying taco shells, these shells being made from the thin pan-cake-like [*sic*] corn products known as tortillas which when folded and fried to crispness and stuffed with various comestibles form a sort of sandwich known as a taco, popular in Mexico and in the southwest portion of the United States. The art of frying tortillas into taco shells as practiced by hand by the Mexican Indians throughout historic time involves holding a tortilla at opposite peripheral

United States Patent Office

Des. 217,593
Patented May 19, 1970

217,593
TACO HOLDER

James R. Loven, San Fernando, Calif.
(10965 Glenoaks Blvd., Pacoima, Calif. 91331)
Filed Mar. 19, 1969, Ser. No. 16,321
Term of patent 3½ years
Int. Cl. D9—04
U.S. Cl. D9—242

FIG. — I

FIG. —2

Illustration from James R. Loven's patent application.

UNITED STATES PATENT OFFICE, NO. D217593 S,
JAMES R. LOVEN, "TACO HOLDER," MAY 19, 1970.

points by forks or sticks and dipping it in hot fat, a process obviously requiring the undivided attention of the person practicing it and subjecting the person to heat and possible burns.

There was still trouble in taco town. How could a cook prevent the shell from falling over and consequently cracking? And how to increase the appeal of the taco to Americans? A solution came with the creation of the tabletop taco holder. The earliest patent application for such an accessory was filed by James R. Loven of San Fernando, California, in 1969 and granted the following year. Loven's invention, an "ornamental design for a taco holder," resembles a winged butter dish. From the beginning, the taco holder has been about aesthetics.

Presaging the modern multi-slot taco holder, Lois L. Guerrero of Hilo, Hawaii, filed her patent application in 1977. She described her invention in detail:

A taco holding tray to support "V"-shaped taco shells for filling and serving, comprising a tray having a linear trough for supporting taco shells, the length of which trough is at least as along as the length of the taco shell, said linear trough having a rounded bottom to support the normal bending radius of the formed taco shell and outwardly inclined side walls forming an open "V" of about 30.degree. to 45.degree. [*sic*], the depth of which trough is such that the side walls will support all but enough of the sides of the taco shell for removal of the taco shell from the trough by the fingers, and an overflow catching means at each end of the trough to catch and hold excess filling material from said taco shells.

In a clever turn, O. Ray Conder Jr.'s TACOSIT resembles a sombrero, although it hews more closely to the favorite headpiece of the *Curious George* Man with the Yellow Hat—or newly hatched chicks ravenous for tortilla product.

Just as odd is the list of references cited by the patent applicants, which includes an epiphanic hodgepodge of objects: napkin holders, frying implements, an ice cream cone stand, an ashtray. Guerrero's USPTO application includes "Clam-Bakers," which were patented in 1878.

Peculiar references and patent applications for the receptacles continued—and continue—to inundate the USPTO, with a narrow (and incorrect) concept of the taco evident through use of standard language like "a taco is a sandwich made of a tortilla rolled up with or folded over a filling and then usually fried" common in the applications. In 1984, inventor Howard J. Kotliar writes about his tray: "If the shell is folded to form a V-shape, which is a common type of sandwich becoming quite popular in this country, there is great difficulty in retaining all of the food within the partially eaten sandwich when it is placed on a plate or a tray, and the problem is worsened by the tendency of the sandwich to roll over on its side." A lot of people were having the problem of not knowing how to eat a taco and a misconception of what a taco is.

But this marketable idea of the taco and container barreled through American culture alongside the rise of supermarket Tex-Mex or "Hispanic" brands in the mid-twentieth century, and it shows no sign of abating. Take, for example, the terracotta Wieland Ware Hot Taco set, advertised in the September 15, 1983, issue of the *Index-Journal* newspaper of Greenwood, South Carolina, as costing $15 for a set of two, but on sale at $10.88. Bentson-West Designs offered a four-compartment holder made in Italy that promises to "make any meal a fiesta." At each end of the accessory was a half-face with hair-like sunbeams that could have been Mesoamerican or Etruscan in origin. Myriad renditions, including those playing on cultural signifiers and stereotypes—Chihuahuas, for example—flooded the market. The taco, once the province of street stalls, catering trucks, Mexican and Tex-Mex restaurants, and fast-food franchises, was firmly wedged into the domestic sphere.

Family taco night and fine dining

At the beginning of the twenty-first century, the taco garnered the attention of chefs with an upscale bent, among them, Jean-Georges Vongerichten at ABC Cocina in New York, Stephan Pyles at Stampede 66 in Dallas, Mexico City native chef-restaurateur Richard Sandoval at Maya in New York City, as well as John Franke at Velvet Taco. These chefs—and many others—have detached the proletarian food from its modest origins in order to exhibit their creations in their venues, sometimes in a taco holder shaped in a zigzag form. When asked why they use a taco holder for plating, chefs explain how modern, attractive, and different it is. But its function remains important.

"I wanted a holder that makes it easy to pick the taco up," Pyles explains. "It makes me laugh when I see folks eating tacos with a knife and fork. This way, they are not tempted. I think it's a cool presentation." Sandoval, who uses holders at most of his restaurants, including Latin Asian fusion concept Zengo, echos Pyles's sentiments. "Taco holders create the perfect angle for holding each of the intended ingredients in a taco. They also keep things uncluttered on the plate and create a unique form of presentation." Velvet Taco executive chef John Franke says his Texas-based team uses custom holders. "The taco holders we use are made by hand by a kitchen equipment company we use for our concepts."

Uncanny in its resemblance to the holder used at Velvet Taco is American Metalcraft's brushed stainless steel model. It hit the market in 2012, a product of a fortuitous accident. As Lee Ann Kelly, vice president of sales, says, "The American Metalcraft taco holder was actually created for another use. One of our chain customers asked us to develop the product to be used in the kitchen to make flatbread sandwiches. This was the use for a few years before we realized that it could be used for taco presentation." Now the Illinois-based company counts Stephan Pyles among its wide range of customers, including "fast food restaurants, hotels, caterers, the list goes on and on," says Kelly.

Evoking Juvencio Maldonado's ingenuity is the Taco Rack, which works double duty as oven utensil and tabletop accessory. Elain De Luca Byrnes, chief marketing officer of La Cook-a-Rack-a Ltd., maker of the Taco Rack, explains: "The Taco Rack is an invention of my business partner Nicolas Stanco. He designed it and had prototypes made to provide a better taco dinner experience for his family. The stress and mess of filling breaking taco shells was too tiresome for them. That led to having it patented and marketed to the home chef and commercial chef." Among the company's clients are Royal Caribbean Cruises, Dave & Buster's, Whole Foods Markets, and restaurants across four continents—including the Hawaii location of international Japanese BBQ chain Gyu-Kaku, where the Taco Rack is used to serve smoked pork belly tacos with yuzu pico de gallo and sake miso salsa. The Taco Rack is available as Chef Series Six Shooters, Triples, Mini Six Shooters, Mini Triples, and as a solo holder.

The spacing between walls of the taco holder wedges varies by manufacture. Some are so tight as to make lifting a taco from the holder difficult. Failed attempts at picking up a taco from a holder inset can result in tiny fissures spreading toward the tortilla's interior. Salsa can stream from the bottom of the taco. It can be a mess. The taco holder is supposed to eliminate that scenario while being visually seductive. One reason could be the amount of filling tucked into the tortilla. As Sandoval notes, "One drawback may be limitations on the amount of ingredients that can be added to the tortilla." If overstuffed, the filling could scatter on to the table and the diner.

"I bought them initially to display our tacos or any specialty taco of the day," says Richard Garcia of the American Metalcraft taco holders he uses at Classic Tacos, a pair of Santa Ana, California, taco trucks that he initially established as a catering business in 2011. In 2013, Garcia, his Mexico-born parents, and other family members rolled out their first truck with a second rig going into service in 2014. He considers taco holders as lures. "They set the perfect viewing angle. Our customers get to see how the taco is assembled and the quantity of fillers," Garcia says. "Most people who see the taco on display, order it. Seeing a beautiful set of tacos just makes it much more appealing than seeing it on a picture, in our opinion."

Nicholas T. Dominguez found inspiration from his family for his Taco-StandUp holders. In the 1960s, he worked at his aunt and uncle's Kansas City Mexican restaurant, Casa De Tacos. There, aluminum foil and crossed fingers buoyed the go-to orders, crunchy tacos with all the trimmings. Some twenty years later, Dominguez's mother gave him Tupperware taco holders (not to be confused with Tupperware's October 1991 limited-release taco holders currently available through tertiary outlets like eBay). "All tacos deserve uprightness," Dominguez says. "I'd imagined a better holder and the interlocking design for several years, drew some pictures. One day in talking with my daughter about it, I realized I should go for it—so she'd know her Dad was more than talk!" The TacoStandUp has since been sold through Avon's catalog and is closing in on 1 million units purchased, according to Dominguez, who says he has received orders from Japan and Australia.

As previously mentioned, taco holders take festive and comical turns. An edible model resembles athletic protection and is described as providing "improved ergonomic fit relative to a user's hand." Another, the colorful

TacoProper, aims once and for all to show consumers the only way to eat a taco, advertising the product, a "kitchen helper," as a "truly revolutionary way to make, serve and eat UNBROKEN tacos" [emphasis in original].

In 2013, Scott M. Bahnsen was granted the rights to his school project–spurred invention, the Taco Susan. The county multi-trades worker in Florida says: "The Taco Susan was conceived from my son's school project when he had to invent something to make life easier. We were having taco night when we were thinking of what to invent, and after passing everything around dozens of times, we had our A-ha moment!" He explains that his research showed no complete taco-serving kit for the family table on the popular taco night existed. Bahnsen also cites a problem commonly used as incentive for the application of taco holders. "Tacos are just naturally messy, to make and eat, and that's half the fun! The [Taco Susan's] taco plates catch some of the mess, though."

But, for Bahnsen, there's more to his invention than containing what a plethora of Anglo Americans perceive as sloppy Mexican food. "Taco Susan is more than keeping taco night tidy. The Taco Susan takes an ordinary meal and makes it an event! Family Taco Night! When you have the Taco Susan set up on the table, and the kids come home from school and see it, there is no mistake what is for dinner!" The Taco Susan transports the entire clan to an unthreatening dimension where fiery handheld pockets can be safely consumed.

It's a wonder every home isn't without one. Yet, while taco holders are used at restaurants and mentioned in cookbooks, magazines, and domestic guides—including *The Polished Woman: Hints, Tips, and Tricks to Getting Organized*, in which the author recommends substituting a muffin tin for a taco holder—entrepreneurs like Bahnsen often have difficulty getting their products on family dining tables. The internet helps, but not much. "The biggest obstacle that I have is the finances it took to bring this invention from idea to a finished product and then trying to market it all on my own. Money runs out just when you want to bring it to the people, and that is the most expensive part, so I submitted it to 'As Seen On TV' crowdfunding," Bahnsen says. "The Taco Susan did great on the crowd-funding site. It sold out very quick. We are hoping they take it on!" However, the Taco Susan isn't available at retail stores. "We are going through this process," he adds.

Wrapping it up

Whether the Taco Susan becomes the commercial hit Bahnsen hopes it will be, his invention has joined the bright and busy history of the taco holder that, since Loven's handiwork, has given consumers and businesses a plethora of options for those taco holders, trays, and stands. The paraphernalia endure in stainless steel, plastic, and ceramic with whimsical names. They are fashioned into the shape of a chile, a Chihuahua, a see-saw, monkey bars, and a sombrero. Unique designs, such as the handmade stoneware with lace pattern from arts-and-crafts marketplace Etsy, are also available. Hart Family Innovations created a holder that rests in a briefcase, facilitates drainage, and, in its patent application, cites Montezuma's feast held in honor of Hernán Cortés and his conquistadores. Even high-end kitchen retailer Williams-Sonoma offers chic contraptions for table, oven, or grill. These products provide diners not well acquainted with traditional tacos a comfortable entry point for culinary tourism on taco night or date night. Some, like TacoProper, claim salvation with mottos such as "Sudden Relief For Taco Lovers." Some are edible. They provide cachet and kitsch folded into one. And with the enduring popularity of the taco—from Taco John's trademarking of Taco Tuesday and highfalutin renditions in four-star epicurean palaces to the latest gourmet taco truck, as well as internet memes (e.g., "I Hate Tacos Said No Juan Ever")—the taco holder's use will continue. If for no other reason than it looks cool.

Entrance to Arizona Taco Festival.

Taco Parties

TACO FESTIVALS HAVE BECOME AN ESSENTIAL PART OF THE TACO experience. They go down in small cities like Greenville, South Carolina, as well as in the prime taco capital of the United States, Los Angeles. And the number of events across the country continues to rise annually. If your town doesn't have a taco festival or hasn't had one yet, odds are good it will have one in the next couple of years. Here is a sampling of festivals nationwide.

Arizona Taco Festival
aztacofestival.com

Perhaps the largest celebration of tacos nationwide, this annual Scottsdale happening welcomes more than forty taco vendors slinging two-dollar parcels for all taco lovers—with plenty of tequila, luchadores, eating contests, and Chihuahuas to boot. Don't worry about the temperature. The Arizona Taco Festival is held in October.

Austin Food & Wine Festival
austinfoodandwinefestival.com

The Lone Star State's capital is captivated by tortilla-wrapped bites. So it's no wonder this happening includes a taco competition that draws fine-dining chefs from across the United States. In the Rock Your Taco event, chefs such as Tim Love (Lonesome Dove/Woodshed Smokehouse), Ming Tsai (Blue Ginger/Blue Dragon), Monica Pope (Sparrow/Beaver's), Aarón Sánchez (Johnny Sánchez), Rick Bayless (Xoco/Topolobampo/Frontera Grill/Cruz Blanca), Fermín Núñez (Suerte), and Tyson Cole (Uchi/Uchiko) show off their taco skills before judges such as Graham Elliot (Graham Elliot Restaurant/Graham Elliot Bistro) and Andrew Zimmern (Lucky Cricket and host of *Bizarre Foods America*).

Barbacoa & Big Red Festival
barbacoabigredfestival.com

The pairing of barbacoa and Big Red soda is a sacred one, one important enough to warrant a huge celebration in San Antonio. Established in 2010, the Barbacoa & Big Red Fest welcomes more than ten thousand attendees annually, all of whom go for the namesake preparation in forms familiar (tacos) and curious (pasta). They're washed down with Big Red in its standard carbonated formula, in a float, or in Krispy Kreme's Big Red Chiller slushie, which matches perfectly with a Krispy Kreme Big Red doughnut.

Connecticut Taco Festival
cttacofestival.com

Like most contemporary taco festivals, this central Connecticut event includes an eating competition, Mexican masked wrestling (lucha libre), and a contest for best taco. The event draws vendors from cities across the state, including Hartford and Stamford, and cities in neighboring states, including Brooklyn and Patchouge, both in New York, and Springfield, Massachussetts. It's not surprising that the festival organizers have to go so far for vendors; Bloomfield is a burg of fewer than twenty-one thousand residents.

The Food Network New York City Wine & Food Festival Presented by *Food & Wine*
nycwff.org/tacos

"Tacos & Tequila," hosted by celebrity TV chef Aarón Sánchez, is a huge draw at this Big Apple bash, which is among the nation's glitziest food festivals.

The Fresno Taco Truck Throwdown
milb.com/fresno

Perhaps the greatest minor league baseball team of all time (let's say it's a time without the San Antonio Missions), the Fresno Grizzlies, aka the Fresno Tacos during Tuesday home games, host the Taco Throwdown in

Festival vendor serving a taco.
COURTESY TACO LIBRE DALLAS.

July. The two-day fiesta draws more than thirty trucks and includes a Fresno Tacos baseball game, musical entertainment, and a taco-eating contest.

The Great Las Vegas Taco Festival
thegreatlasvegastacofestival.com

C'mon, how can Sin City not have a taco festival? Of course, this one goes down during Dia de los Muertos. Lucha libre matches, a taco-eating contest, and carnival rides give festivalgoers breaks between tacos. A car show is thrown in for good measure.

Los Angeles Taco Festival
latacofestival.com

As expected, the US taco capital hosts quite a few taco festivals, including this East Side fete that is part fundraiser for homeless youth service Jovenes Inc.

River's Edge Taco Fest
riversedgetacofest.com

Tacos and taco lovers are everywhere—even in the sister cities of Omaha, Nebraska, and Council Bluffs, Iowa. The inaugural River's Edge Taco Fest in 2018 featured twenty taco vendors, including the local outpost of Dallas-based Rusty Taco, and musical headliner Sir Mix-a-Lot. Luchadores from the Omaha Midwest Mexican Wrestling and Midwest Wrestling Alliance organizations provided the ring entertainment.

Taco Libre Dallas
tacolibrefest.com

Although there are older and bigger taco festivals, none is more important to me than Taco Libre Dallas. It should be. Since 2015, I have curated the taco vendor lineup that has brought the finest taquerias to thousands of festival attendees. Vendors have included the great Revolver Taco Lounge, nationally renowned Trompo, breakfast taco king Tacodeli, neighborhood linchpin El Padrino, guest vendors from Mexico City, and so many more. Taco Libre Dallas goes down the last weekend in April at the Shed at the Dallas Farmers Market. Partially covered, the event is protected from the elements, with space for taco trucks and more vendors. Each year sees a mix of veteran festival vendors, like El Come Taco and Ki'Mexico, alongside new additions, like vegan taqueria Nuno's Tacos & VegMEX Grill and Easy Slider, a burger truck that in 2019 sold a cheeseburger taco. And then, of course, there are the luchadores! Get tickets early. The festival sells out each year.

Taco Madness
lataco.com

Brought to the masses from the crew of L.A. Taco, a website celebrating all aspects of the taco lifestyle (including urban art and music), which turned into an important local journalism outlet, this extension of the annual bracket competition is the coolest taco party in SoCal.

Luchadores at Taco Libre.
COURTESY TACO LIBRE DALLAS.

Taco Fest: Music y Mas
tacomusicfest.com

More than thirty vendors (trucks, restaurants, taquerias) gather at San Antonio's La Villita Historic Arts Village, the site of the city's first settlement. Even before Spanish soldiers and their families called the plot of land home, La Villita was home to Native Americans. The taco styles represented by the vendors include San Antonio's iconic breakfast and puffy tacos, as well as gussied-up selections and longstanding classic styles. The inaugural Taco Fest in 2018 had a banging soundtrack provided by the likes of Piñata Protest, Girl in a Coma, Brown Sabbath, and headliner La Santa Cecilia.

Tacofest

slctacofest.com

From local institutions to late-night taco trucks, Salt Lake City has a vibrant taco scene. It's feted at this event collecting more than twenty vendors at the Mexican Civic Center downtown and raising funds for organizations such as Meals On Wheels and the Boys and Girls Club.

Tacos 'N Tequila

tacotequilafiesta.com

Greenville, South Carolina, is developing into a small but impressive taco town, joining other Southern cities in the category of minor taco destination. This is a good thing. I want to see more of this. You can see more of it at Tacos 'N Tequila. Local favorites Willy Taco, Papi's Tacos, and Tipsy Taco are among the participating restaurants.

Taco Week

local.thepitchkc.com/event/taco-week

This isn't a taco festival so much as a celebration of tacos. Hosted by *The Pitch*, an alt-weekly in Kansas City, Missouri, Taco Week lassos a bunch of local taquerias, bars, and restaurants to offer 50 percent discounts on their tacos. Some participating businesses even create tacos just for Taco Week. It's become an eagerly anticipated annual event, which might be surprising for people unacquainted with Kansas City history. But since you're reading this book, you're not one of them! Make sure to read the #KCTacoWeek-Commandments for expert tips and best practices.

Top Taco NOLA

toptaconola.com

The last several years have seen a spike in taco options in New Orleans, and the Crescent City finally hosted its own taco festival in 2017. Top Taco Nola features tacos from an incredible range of NOLA taco and non-taco shops, including Johnny Sánchez, Araña, Cochon Butcher, Del Fuego, Jacques

Imo's Café, and Los Jefes. As the festival has grown, the organizers have turned the weeklong soiree of mezcal dinners, parties, and shindigs into the kind of event only a city like New Orleans could host.

Twisted Taco Truck Throwdown
facebook.com/TacoTruckThrowdownSA

Before San Antonio's first taco festival, the 2018 Taco Fest: Music y Mas, the taco capital of Texas had only this tournament for dozens of taco trucks. The annual event is free and features dollar tacos al pastor.

Virginia Beach Taco Festival
virginiabeachtacofest.com

I like to think the Virginia Beach Taco Festival attendees show up as much for the myriad taco options and tequila tastings as for the chance to witness the pained expressions of the competitors in the chile-eating contest. Those poor souls.

Wichita Taco Festival
festiveict.com/taco-fest

Thousands of folks flock to the Wichita Taco Festival in Kansas for tacos from family-run shops all the way to the tortilla-wrapped specialties of upmarket concerns. We're talking local Mexican food standard-bearers such as El Patio Café, opened in 1950; Hawaiian-style Filipino lumpia from the LumpiaPalooza food truck; barbecue specialists Angry Elephant; and District Taqueria, done up with urban industrial design.

Acknowledgments

THIS BOOK IS THE CULMINATION OF NEARLY TEN YEARS OF research on the taco on both sides of the border. Since my days of blogging about tacos and any tortilla-related subject, I've darted across the three North American nations for tacos. I've made annual visits to Mexico for tacos; eaten my fill of tacos in Dallas-Fort Worth, where I live with my family; made taco stops across the United States; and encountered pretty great tacos in Vancouver, Canada. Everywhere I traveled, I spoke to people about tacos; it was like living a dream come true. People, often strangers at first, trusted me with their stories and gave me their time. To all who did so, I am grateful, I am honored, and I hope I've done your stories justice. The stories in this book are the stories of our country and of home. They're stories of difficult decisions and hard work. They're stories of solitude and family. They're stories of friends. I owe a big ol' gracias to everyone who contributed to the publication of this book.

First, there are my dear friends Jon Daniel and Robert L. Strickland, the two greatest taco-traveling companions I could ask for. Not only did they provide excellent and expedient driving across Texas and state lines, Jon and Robert also provided hours of laughter, bad jokes, dad jokes, counsel, insight, and care, especially when my epilepsy got the better of me. They've also offered me their stomachs to potentially torture but more often than not to gratify. To Pat Sharpe and Kathy Blackwell, who have put up with my taco antics and given them direction in the pages of *Texas Monthly*, and Daniel Vaughn, the magazine's barbecue editor, for the tips and recommendations and favors throughout the years. To Helen Hollyman, my former editor at *Munchies*, whom I somehow persuaded to let me write about kosher taco art installations, Scandinavian Taco Friday, and more. To Caroline Parkes of Memphis Travel, my gracious driving host in my favorite Tennessee city. To Deb Park of Turner PR in Denver who has repeatedly pointed me in the right direction in the Mile High City. To Dan Gibson of Visit Tucson, who, when I asked for help connecting with another food writer in The Old Pueblo, came through big time with Andi Berlin of the *Arizona Daily Star*. Thank you, Andi, for spending a day eating tacos and Tucsonan food with me. Those burritos at Anita Street Market were fantastic. To Dave Tyda, of the Arizona Taco Festival, for driving me around Phoenix for a day and a half of taco eating and for eschewing the itinerary at the right times. It took years to break tortillas together, but at last we did, and I'm glad we did.

I owe thanks to my dear friends from New York, John and Jenene Bernstein, for allowing me to crash on their couch while they were going through daily life as a young family. Ben Haas and Matt Levy, gracias for being you and for humoring me. There are other New Yorkers. There is El Profe, Steven Alvarez, whose "Taco Literacy" courses have opened minds to the complexity of the taco and who has offered advice and encouragement while sharing jokes and gifts. To Lesley Téllez, for her insight and encouragement. Both Steve and Lesley took time to read chapters of *American Tacos*. To Lisa Fain, the Homesick Texan, for being an early and consistent cheerleader.

Chicago and its taco booster Titus Ruscitti deserve a shout-out. Titus is an unwavering advocate for great tacos, acknowledging Chicago as a taco city deserving of a place next to Los Angeles and San Antonio. He drove Robert Strickland and me around Chicago and put us up for the night during our twenty-six-hour taco tour of his hometown. (Sorry that your car battery died, man.) Nick Kindelsperger, another champion of the Windy City's taco scene and a food and dining reporter for the *Chicago Tribune*, also deserves a tip of the hat for adding his expertise and for joining the hunt for parking in the two feet of snow dropped by Winter Storm Harper during our 2019 trip to his city.

On the subject of San Antonio, the cultural and culinary capital of Texas is sprawling, boiling, and filled with kind people and enlightening foods. I was honored to participate in the 2015 Foodways Texas symposium in San Antonio and connect with scores of people who care for the culinary diversity of the Lone Star State. It was there that I met Gustavo Arellano, a compa who has offered both engaging, often hilarious conversation on Mexican food and loads of encouragement. There is a whole SoCal crew that deserves props, including the homie Javier Cabral, whose endless energy, *Dragon Ball* fandom, and love of LA punk rock is inspiring; Bill Esparza, the fierce chronicler of Mexican cuisines and the one to frame Alta California cuisine for the rest of us; and Daniel Hernandez and everyone at the L.A. Taco website for doing God's work. I ran into Jeffrey Pilcher, author of *Planet Taco*, at the last Esparza-curated *L.A. Weekly* Tacolandia. In the rush and immediacy of our mutual judging responsibilities, I don't recall thanking him for his early support. So, Jeffrey, this is overdue, but thank you.

To Nick Zukin and Scott Craig, thank you for the generosity with your time, money (meals, airfare, books, tacos), and knowledge. I wish you could have been with Robert and me when we ate our way through Salt Lake City with a stop at Crown Burgers. Nick introduced me to Francisco de Santiago, an ebullient culinary guide, who seemingly knows everyone in Mexico City, and his wife Lourdes. We had an incredible night of tacos that featured suadero and a stop on Calle de los Tacos. That time is owed to Nick, yes, but it's also owed to Alejandro Escalante. My friend, author of *La Tacopedia*, the first comprehensive encyclopedia of the taco in Mexico, convinced the organizers of Foro Mundial de la Gastronomía Mexicana to invite me to give a presentation on American tacos in 2017. The symposium was enchanting. I will never forget mole de manzana. I was terrified to be on a stage in front of some of the most passionate culinary minds in North America, arguing that tacos north of el Rio Bravo are as legitimate as those in Mexico. I was convinced that bags of tortillas and cazuelas would be catapulted my way when I uttered the words "not all tacos are Mexican." No injuries were sustained. In fact, I was surprised by how well the topic was received. During my interview with Ray Garcia, the chef-owner of B.S. Taqueria and Broken Spanish, he told me, "It's exciting that there's an actual connection between chefs in the United States and chefs in Mexico around the common idea of influence in all its various stages of evolution." Indeed, Mexican chefs and food writers and academics are approaching American Mexican food with equal seriousness. The dialogue is exciting! And the organizers of el Foro deserve loads of gratitude.

Back in Texas, I owe much appreciation to Alex Flores, the original graphic designer for *Taco Trail*, and to M. Brady Clark, the current designer responsible for the rebranding. Thanks to Marvin Bendele, executive director of Foodways Texas; Agradezco a Four Corners Brewing Company, for offering me space to work when I needed to get the hell out of my house; and Tami Thomsen and Dale Brock, for your patience while I juggled curating Taco Libre and writing this book. Thank you to my editors at the University of Texas Press, including Casey Kittrell for his dedication and guidance, and to my editors and all the staff at *Cowboys & Indians* for their endless pats on the back and for the couch! I can't forget the couch. To Mark Donald, the editor at *Dallas Observer*, who looked out for me when I was the new kid in Dallas and believed in me, I owe the *Taco Trail* to you.

Finally, I will never be able to thank my wife Jessica, and my son, Diego—"Taquito" as he is sometimes called—enough. Diego was my first taco wing man. He continues to be the most brutally honest and surprising of all those I've had the pleasure of sharing tortillas with—and that's even considering Robert's "rabbit's colon" assessment of a vegetable taco in Nashville. To la esposa, mi Alma, you have been more than patient and understanding. You have given me words of encouragement. You have cared for me without complaint when, during breakthrough seizures, I needed it the most. Without you, none of this would be possible. I wouldn't have learned the magic of breakfast tacos or how the smooth, grassy taste of lengua de res can alter the direction of one's life. Gracias, mi amor.

And, thank you, dear readers. What are you waiting for? ¡It's taco time, amiguitos!

Notes

UNLESS OTHERWISE SPECIFIED HERE, QUOTES ARE FROM INTER-views—conducted in person, over the phone, or via email—between the individuals discussed in the book and myself.

Introduction. Your Taco Country Guide

Part of this introduction adapts my *Texas Monthly* essay "Buen Provecho," which ran as part of the November 2015 "120 Tacos to Eat Before You Die" feature.

Chapter 1. Breakfast Tacos

18 *a spat over breakfast tacos*: Matthew Sedacca, "How Austin Became the Home of the Crucial Breakfast Taco," *Eater Austin*, February 19, 2016.

18 *"The subject of tacos"*: "Exile Matthew Sedacca from Texas for Taco Negligence," online petition, Change.org, https://www.change.org/p/city-of-austin-texas-exile -matthew-sedacca-from-texas-for-taco-negligence.

18 *The hostilities made the newswires*: Gustavo Arellano, *Taco USA: How Mexican Food Conquered America* (New York: Scribner, 2012).

18 *posted the date of the earliest newspaper print mention*: "A Texas Tasting Tour through San Antonio," *Arizona Republic*, July 23, 1975.

19 *Wasting no time*: James Barragan, "Austin Mayor Declares 'Taco War' on San Antonio," *Austin American-Statesman*, February 27, 2016.

19 *A treaty summit was held*: Jackie Wang, "Austin, San Antonio End Taco War, Share Breakfast in Peace," *Austin American-Statesman*, March 10, 2016.

19 *It wasn't the first time breakfast tacos have been used*: Part of this chapter originally appeared as "The Real Texas Breakfast Taco History Involves Cannibalism, Ted Cruz, and War" on the *Vice* food vertical, "Munchies," August 6, 2016. The feature includes the vignette about the Texas congressional delegation and Rep. Brady's quote. Gary Martin, "Can Breakfast Tacos Reunify Texans on the Hill?" *San*

Antonio Express-News, May 24, 2013, and reference to Gustavo Arellano's inclusion of breakfast tacos in *Taco USA: How Mexican Food Conquered America* (New York: Scribner, 2012).

20 *Fall 2018 saw a flare-up*: José R. Ralat, "Dallas Is a Taco City," *D Magazine*, September 2018.

20 *"Can we not?"*: Jessica Elizarraras, "Journalists Need to Stop Claiming Tacos, and Mayors Need to Stop Championing the Wrong Thing," *San Antonio Current*, September 5, 2018.

21 *Everybody seemed to take a deep breath*: Travis Snyder, *"Food & Wine* Potentially Reignites Breakfast Taco War Between San Antonio and Austin," *San Antonio Current*, January 31, 2019.

21 *worldwide survey of the history of Mexican food*: Jeffrey M. Pilcher, *Planet Taco: A Global History of Mexican Food* (Oxford and New York: Oxford University Press, 2012). There is a plethora of theories about the etymology of the word "taco." The most commonly accepted is Pilcher's miner theory. Others, including that of David Bowles, a scholar of Nahuatl, the language of the Aztecs, are linguistically based. Bowles makes the case that "taco" and forms of the word once referred to myriad cylindrical objects, like billiards sticks and dowels, and have Proto-Indo-European roots. He connects "taco" to the Nahuatl word *"tlaxcalmimilli,"* which translates to "tortilla cylinder." David Bowles, "Mexican X-plainer: Tacos, Not Tlahcos," *Medium* (website), December 12, 2018.

22 *alongside enchiladas, tamales, and cabrito asado*: Menu, *San Antonio Light*, June 5, 1904.

22 *"Candelario Oropeza of Mexico City, a* semi-cannibal*"*: "Mexican Matters," *El Paso Daily Times*, March 27, 1906.

23 *"typical kitchen in Mexico"*: "Real Mexican Cooking: What Is Served on the Table in the Home of Mexican Family," *San Antonio Express*, March 23, 1913.

23 *"macaroni sandwiches"*: "Originales Teorias de Isidora Duncan Acerca del Desarrollo de los Ninos," *El Paso Morning Times*, February 5, 1915.

23 *"small 'taco hut'"*: Ed Castillo, "About Town," *San Antonio Express and News*, May 24, 1959.

24 *consuming tacos for breakfast*: Associated Press, "Politickin' in Texas," *Baytown Sun*, May 28, 1962.

24–25   *"South Texas breakfast tacos"*: "Expect 1200 Bicyclists for 12th Easter Tour," *Kerrville Mountain Sun*, April 3, 1985.

25   *"Barbeque Tacos"*: Advertisement, *Del Rio News Herald*, March 16, 1973.

26   *"One customer has grown a liking for them"*: "And Now: The Jimmy Carter Peanut and Egg Taco," *Abilene Reporter-News*, December 16, 1976.

26   *"Tacos for breakfast? Yes"*: advertisement, *Port Aransas South Jetty*, September 19, 1975.

26   *offered a coupon*: advertisement, *Austin American-Statesman*, September 9, 1978.

26   *"If You're Not in San Antonio"*: Alison Cook, "The Great Texas Taco Tour," *Texas Monthly*, April 1986.

27   *"Had no regular supper"*: James G. Bell and J. Evetts Haley, "A Log of the Texas-California Cattle Trail, 1854, I," *Southwestern Historical Quarterly* 35, no. 3 (1932): 208–237.

28   *"under the most sanitary conditions"*: Advertisement, *Bryan Eagle*, December 2, 1970.

28   *Specificity is critical here*: Daniel D. Arreola, *Tejano South Texas: A Mexican American Cultural Province* (Austin: University of Texas Press, 2010).

28   *"How they came to be called mariachis"*: Mando Rayo and Jarod Neece, *The Tacos of Texas* (Austin: University of Texas Press, 2016).

28   *the Laredo breakfast taco's origins*: Norma E. Cantú, "Being Tejana: Thoughts on Land, Language and Culture," *Puentes: Revista México-chicana de literatura, cultura y arte*, 1–6 (2007–2010).

30   *as we see in reports from South Texas*: Hector Galan, dir., *Children of Giant* (Galan Productions, 2015).

31   *"A neighbor down the street"*: Mando Rayo and Jarod Neece, *Austin Breakfast Tacos: The Story of the Most Important Taco of the Day* (Mt. Pleasant, SC: The History Press, 2013).

32   *names like Space Cowboy*: Patricia Sharpe, José R. Ralat, et al., "The 120 Tacos You Must Eat Before You Die," *Texas Monthly*, December 2015.

34–35   *"While countless non-Texans get introduced"*: Dan Solomon, "Can Any Texas City Claim the Breakfast Taco as Its Own?" *Texas Monthly*, February 22, 2016.

35 *"Austin trumps all other American cities"*: John T. Edge, "Tacos in the Morning? That's the Routine in Austin," *New York Times*, March 10, 2010.

Chapter 2. Golden and Crunchy

46 *"The traditional taco has to be fried"*: "Spiced Food Is Part Of Local Fiesta," *Brownsville Herald*, February 12, 1950.

46 *from a travelogue printed a few years earlier*: Bertha Haffner-Ginger, *California Mexican-Spanish Cook Book: Selected Mexican and Spanish Recipes* (Los Angeles: Citizen Print Shop, 1914).

46 *a taco recipe that called for frying*: Castelar Crèche, *Castelar Crèche Cook Book* (Los Angeles, Times-Mirror Printing and Binding House, 1922). This cookbook was edited and assembled by the Castelar Crèche board of directors in an effort to raise funds for the Castelar Crèche, an orphanage for infants.

46 *Scads of published materials*: This is an abbreviated rundown of early recipes and mentions. An extended history can be found in Gustavo Arellano's *Taco USA: How Mexican Food Conquered America* (New York: Scribner, 2012). Arellano writes of the storied Mitla Cafe, which opened in 1937 in San Bernardino, California, noting that it is the restaurant that "inspired" Glenn Bell (of Taco Bell infamy), who "ripped off" the Mitla taco to create his crunchy taco.

46 *"echando tacos"*: "Los Niños del Dia," *El Fronterizo*, December 17, 1887. On the subject of echando tacos, I once came across a truck in Mexico City emblazoned with the stenciled words: EL MEXICANO NO COME/"SE ECHA UN TACO." The English translation of the first part—a Mexican doesn't eat—frames eating a taco as a distinct form of consumption, above and beyond the necessary act of eating. There is no precise translation for "se echa un taco." It means "throws tacos onto oneself." It's a quirky statement that gets to the importance of tacos in Mexican culture.

46 *a recipe for a soup*: "Recetas Utiles," *El Fronterizo*, May 5, 1887.

47 *"It was new. It was different"*: Advertisement, *Amarillo Globe-Times*, January 12, 1965.

47 *"cocktail tacos"*: Melanie De Proft, "Shortcuts to Mexican Cookery," *Waco Tribune-Herald*, March 21, 1971.

47 *"Although the fold-over model is standard fare"*: "¡El Mucho Gusto Cookbook!" *Arizona Republic*, October 21, 1973.

48   *technological advancement in the kitchen*: United States Patent Office, No. 2,506,305, Juvencio Maldonado, "Form for Frying Tortillas to Make Fried Tacos," May 2, 1950.

48   *began to tinker*: José R. Ralat, "The Demand for 'Authenticity' Is Threatening Kansas City's Homegrown Tacos," *The United States of Mexican Food, Eater*, April 23, 2019.

49–50   *Then there's Lucy's Café*: This section originally appeared as "Lucy's Café and a Brief History of the First Gourmet Tacos," published on my website *Taco Trail* (thetacotrail.com), April 9, 2017. For a taste of classic El Paso Mexican food, Lucy's Café (aka Lucy's Restaurant) is a must-visit.

51   *And then we're back to El Paso*: Portions of this section originally appeared as "Flautas Are Tacos Too," *Texas Monthly*, December 2017.

51   *on the restaurant's fiftieth anniversary*: Resolution H.R. no. 84, Texas Legislature, July 18, 2003.

53   *born from one of the darkest periods*: Sections on the history of fry bread are adapted from my article, "More Than Fry Bread," *Cowboys & Indians* (October 2013). It's in this article that artist Steven Deo's Art of Indian series is mentioned as well as the USDA data.

53   *Hopi women grinding maize*: Edward S. Curtis, *The Mealing Trough—Hopi* (photograph), Arizona, ca. 1906, www.loc.gov/item/92519541.

53   *wafer-thin, tortilla-like blue corn piki bread*: "Ruby Chimerica Makes Piki Bread," Autry Museum of the American West, 2012, www.youtube.com/watch?v=6SENR9jIrHI.

53–54   *The blue corn powder is nixtamalized*: Lois Ellen Frank, "Piki Bread," ieveryware.com. Frank, who is enrolled in the Kiowa Nation, also writes about piki in *Foods of the Southwest Indian Nations: Traditional and Contemporary Native*, her 2002 cookbook published by Ten Speed Press.

54   *made for important rituals*: Robert Boissiere, *The Hopi Way: An Odyssey* (Santa Fe: Sunstone Press, 1985).

54   *What we know as fry bread*: Johnson Broderick, *Navajo Stories of the Long Walk Period* (Tsaile, AZ: Diné College Press, 1973).

54   *An alternate fry bread creation theory*: Dahlia Cordova, *The Navajo Way of Life: A Resource Unit with Activities for Grades 4–6* (Salt Lake City School District, 1982), microform.

56   *originally at the Ranch Kitchen*: Marian Clark, *The Route 66 Cookbook* (San Francisco: Council Oak Books, 1995).

56   *the film based on a short story*: Chris Eyre, dir., *Smoke Signals* (Miramax, 1998).

57   *a whimsical mockumentary*: Travis Holt Hamilton (as Holt Hamilton), dir., *More than Frybread* (Better World Distribution, 2011).

58   *Denver-based fast-casual restaurant*: Tocabe was featured in the Food Network *Diners, Drive-Ins and Dives*, Season 0, Episode 20 ("Crazy for Chicken") and Season 12, Episode 4 ("Grillin' and Smokin'"). A Tocabe recipe was printed in Guy Fieri, *Diners, Drive-Ins, and Dives: The Funky Finds in Flavortown—America's Classic Joints and Killer Comfort Food* (New York: William Morrow Cookbooks, an imprint of HarperCollins, 2013).

58   *from the Yocha Dehe Wintun Nation*: While visiting Denver during book research, I visited Tocabe and attempted to meet with co-owner Ben Jacob to discuss indigenous cuisines. My attempts took place before, during, and after my visit and included working through a mutual friend. Alas, I was never able to connect with Jacobs. Thanks to increased interest in pre-European-contact Native American foodways, there is much reference material available. It includes Gowri Chandra, "Native American Cuisine Is on the Rise—But Please Don't Call It a Trend," *Food & Wine*, February 1, 2018. See also Elizabeth Dahl, "How One Denver Restaurant Is Introducing Native American Food to the Hungry Masses," *The Manual*, February 21, 2018, www.themanual.com/food-and-drink/tocabe-native-american-food-interview-ben-jacobs/. Also, see the work of the Sioux Chef (sioux-chef.com)—which I have written about in *Cowboys & Indians* magazine—and the I-Collective (icollectiveinc.org).

63   *No matter the arena*: "300 Navajo Rugs Expected At April Crownpoint Auction," *Albuquerque Journal*, March 18, 1973.

63   *the importance of community*: A section of this chapter was originally published in "Taste of the West: Fried Pride in Pawhuska," *Cowboys & Indians*, October 2017.

65   *built into and around a former Dairy Queen*: A segment of this section is adapted from "In Search of Puffy Tacos," an article I originally wrote for the *Dallas Morning News*, January 18, 2013.

66   *Tex-Mex scholar Robb Walsh argued*: Robb Walsh, "The Puffy Taco Invasion," *Austin Chronicle*, April 30, 2004.

70   *Discrepancies in this timeline exist*: Advertisement, *Monroe News-Star*, November 23, 1970, advertisement, *Monroe News-Star*, February 1, 1971.

70   *"Mexican health food"*: Advertisement, *San Antonio Express*, June 17, 1977.

72   *"I'm the first to say I'm not a culinary-trained chef"*: Elizabeth Castillo and Karen Haram, "Puffy Tacos a Hit at the White House," *San Antonio Express-News*, June 16, 2010.

Chapter 3. Barbacoa and Barbecue Tacos

82   *Europeans in the Caribbean basin*: Gonzalo Fernández de Oviedo y Valdés, *Historia general y natural de las Indias* (Madrid: Imprenta de la Real Academia de la Historia, 1851), https://archive.org/details/generalynatural01fernrich/page/n6.

82   *culinary traditions continue to prevail*: Mario Montaño, *The History of Mexican Folk Foodways of South Texas: Street Vendors, Offal Foods, and Barbacoa de Cabeza* (PhD diss., University of Pennsylvania, 1992), https://repository.upenn.edu/dissertations/AAI9308630.

82   *Barbacoa is barbecue*: Alexandra Y. Aikhenvald, *Languages of the Amazon* (Oxford and New York: Oxford University Press, 2012).

82   *a grain store or a stick framework*: Heriberto García Rivas, *Cocina prehispánica Mexicana: La comida de los antiguos Mexicanos* (Mexico City: Panorama Editorial, 1991).

82   *among the meats suitable for barbacoa*: Álvar Núñez Cabeza de Vaca and Pedro Hernández, *Relación de los naufragios y comentarios de Álvar Núñez Cabeza de Vaca*, vol. 5 (Librería General de Victoriano Suárez, 1906).

82   *left barbacoa with a "barbaric" connotation*: Andrew Warnes, *Savage Barbecue: Race, Culture, and the Invention of America's First Food* (Athens: University of Georgia Press, 2018).

82   *sweeping reforms of the food science movement*: Marvin Bendele, "*Barbacoa*? The Curious Case of a Word," in *Republic of Barbecue: Stories Beyond the Brisket*, ed. Elizabeth S. D. Engelhardt (Austin: University of Texas Press, 2009). Here is a choice quote from Bendele's excellent essay: "Apparently, dirt is too dirty to use as an oven, but clean enough for mud pies in the playground."

83   *"Nothing would make that obstinate ass move"*: Gustavo "Gus" Arriola, "Gordo," *Freeport Facts*, July 21, 1953.

83   *"fit for the table of a king"*: Fanny Chambers Gooch Iglehart, *Face to Face with the Mexicans: The Domestic Life, Educational, Social, and Business Ways, Statesmanship and Literature, Legendary and General History of the Mexican People, as Seen and*

Studied by an American Woman During Seven Years of Intercourse with Them (London: Sampson Low, Marston, Searle & Rivington, 1887).

85   *the last of his kind*: The first section of this chapter is adapted from "Vera's Backyard Bar-B-Que," my article published in *Cowboys & Indians*, April 2014. The quote from the Brownsville Public Health Department supervisor also appears in the article. The city worker to whom I attribute the quote is Roberto Garcia.

88   *"the Mexican 'barbacoa' has been adapted and taken over"*: "Marinade Provides Secret Of Tasty Broiled Chicken," *Sheboygan Press*, August 4, 1966.

88   *Taco Village*: Advertisement, *The Monitor* (McAllen, Texas), February 23, 1967.

88   *for a dime*: Advertisement, *Brownsville Herald*, June 5, 1964.

89   *afforded candidates a chance*: "Candidates Gather At 'Botana' Saturday," *Del Rio News-Herald*, April 29, 1974.

94   *In South Philly Barbacoa's first year*: Andrew Knowlton, "America's Best New Restaurants 2016," *Bon Appetit*, August 2016.

95   *Netflix dedicated an episode*: "Cristina Martinez," *Chef's Table*, Season 5, Episode 1 (Netflix).

95   *the same luscious lamb barbacoa*: Myrna I. Martinez, "Cristina Martínez, la chef indocumentada que ha conquistado EEUU," *Gourmet de Mexico*, gourmetdemexico.com.mx.

100   *an occasional special at Davila's BBQ*: Davila's BBQ Advertisements, *Seguin Gazette-Enterprise*, February 20, 1991, and June 18, 1993.

100   *The lamb barbacoa, prepared in a pozo*: "Barbecue and Barbacoa," *Man Fire Food*, Season 7, Episode 5 (Cooking Channel).

Chapter 4. K-Mex

113–118   *is linked to Kogi BBQ and Kogi's chef, Roy Choi*: Roy Choi with Tien Nguyen and Natasha Phan, *L.A. Son: My Life, My City, My Food* (New York: Anthony Bourdain/Ecco, 2013). My attempts to connect with Roy Choi for an interview were in vain. Therefore, my research and writing relied on his autobiographical cookbook, *L.A. Son*, and newspaper and online sources, including: Andrew Romano, "Thanks to Twitter, America's First Viral Eatery," *Newsweek*, February 27, 2009; "I am Roy Choi. I make Korean BBQ tacos and worked with Jon Favreau on the movie *Chef*. You may have seen me on TV, but not in a Humvee, or on the streets serving it up. Now I'm on CNN. AMA!" Reddit AMA, October 21, 2014,

www.reddit.com/r/IAmA/comments/2jwvon/iama_roy_choi_i_make_korean
_bbq_tacos_and_worked/; L.A. Taco Roy Choi archives, *L.A. Taco*, www.lataco
.com/tag/roy-choi/; Jessica Gelt, "A Street Sensation Is Born; Answering Twitter's
Call, Hip Angelenos Flock to the Kogi Korean BBQ Truck, Wherever It Might
Park," *Los Angeles Times*, February 11, 2009; Roy Choi, "A Gateway to Feed
Hunger: The Promise of Street Food," MAD3, August 25–26, 2013, www
.informedmeateater.com/watch-roy-choi-a-gateway-to-feed-hunger-the-promise
-of-street-food/; Oliver Wang, "To Live and Dine in Kogi L.A.," *Contexts*, Fall 2009;
Daniel Patterson and Roy Choi, "Roy Choi and Daniel Patterson Announce loco'l,"
MAD4, August 24–25, 2014, www.madfeed.co/video/roy-choi-and-daniel
-patterson-announce-locol/; "*Roy Choi's Tacos Channel LA and the Immigrant
Experience*," *Fresh Air*, NPR, November 7, 2013; Jennifer Steinhauer, "For a New
Generation, Kimchi Goes with Tacos," *New York Times*, February 25, 2009.

119 *Tacos weren't on the menu*: Lara Rabinovitch, "Four Unforgettable, Weird Places to
Eat in Los Angeles," *Saveur*, January 16, 2018.

119 *when the size of the Korean community*: Korean American Coalition-Los Angeles,
"Top 10 Counties Ranked By Total Korean Population," www.kacla.org/census
-demographics-and-citizenship.html.

119 *Korean immigration to the United States was sporadic*: Jie Zong and Jeanne Batalova,
"Korean Immigrants in the United States," Migration Policy Institute, February 8,
2017.

120 *"frilly lettuce cups"*: S. Irene Virbila, "New Kids on the Block," *Los Angeles Times*,
September 1, 1996.

120 *Years later, in a review*: Carey Sweet, "A Pretty Pickle: You'll Find Raw Fish but
No Raw Deals at the West Valley's Tabletop Grill," *Phoenix New Times*, August 15,
2002.

Chapter 5. Sur-Mex

132 *the Memphis population clocked in at*: Memphis Quick Facts, US Census (1980, 1990,
2000, 2010).

135–137 *I visited the soft-spoken Hernandez*: Although the majority of biographical and
historical information about Taqueria del Sol, Mike Klank, and Eddie Hernandez
was gathered during the interview process, I referred to Hernandez's cookbook,
Turnip Greens & Tortillas, to fill in the gaps and check facts. Eddie Hernandez and
Susan Puckett, *Turnip Greens & Tortillas: A Mexican Chef Spices Up the Southern*

Kitchen (Boston, MA: Rux Martin/Houghton Mifflin Harcourt Publishing Company, 2018).

135 *Towne Crier Chicken restaurant*: Advertisement, *The H-SU Brand* (Abilene, Texas), October 6, 1972.

136 *the pair opened Sundown Café*: Yvonne Zusel, "Remember this Restaurant? Sundown Cafe on Cheshire Bridge," *Atlanta Journal-Constitution*, February 25, 2016.

137 *the Crescent City saw an influx*: Elizabeth Fussell, "Constructing New Orleans, Constructing Race: A Population History of New Orleans," *Journal of American History* 2007, 94 (3), 846–855.

137 *the sudden surge of a Latino low-skilled workforce*: Elizabeth Fussell, "Hurricane Chasers in New Orleans: Latino Immigrants as a Source of a Rapid Response Labor Force," *Hispanic Journal of Behavioral Sciences* 2009a, 31 (3), 375–394.

137 *the US government temporarily suspended*: Elizabeth Fussell, "Post-Katrina New Orleans as a New Migrant Destination," *Organization and Environment* 2009b, 22 (4), 458–469.

137 *the city's population shrank*: Allison Plyer, "Facts for Features: Katrina Impact," Data Center, August 26, 2016.

138 *in adjacent Jefferson Parish*: "Who Lives in New Orleans and Metro Parishes Now?" Data Center, July 9, 2018.

138 *a long history with Latin American cultures*: Julie M. Wiese, *Corazón de Dixie: Mexicanos in the U.S. South since 1910* (Chapel Hill: University of North Carolina Press, 2015).

138 *tamales and their vendors*: "Hot Tamale Man Knocked on Head and Robbed," New Orleans *Times-Picayune*, August 23, 1897.

138 *crime beat pages of newspapers*: "Stabbed by a Mexican," New Orleans *Times-Picayune*, December 26, 1900.

139 *"a new breed of serious New Orleans taquerias"*: Brett Anderson, "Del Fuego Taqueria," New Orleans *Times-Picayune*, October 18, 2014.

140 *"Mexican dishes from Sánchez's heritage"*: Todd A. Price, "7 Things to Know about Johnny Sanchez: The New John Besh and Aaron Sánchez Taqueria Opens Thursday in CBD," New Orleans *Times-Picayune*, October 8, 2014.

140 *where such behavior was permissible*: Brett Anderson, "John Besh Restaurants Fostered Culture of Sexual Harassment, 25 Women Say," New Orleans *Times-Picayune*, October 21, 2017.

140 *In February 2019, Sánchez gained new partners*: Ian McNulty, "John Besh Out at Johnny Sanchez; Chef Aaron Sanchez, Partners to Run New Orleans Restaurant," *New Orleans Advocate*, February 16, 2019.

140 *On the mobile front*: Todd A. Price. "Taceaux Loceaux, Long-Running Food Truck, Will Open Uptown Restaurant," New Orleans *Times-Picayune*, April 23, 2019.

141 *"If there's one thing that rubs me the wrong way"*: Gwendolyn Knapp, "Three Ways Dining in Nola Has Changed Since Katrina," *Eater New Orleans*, February 25, 2016.

145 *no good tacos in Charleston*: Robert F. Moss, "From Humble Ingredients to His Love of Valentina Hot Sauce, Sean Brock Gives an Inside Look at Minero," *Charleston City Paper*, October 16, 2014.

146 *Chutneys can be added*: Veronica Meewes, "The Spice Is Right with These Indian Tacos," *Austin Chronicle*, May 4, 2018.

148 *connects West African foodways*: Adrian Miller, *Soul Food: The Surprising Story of an American Cuisine One Plate at a Time* (Chapel Hill: University of North Carolina Press, 2013).

149 *There is a possibility of such a thing*: Maria Yagoda, "Sean Brock Leaves Restaurant Group to Focus on Nashville Projects," *Food & Wine*, August 1, 2018.

149, 151 *"Latinas/os are moving to the South"*: Perla M. Guerrero, *Nuevo South: Latinas/os, Asians, and the Remaking of Place* (Austin: University of Texas Press, 2017).

150 *West Indian tacos are gaining momentum*: "Detailed Look at Sub-Saharan African and Caribbean Ancestry," US Census Bureau, December 2017.

152 *tacky Mexican-inspired South of the Border theme park*: Robin Schafer with Evelyn Schafer Hechtkopf, "South of the Border," Jewish Historical Society of South Carolina, jhssc.org.

152 *Confederate Kosher Mexican motel*: Nicole King, "Behind the Sombrero: Identity and Power at South of the Border, 1949–2001," in *Dixie Emporium: Tourism, Foodways, and Consumer Culture in the American South*, ed. Anthony J. Stanonis (Athens: University of Georgia Press, 2008).

Chapter 6. Jewish and Kosher Tacos, or Deli-Mex

158 *And that tale begins*: Parts of this chapter originally appeared as "This Texan Jew Is Bringing Kosher Tacos to the Border" on the *Vice* food vertical, "Munchies," November 28, 2015.

159 *"a load of junk"*: Letter to the Editor, "Don Pedro Says," *Brownsville Herald*, September 9, 1959.

159 *"Confederate Kosher Mexican motel"*: Advertisement, Vidette-Messenger (Valparaiso, Indiana), October 26, 1961.

159 *"ZE ONLEE"*: Advertisement, *Carolina Israelite* (Charlotte, North Carolina), January–February 1968.

159–160 *But it was par for the course*: Nicole King, "Behind the Sombrero: Identity and Power at South of the Border, 1949–2001," in *Dixie Emporium: Tourism, Foodways, and Consumer Culture in the American South*, ed. Anthony J. Stanonis (Athens: University of Georgia Press, 2008).

160 *"where AAA uses Jaguar tow-trucks"*: Between Channels, "Comic Quotes," *Salem News* (Salem, Ohio), October 17, 1966.

160 *peculiar lunches consumed*: Bettelou Peterson, "Boonesborough: Is There a Feud?" *Detroit Free Press*, July 6, 1967. This TV column includes an anecdote about Kosher Burrito, a kosher taco stand chain in Los Angeles, which appears in the 1960s TV show *Dragnet*. The chain grew to include a location in Las Vegas, covered in "Some Pots Shouldn't Melt," *Chicago Tribune*, November 20, 1977. The Kosher Burrito closed in 2000.

160 *"Kosher Tacos Aren't Religious"*: Paul Dean, "Sometimes Hot Lines Can Be Chilled," *Arizona Republic*, September 7, 1970.

161 *The presence of Crypto-Jews*: Stephen Leon, *The Third Commandment and the Return of the Anusim: A Rabbi's Memoir of an Incredible People* (Santa Fe: Gaon Books, 2017).

161 *Leon received a call*: María Cortés González, "Texan Rabbi on the Trail After the Jewish History of El Paso," *El Paso Times*, July 29, 2018.

164 *This kosher spin on tacos al pastor*: José Toribio Medina, *Historia del Tribunal del Santo Oficio de la Inquisicion en Mexico* (Mexico DF: Ediciones Fuente Cultural, 1952).

164 *"forty thousand leagues of territory"*: Robert S. Weddle, "Carvajal y de la Cueva, Luis de," *Handbook of Texas Online*.

165 *The disgraced governor was sentenced to exile*: Alfonso Toro, *La familia Carvajal: Estudio histórico sobre los judíos y la Inquisición de la Nueva España en el siglo XVI*, 2 vols. (Mexico City: Patria, 1944).

166 *"There's nothing like kosher Mexican"*: Tom Fesperman, "The Great Equalizer," *Redlands Daily Facts* (Redlands, California), April 20, 1977. The company Fesperman convinced in his newspaper story wasn't the only manufacturer to produce Kosher Mexican products for mass consumption. In the late 1990s, Manischewitz—a kosher food brand famous for its wine and matzo—produced and advertised a complete taco dinner box, much like notable companies such as Old El Paso.

166 *tacos were served at special events*: "Tidbits," *Southern Illinoisan* (Carbondale, Illinois), April 16, 1997, and *Jewish News* (Whippany, New Jersey), January 18, 2007.

169 *include a rye tortilla recipe*: Alex Stupak and Jordana Rothman, *Tacos: Recipes and Provocations* (New York: Clarkson Potter, 2015).

Chapter 7. Alta California Tacos

Although I conducted interviews for this chapter, not all subjects were forthcoming about (or had time to get into) the nitty-gritty of their résumés. In those cases, I consulted the *L.A. Mexicano* and *Guerrilla Tacos* cookbooks.

174 *Its inspiration is found in the mashed potato-packed tacos*: Wesley Avila and Richard Parks III, *Guerrilla Tacos: Recipes from the Streets of L.A.* (Berkeley, CA: Ten Speed Press, 2017).

178–179 *cultivating the genre of Alta California cuisine*: Bill Esparza, *L.A. Mexicano: Recipes, People & Places* (Altadena, CA: Prospect Park Books, 2017).

180 *"those early days that preceded the American occupation"*: Encarnación Pinedo, *El cocinero español* (The Spanish Cook), E. C. Hughes, 1898 (Santa Clara University Library's Archives & Special Collections).

180 *recounted a life of religious ceremonies*: Encarnación Pinedo, *Pinedo Reminiscence*, Santa Clara College, 1901 (Santa Clara University Library's Archives & Special Collections).

Chapter 8. El Taco Moderno

Parts of this chapter originally appeared as "This Legendary Gunmaker Moonlights as a Restaurant Dishwasher" on the *Vice* food vertical, "Munchies," September 28, 2017, and as "Does a Great Taco Require a Handmade Tortilla?" in *Texas Monthly*, March 2018.

194 *This isn't a white people thing*: Wesley Avila with Richard Parks III, *Guerrilla Tacos: Recipes from the Streets of L.A.* (Berkeley, CA: Ten Speed Press, 2017).

Appendix 1. Signs of a Truly Outstanding Taco Joint

This appendix is adapted from an article that originally appeared as "The 6 Signs of a Truly Outstanding Taco Joint" on *Thrillist*, June 9, 2017.

Appendix 2. A Brief History of the Taco Holder

224–225 *these hard-shell vittles*: Gustavo Arellano, *Taco USA: How Mexican Food Conquered America* (New York: Scribner, 2012).

225 *reviled by Mexicans as aberrations*: Jeffrey M. Pilcher, *Planet Taco: A Global History of Mexican Food* (Oxford and New York: Oxford University Press, 2012).

225 *touted the taco as acceptable and safe*: Myrtle Richardson, *Genuine Mexican and Spanish Cookery for American Homes* (Cookeville, TN: Putnam Printing Company, 1934).

226 *To solve that dilemma*: United States Patent Office, No. 2,506,305, Juvencio Maldonado, "Form for Frying Tortillas to Make Fried Tacos," May 2, 1950.

226 *"utensil for cooking tacos"*: United States Patent Office, No. 2627222 A, Santiago M. Luna, "Utensil for cooking tacos," February 3, 1953.

226 *"The preparation of tacos involves frying"*: United States Patent Office, No. 2,635,528, Victor P. Torres, "Frying utensil," April 21, 1953.

226–227 *"A device for frying taco shells"*: United States Patent Office, No. 2792774 A, Joseph P. Veach, "Taco shell fryer," May 21, 1957.

227 *"ornamental design for a taco holder"*: United States Patent Office, No. D217593 S, James R. Loven, "Taco holder," May 19, 1970.

228 *"A taco holding tray"*: United States Patent Office, No. 4004501 A, Lois L. Guerrero, "Taco holding tray," January 25, 1977.

228 *resembles a sombrero*: United States Patent Office, No. 5065870 A, O. Ray Conder Jr., "Taco holder," November 19, 1991.

228 *"If the shell is folded"*: United States Patent Office, No. 4603825 A, Howard J. Kotliar, "Taco holder," August 5, 1986.

232 *"The Taco Susan was conceived"*: United States Patent Office, No. 8402901B1; Scott M. Bahnsen, "Lazy Susan device and accessories," March 26, 2013, United States Patent Office, No. US8544930 B1; Scott M. Bahnsen, "Lazy Susan device with snap fit top and base," October 1, 2013.

232 *substituting a muffin tin*: Angie Massengill, *The Polished Woman: Hints, Tips, and Tricks to Getting Organized* (Bloomington, IN: Xlibris, 2010).

233 *Some are edible*: United States Patent Office, No. 20110256275 A1, John P. Gillig, "Edible taco style food shell," October 20, 2011.

233 *trademarking of Taco Tuesday*: E. Scott Reckard, "'Taco Tuesday' Trademark Tussle," *Los Angeles Times*, July 23, 1997. This is just one of many possible references applicable here. A simple database search of newspaper archives—or, heck, Google—will give you excellent pickings, including legal documents.

Further Reading

Arellano, Gustavo. *Taco USA: How Mexican Food Conquered America*. New York: Scribner, 2012.

Avila, Wesley, and Richard Parks III. *Guerrilla Tacos: Recipes from the Streets of L.A.* Berkeley, CA: Ten Speed Press, 2017.

Choi, Roy, with Tien Nguygen and Natasha Phan. *L.A. Son: My Life, My City, My Food*. New York: Anthony Bourdain/Ecco, 2013.

Edge, John T. *The Potlikker Papers: A Food History of the Modern South*. New York: Penguin Press, 2017.

Escalante, Alejandro. *La Tacopedia: Enciclopedia del taco*. Mexico City: Trice Ediciones, 2013.

Esparza, Bill. *L.A. Mexicano: Recipes, People & Places*. Consortium Books, 2017.

Fain, Lisa. *The Homesick Texan Cookbook*. New York: Hachette Books, 2011.

———. *The Homesick Texan's Family Table: Lone Star Cooking from My Kitchen to Yours*. Berkeley, CA: Ten Speed Press, 2014.

———. *QUESO! Regional Recipes for the World's Favorite Chile-Cheese* Dip. Berkeley, CA: Ten Speed Press, 2017.

Forbes, Paul. *The Austin Cookbook: Recipes and Stories From Deep in the Heart of Texas*. New York: Harry N. Abrams, 2018.

Fussell, Betty. *The Story of Corn*. Albuquerque: University of New Mexico Press, 2004.

Martin, Jacqueline Briggs, and June Jo Lee. *Chef Roy Choi and the Street Food Remix (Food Heroes)*. Illustrated by Man One. Bellevue, WA: Readers to Eaters, 2017.

Miller, Adrian. *Soul Food: The Surprising Story of an American Cuisine One Plate at a Time*. Chapel Hill: University of North Carolina Press, 2017.

Morton, Paula E. *Tortillas: A Cultural History*. Albuquerque: University of New Mexico Press, 2014.

Pilcher, Jeffrey M. *Planet Taco: A Global History of Mexican Food*. Oxford and New York: Oxford University Press, 2012.

————. *Que vivan los tamales! Food and the Making of Mexican Identity*. Albuquerque: University of New Mexico Press, 1998.

Rubin, Adam. *Dragons Love Tacos*. Illustrated by Daniel Salmieri. New York: Dial Books, 2012.

————. *Dragons Love Tacos 2*. Illustrated by Daniel Salmieri. New York: Dial Books, 2017.

Stupak, Alex, and Jordana Rothman. *Tacos: Recipes and Provocations*. New York: Clarkson Potter, 2015.

Téllez, Lesley. *Eat Mexico: Recipes and Stories from Mexico City's Streets, Markets & Fondas*. London: Kyle Books, 2015.

Vaughn, Daniel. *The Prophets of Smoked Meat: A Journey through Texas Barbecue*. New York: Anthony Bourdain/Ecco, 2013.

Walsh, Robb. *Legends of Texas Barbecue Cookbook: Recipes and Recollections from the Pitmasters, Revised & Updated with 32 New Recipes!* San Francisco: Chronicle Books, 2016.

————. *The Texas Cowboy Cookbook: A History in Recipes and Photos*. Berkeley, CA: Ten Speed Press, 2007.

————. *Texas Eats: The New Lone Star Heritage Cookbook, with More Than 200 Recipes*. Berkeley, CA: Ten Speed Press, 2012.

————. *The Tex-Mex Cookbook: A History in Recipes and Photos*. Berkeley, CA: Ten Speed Press, 2004.

Weise, Julie M. *Corazón de Dixie: Mexicanos in the U.S. South since 1910*. Chapel Hill: University of North Carolina Press, 2015.

Zurita, Ricardo Muñoz. *Larousse Diccionario Enciclopedico de la Gastronomia Mexicano*. Mexico City: Larousse Mexico, 2013.

Index

Note: Page numbers in italics indicate images and captions.